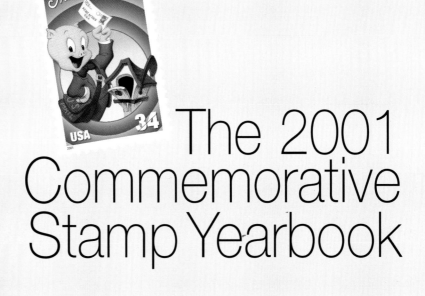

The 2001 Commemorative Stamp Yearbook

USA
34

Venus Flytrap
2001

2001

Other books available from
the United States Postal Service:

An American Postal Portrait

The 2000 Commemorative Stamp Yearbook

The Postal Service Guide to U.S. Stamps
Twenty-Seventh Edition
Twenty-Eighth Edition

The 2001 Commemorative Stamp Yearbook

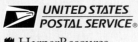

UNITED STATES POSTAL SERVICE®

HarperResource
An Imprint of HarperCollins Publishers

Leonard Bernstein

2001 COMMEMORATIVE STAMP YEARBOOK.
Copyright © 2001 by the United States Postal Service.
All rights reserved. Printed in the United States of America.
No part of this book may be used or reproduced in any manner
whatsoever without written permission except in the case of
brief quotations embodied in critical articles and reviews.
For information address HarperCollins Publishers, Inc.,
10 East 53rd Street, New York, NY 10022.

The designs of stamps and postal stationery are the subject
of individual copyrights by the United States Postal Service.
UNITED STATES POSTAL SERVICE, the eagle logo, and
POSTAL SERVICE are trademarks of the United States
Postal Service.

HarperCollins books may be purchased for educational,
business, or sales promotional use. For information please write:
Special Markets Department, HarperCollins Publishers, Inc.,
10 East 53rd Street, New York, NY 10022.

Library of Congress Cataloging-in-Publication Data
has been applied for.
ISBN: 0-06-019897-4

34 USA

Contents

Introduction

The art of illustration has long illuminated books, magazines, and murals. This year, the U.S. Postal Service focuses on the work of great illustrators—and their important role in the commemorative stamp program.

MAXFII

Every stamp illustrates a story in miniature. Just look at this year's American Illustrators stamps and you'll see 20 moments frozen in time, from depictions of history and daily life to dreamscapes from the minds of some of our country's finest creative talents. Life on the Dakota prairie, the antics of college students in the 1920s, the adventures of pirates and knights—as we encounter these and other colorful scenes, we stop and imagine the story behind each one, delighted to be drawn into their fascinating worlds.

But there's one story that the stamps alone don't tell: the many awards that stamp artists and their artwork frequently receive from prestigious organizations such as the Art Directors Club of Metropolitan Washington and the Society of Illustrators. These organizations honored two 1999 stamp issuances featuring illustrations by Steve Buchanan: the exotic Tropical Flowers and the lively and colorful Insects and Spiders. Buchanan, who creates his artwork digitally, cultivates his talents once again with the beautifully eerie botanical drawings on this year's Carnivorous Plants stamps.

The Nature of America series of stamp panes has also received numerous accolades for its wonderfully detailed illustrations. Featuring artwork by John D. Dawson, the 1999 Sonoran Desert issuance won an Award of Excellence at the Society of Illustrators' 42nd Exhibition, and last year's Pacific Coast Rain Forest stamp pane received a Creativity 30 Award of Distinction. These stamp panes have proven highly popular

PEANUTS

USA 34

2001

ARRISH

not only with collectors, but also with anyone awed by the diversity and incredible beauty of nature. Well known as a natural history artist, Dawson returns this year to continue his acclaimed work on the third stamp pane in the series. This new pane places us right in the middle of the Great Plains Prairie—a distinctly American landscape that serves as a backdrop for natural history, human history, and now philatelic history as well.

The 2001 holiday stamps feature a wide range of visual styles that illustrate the nation's many diverse traditions. The Eid stamp, graced with an elegant design by renowned calligrapher Mohamed Zakariya, calls to mind great Islamic manuscripts, while the machine-appliquéd needlework by Margaret Cusack on the Thanksgiving stamp evokes the gentle designs of American folk art stitchery. This year's Holiday

FACING PAGE: Charles M. Schulz brought us Snoopy's adventures for decades in the comic strip "Peanuts." ABOVE LEFT: This Maxfield Parrish painting was originally created as a mural for the Eastman Theatre in Rochester, New York. LEFT: J. C. Leyendecker's famous Arrow Collar Man was an advertising icon who won the hearts of countless women. ABOVE RIGHT: Margaret Cusack designed and created the machine-appliquéd needlework that appears on this year's Thanksgiving stamp.

Traditional stamp, featuring art by Italian Renaissance painter Lorenzo Costa, evokes a long tradition of devotional imagery, and the Holiday Contemporary stamps help tell the tale of a beloved cultural icon: Santa Claus.

This year's stamps also illustrate the great diversity of artistic approaches that are used to create the commemorative program. Award-winning Hollywood artist Drew Struzan portrays Lucille Ball in his own inimitable style, while James Steinberg's striking acrylic-and-gouache illustration for the Diabetes stamp highlights the importance of awareness and early detection of the disease. With its paper-cut design and grass-style calligraphy, the Lunar New Year stamp again reminds us of venerable artistic traditions. The meticulous and time-honored art of engraving is represented this year as well, with a stamp honoring the centennial of the Nobel Prize by world-famous engraver Czeslaw Slania.

From the comic-strip world of "Peanuts" to the traditional designs of Amish quilts, this year's stamps tell stories. *The 2001 Commemorative Stamp Yearbook* collects these compelling images all in one place, where they illustrate what happens when award-winning artists bring talent, tradition, and great imagination to their work—allowing each stamp to tell its unique story again and again.

Year of the Snake

It begins not just with a bang, but with a whole series of eye-popping sights and percussive sounds: the crackle of fireworks, the flashing colors of beautiful decorations, and performers in lion and dragon costumes dancing to the relentless rhythms of drums. From New York to San Francisco, streets light up with parades and revelry as Asian Americans joyously celebrate Lunar New Year.

Also called the Spring Festival, the traditional Chinese New Year celebrates the beginning of a new season, a time of renewed hope for a prosperous future. During the festivities, everyone concentrates on the year to come. Bright red clothing and window decorations get the year off to an auspicious beginning, and a sense of reconciliation and neighborly peace abounds.

The festivities themselves are steeped in history. Window and door decorations that feature Chinese couplets on red

Oakland, CA
January 20, 2001
Place and Date of Issue

Clarence Lee
Illustrator, Designer

Terrence W. McCaffrey
Art Director

paper belong to a tradition that goes back more than 1,000 years, to a time when similar good-luck messages were written on peach wood. Meanwhile, the firecrackers that explode along city streets are more than mere noisemakers; it has long been believed that they frighten away unlucky spirits. In preparation for the new year, people also clean their homes thoroughly in order to begin the new season with a clean slate and renewed prospects.

This ninth stamp in the award-winning Lunar New Year series commemorates the Year of the Snake, which runs from January 24, 2001, to February 11, 2002.

A symbol of wisdom and charm, the snake is the sixth of twelve animals associated with the Chinese lunar calendar. Chinese folklore traditionally assigns particular characteristics to people based on the animal associated with their birth year. People born during the Year of the Snake are said to be elegant, intelligent, and romantic and are often suited to careers as philosophers and teachers.

With its emphasis on new and auspicious beginnings, the tradition of Lunar New Year offers an enjoyable, hopeful experience—good reason for all Americans to join in the celebration.

Roy Wilkins

Principled determination and a belief in the power of legislative action made him a vital force in the civil rights movement.

On a hot August afternoon in 1963, Roy Wilkins stood at the Lincoln Memorial in Washington, D.C. Assembled before him were more than 200,000 Americans who had come from all over the country to attend the March on Washington for Jobs and Freedom—a powerful moment in the civil rights movement that Wilkins himself helped organize.

"Now, we expect the passage of a civil rights bill," he told them. "We commend those Republicans in both Houses who are working for it. We salute those Democrats in both Houses who are working for it. In fact, we even salute those from the South who want to vote for it but don't dare to do so, and we say to those people: Just give us a little time, and one of these days, we'll emancipate *you*." This was quintessential Wilkins, a man whose methods lay not in fiery oratory, but in principled determination and a belief in the power of legislative action—traits that made him a vital force in the civil rights movement.

Born August 30, 1901, in St. Louis, Missouri, Wilkins graduated from the University of Minnesota in 1923. He joined the staff of the National Association for the Advancement of Colored People (NAACP) as assistant secretary in 1931, also serving as the editor of the organization's official magazine, *The Crisis*, from 1934 to 1949. In 1950 he became the administrator of the NAACP and in 1955 he assumed the leadership, serving until 1977 as executive secretary and executive director.

Advocating nonviolent means and the use of the legal system to achieve racial equality and to advance the rights of African Americans, Wilkins was a skilled administrator and a respected leader. He was consulted by Presidents, including John F. Kennedy and Lyndon Johnson, and under his leadership the NAACP campaigned for the Civil Rights Act of 1964, the Voting Rights Act of 1965, and the Fair Housing Act of 1968.

In 1964, Wilkins received the NAACP's Spingarn Medal, an annual award recognizing outstanding achievement by an African American. Today a monument honoring his accomplishments stands in St. Paul, Minnesota, as a reminder of his unwavering commitment to civil rights.

"But we have never given up—never quit," he wrote in his autobiography, *Standing Fast*. "We have believed in our country. We have believed in our Constitution. We have believed that the Declaration of Independence meant what it said. All my life I have believed these things, and I will die believing them. I share this faith with others— and I know that it will last and guide us long after I am gone."

Minneapolis, MN
January 24, 2001
Place and Date of Issue

Morgan and Marvin Smith
Photographers

Richard Sheaff
Designer, Art Director

ABOVE LEFT: *Wilkins meets with President Johnson in the Oval Office, April 1968.*
ABOVE TOP: *Wilkins alongside Walter White and Thurgood Marshall in the 1950s.*
ABOVE BOTTOM: *An article by Wilkins in the April 1937 issue of* The Crisis.

ROY WILKINS

Love

"A person who can write a long letter with ease," remarked Jane Austen in *Pride and Prejudice*, "cannot write ill." With the issuance of this year's Love stamps, the U.S. Postal Service pays tribute to the timelessness of love letters and the enduring and romantic feelings they symbolize.

Love letters come in all shapes and sizes, but the messages they convey are decidedly universal. An Old English poem found in a tenth-century manuscript describes a lonely traveler inscribing a message on a wooden stave and sending it home to his lover across the sea. "He is waiting in that country," wrote the anonymous poet, "and would keep faith for as long as he lives, as you two often swore in former days." The traveler included on the stave a series of mysterious symbols—perhaps a secret message meant only for the eyes of his beloved.

That same desire to express romantic feelings in a love letter manifests itself throughout the centuries. Poet John Keats fell deeply in love with Fanny Brawne, who lived not across expanses of great oceans, but right next door. "You are always new," he wrote to her in 1820. "The last of your kisses was ever the sweetest; the last smile the brightest; the last moment the gracefullest. When you pass'd my window home yesterday, I was fill'd with as much admiration as if I had then seen you for the first time." Sadly,

Keats died of tuberculosis the following year, but his love for Fanny Brawne remained unwavering.

Featuring correspondence between Abigail Smith and John Adams during their courtship, this year's beautiful Love stamps underscore the lasting nature of profound sentiments expressed in writing. The two were married in 1764, more than thirty years before Mr. and Mrs. Adams would become President and First Lady of the United States. They were married for 54 years—the satisfying outcome of a relationship begun in letters.

Lovejoy, GA
February 14, 2001
Place and Date of Issue

Reneé Comet
Photographer

Lisa Catalone
Designer

Ethel Kessler
Art Director

"I wish I had the gift of making rhymes, for methinks there is poetry in my head and heart since I have been in love with you. You are a Poem. Of what sort, then? Epic? Mercy on me, no! A sonnet? No; for that is too labored and artificial. You are a sort of sweet, simple, gay, pathetic ballad, which Nature is singing, sometimes with tears, sometimes with smiles, and sometimes with intermingled smiles and tears."

— *Nathaniel Hawthorne to his wife Sophia, 1839*

American Illustrators

"Look on this, study it, absorb it," illustrator Howard Pyle would tell students at his highly selective school. "Never again will it be the same. If you see it tomorrow the light will be different and you will be different. This moment is unique." Pyle saw the importance of those moments—and knew that American illustrators could document them with consummate skill.

Advances in printing and publishing made possible by the Industrial Revolution ushered in a new era for American illustrators during the last quarter of the 19th century, allowing their work to be reproduced with increasing fidelity and attracting some of the country's finest talents to the field. Illustrations originally commissioned for books, advertisements, magazines, murals, and posters today serve as an invaluable artistic chronicle of American culture—from fashions and fads to pivotal moments in history. Because of the talents of the illustrators featured on this stamp pane, we can easily imagine ourselves in the worlds they created—moving among the glamorous ranks of high society, undertaking incredible adventures, or visiting fantasy lands that seem too real not to exist.

In a time before television, when magazines were a dominant medium, many illustrators were also celebrities. Neysa McMein, who consorted with members of the Algonquin Round Table, was known to paint portraits, magazine covers, or other commercial assignments while holding lavish parties at her New York studio. The outspoken James Montgomery Flagg befriended Hollywood stars and made the rounds of the New York club scene. He immortalized himself by serving as

LEFT: *Neysa McMein and one of her glamorous portraits.* ABOVE: *Norman Rockwell adapted the pose of Michelangelo's Isaiah from the Sistine Chapel for this "Rosie the Riveter" illustration.*

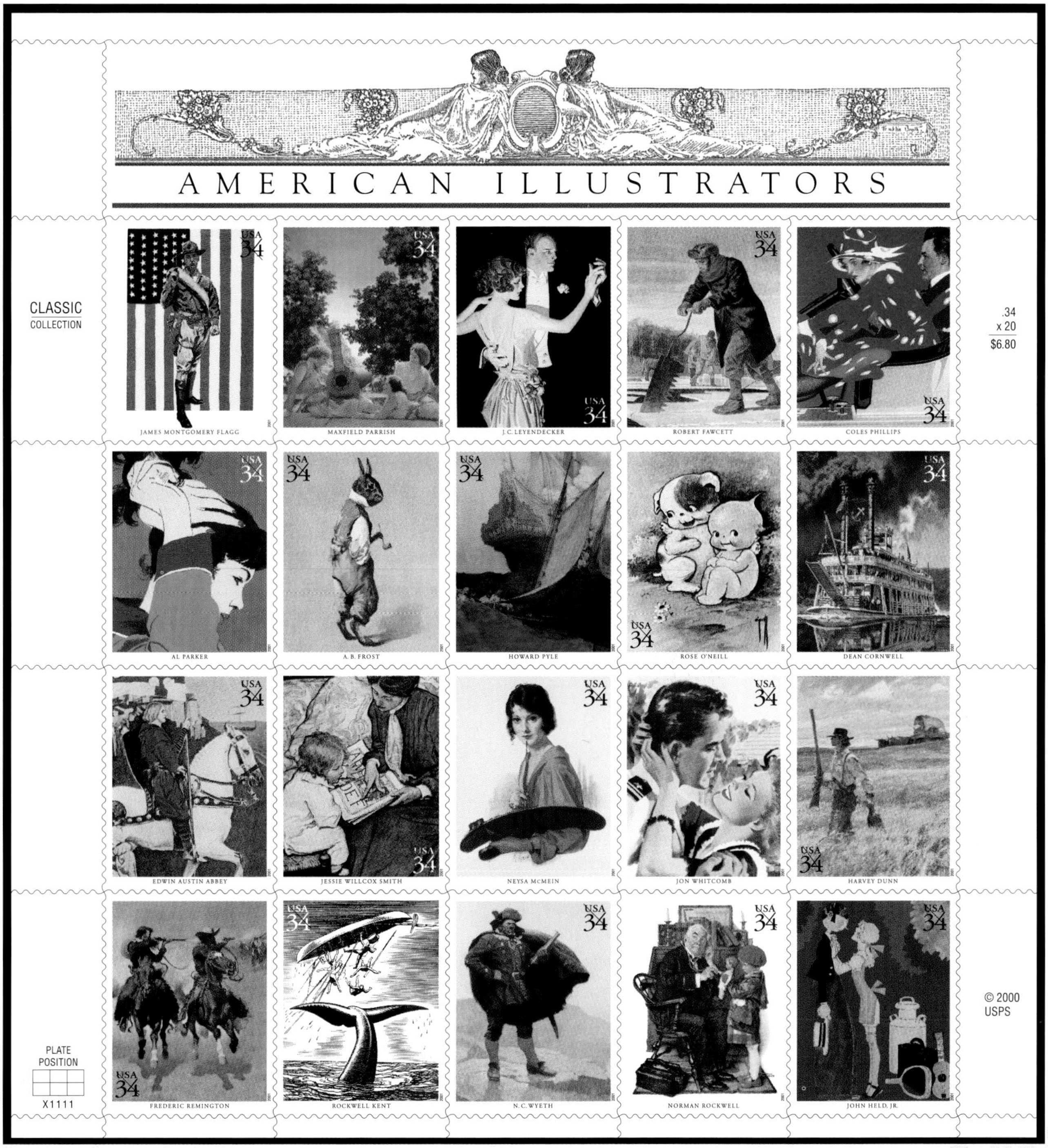

AMERICAN ILLUSTRATORS

CLASSIC
COLLECTION

.34
x 20
$6.80

JAMES MONTGOMERY FLAGG

MAXFIELD PARRISH

J.C. LEYENDECKER

ROBERT FAWCETT

COLES PHILLIPS

AL PARKER

A.B. FROST

HOWARD PYLE

ROSE O'NEILL

DEAN CORNWELL

EDWIN AUSTIN ABBEY

JESSIE WILLCOX SMITH

NEYSA MCMEIN

JON WHITCOMB

HARVEY DUNN

FREDERIC REMINGTON

ROCKWELL KENT

N.C. WYETH

NORMAN ROCKWELL

JOHN HELD, JR.

© 2000
USPS

PLATE
POSITION

X1111

Maxfield Parrish illustration authorized by the Maxfield Parrish Family Trust. Rockwell Kent illustration © Plattsburgh State Art Museum, Rockwell Kent Gallery, Plattsburgh, NY.
Norman Rockwell illustration © 1929 The Curtis Publishing Company. John Held, Jr., illustration courtesy of Judy Held.

N. C. WYETH John Held Jr. M. P
Pyle.
H. Pyle.
DEAN CORNWELL
o'Nei
Pyle.
MONTGOMERY FLAGG

In addition to being out-standing illustrators, the men and women honored on this stamp pane were also writers, teachers, travelers, and poets. Their experiences, as impressive as their artistic abilities, lent depth and authenticity to their work.

his own model for Uncle Sam proclaiming "I Want You"—a magazine cover that became one of the most famous military recruitment posters of the 20th century.

Flagg's distinctive version of Uncle Sam was just one of many enduring American icons to flow from the pens and brushes of these great illustrators. Women swooned over the handsome Arrow Collar Man created by J. C. Leyendecker, and many Americans embraced the fashion styles popularized by artists such as Coles Phillips and Al Parker. Other illustrators charmed us with humor and tender moments: Rose O'Neill's Kewpies delighted generations of children with their whimsical antics; the gawky flappers and sheiks of John Held, Jr., stumbled amusingly through the Jazz Age; and Jessie Willcox Smith's sensitive drawings of mothers and children warmed the hearts of magazine readers for years.

These artists also turned literary masterpieces into illustrated classics. No library is complete without N. C. Wyeth's beautifully illustrated edition of Robert Louis Stevenson's *Treasure Island*, or the 1930 edition of *Moby Dick* featuring the striking designs of Rockwell Kent. To many fans, Robert Fawcett's illustrations for a series of Sherlock Holmes stories in *Collier's* magazine remain highly memorable depictions of the famous sleuth, and Edwin Austin Abbey's renderings of Shakespearean scenes have been enjoyed by countless Anglophiles and theater aficionados.

ABOVE LEFT: *Howard Pyle paints* The Battle of Nashville, *c.1906.* ABOVE: *A painting of French explorers on Frederic Remington's easel, 1906.* LEFT: *A Coles Phillips illustration for the cover of* Life, *September 1911.*

New York, NY
February 1, 2001
Place and Date of Issue

Carl Herrman
Designer, Art Director

COLES PHILLIPS

In addition to being outstanding illustrators, the men and women honored on this stamp pane were also writers, teachers, travelers, and poets. Their experiences, as impressive as their artistic abilities, lent depth and authenticity to their work. Frederic Remington, for example, is best known for recording the end of the Old West in paintings and magazine illustrations, but he also served as an artist and correspondent in Cuba during the Spanish-American War. Similarly, throughout World War I, artists created posters to support the war effort, and some illustrators, such as Harvey Dunn, served as official military artists and documented the grim realities of the battlefield. During World War II, illustrators again answered the call. Some visited veterans hospitals to sketch the wounded for their families and boost morale. Others served as military artists, among them Jon Whitcomb, a Navy artist in the Pacific who also created a dramatic series of advertisements about the postwar homecomings of American soldiers.

In 1901 nine artists and one advising businessman founded the Society of Illustrators. As the society celebrates its centennial, the U.S. Postal Service is pleased to honor the contributions of the men and women who continue to give Americans what Maxfield Parrish once called "windows for their minds." Whether we are delighting in a uniquely American scene by Norman Rockwell or in N. C. Wyeth's depictions of brave knights, the work of these illustrators provides glimpses of worlds we otherwise might never have seen—while offering a fascinating look into our own national past.

ABOVE LEFT: *Caricatures by James Montgomery Flagg.* ABOVE: *A 1944 poster by Jon Whitcomb.* BELOW: *A June 1926 magazine cover by John Held, Jr.* BELOW LEFT: *N. C. Wyeth at work in a detail from his 1913 self-portrait.*

The Nobel Prize

". . . to those who, during the preceding year, shall have conferred the greatest benefit on mankind."

Each year on December 10, the attention of the world falls upon two cities: Stockholm, Sweden, and Oslo, Norway, where the Nobel Prizes are awarded. In 2001, the world celebrates 100 years of the Nobel Prize, the extension and fulfillment of the lifetime interests of one man: Alfred Nobel.

Born in Stockholm in 1833, Alfred Bernhard Nobel received an international education, mastered several languages, and became an inventor and industrialist. Focusing primarily on chemical inventions, he patented dynamite in 1867 and established companies and laboratories throughout Europe. A man of broad interests, Nobel held more than 350 patents, and he also wrote poetry and drama.

On November 27, 1895, Nobel signed his last will and testament in Paris—creating the prestigious award that is now synonymous with his name. He called for the bulk of his fortune to fund the creation of prizes to be given "to those who, during the preceding year, shall have conferred the greatest benefit on mankind." Nobel died in 1896, and in 1900 the Nobel Foundation was established. The first Nobel Prizes were awarded on December 10, 1901, the anniversary of Nobel's death, in Stockholm and Oslo (then known as Christiania). The recipients included Swiss humanitarian Jean Henri Dunant and Wilhelm Conrad Röntgen, the physicist who discovered X rays.

Today, Oslo remains the site of the annual awarding of the Peace Prize, while prizes in Physics, Chemistry, Physiology or Medicine, and Literature, as well as the Bank of Sweden Prize in Economic Sciences in Memory of Alfred Nobel, created in 1968, are still awarded in Stockholm. For many recipients of the Nobel Prize, the presentation of these awards remains a humbling reminder of human achievement. William Faulkner, one of more than 250 Nobel laureates from the United States, summed up his feelings in his 1949 acceptance speech.

Washington, DC
March 22, 2001
Place and Date of Issue

Czeslaw Slania
Engraver

Olöf Baldursdottir
Designer

Terrence W. McCaffrey
and Stephan Fransius
Art Directors

"I feel that this award was not made to me as a man," he said, "but to my work—a life's work in the agony and sweat of the human spirit, not for glory and least of all for profit, but to create out of the materials of the human spirit something which did not exist before."

That sense of striving to realize human potential is a hallmark of the Nobel Prize, a decidedly international award that Nobel himself felt should disregard national borders. He wrote in his will that the nationality of the candidates should not be a consideration, "but that the most worthy shall receive the prize, whether he be a Scandinavian or not." In keeping with the spirit of Nobel's international legacy, the U.S. Postal Service issues this stamp, engraved by Polish-born Swedish stamp engraver Czeslaw Slania, jointly with Sweden Post.

American recipients of the Nobel Prize include Pearl S. Buck (above left) in 1938 and Toni Morrison (above) in 1993. RIGHT: *A posthumous painting of Alfred Nobel by Emil Österman.*

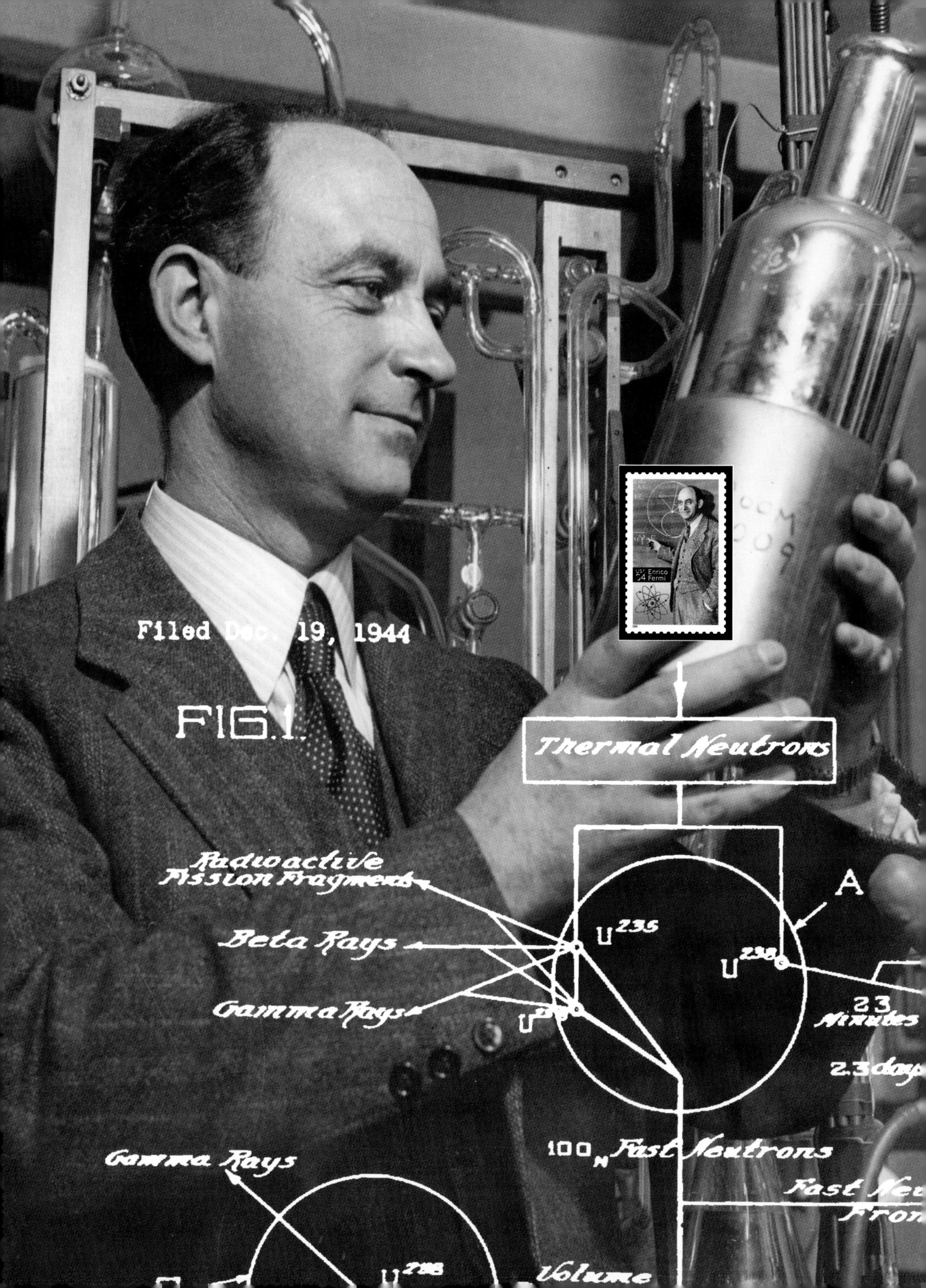

Filed Dec. 19, 1944

FIG. 1.

Thermal Neutrons

Radioactive
Fission Fragments

Beta Rays

Gamma Rays

Gamma Rays

U^{235}

U^{238}

A

23
Minutes

2.3 days

100 Fast Neutrons

Fast Ne
Fro

Volume

Enrico Fermi

For his discovery of nuclear reactions brought about by slow neutrons, Fermi was awarded the Nobel Prize in Physics in 1938.

Praised by the Chairman of the Nobel Committee for Physics in 1938 for "his experimental skill, his brilliant inventiveness and his intuition," Enrico Fermi was one of the preeminent physicists of the Atomic Age.

Born in Rome on September 29, 1901, Fermi received a Ph.D. in physics from the University of Pisa in 1922 and taught theoretical physics at the University of Rome from 1927 to 1938. In 1934, while experimenting with neutron bombardment of uranium, Fermi—without realizing it at the time—became the first physicist to split the atom.

For his discovery of nuclear reactions brought about by slow neutrons, Fermi was awarded the Nobel Prize in Physics in 1938. After accepting the prize in Stockholm, Fermi immigrated to the United States with his wife Laura, who was Jewish, and their two children, in order to escape anti-Semitic persecution in Italy.

In 1939, Fermi joined the faculty at Columbia University, where he taught physics and began conducting experiments with uranium in an attempt to create a controlled nuclear chain reaction. In January 1942, his work was transferred to the University of Chicago, where he supervised the design and assembly of the first nuclear reactor as part of the secret Manhattan Project—the code name for the coordinated U.S. effort to produce the atomic bomb during World War II.

On December 2, 1942, Fermi and his team made history when they achieved the first controlled and self-sustaining man-made nuclear chain reaction. Their success was fundamental to the production of plutonium; thereafter, the actual construction of the atomic bomb became the primary focus of the Manhattan Project. In September 1944, shortly after becoming a naturalized citizen of the United States, Fermi moved to Los Alamos, New Mexico, to assist in directing the project's scientific team there. He was present when the first atomic bomb was tested in the desert near Alamogordo on July 16, 1945.

At the end of the war, Fermi accepted an invitation to teach physics at the University of Chicago's new Institute for Nuclear Studies. There he turned his attention to high-energy physics and helped develop the synchrocyclotron, which at the time was the largest particle accelerator in the world. He also voiced concern over the secrecy of nuclear research, and he advised against the development of a hydrogen bomb on ethical grounds.

Shortly before Fermi died of cancer on November 28, 1954, President Dwight D. Eisenhower and the Atomic Energy Commission gave him a "special award for his lifetime of accomplishments in physics and, in particular, for the development of atomic energy." In 1955, the Institute for Nuclear Studies was renamed the Enrico Fermi Institute for Nuclear Studies (now the Enrico Fermi Institute) in his memory. The Fermi National Accelerator Laboratory (Fermilab) in Batavia, Illinois, was also named for him, as was the element fermium. The Enrico Fermi Award, the U.S. government's oldest science and technology award, was established in 1956 as a memorial to the physicist whose work changed the world, and whose brilliance continues to inspire succeeding generations of scientists.

FACING PAGE: *Fermi inspecting equipment at Columbia University, January 1939, with the overlay of a plan for a neutronic reactor.* ABOVE: *Fermi with an electronics chassis used at the University of Chicago synchrocyclotron, 1948.* LEFT: *Fermi in New York on January 2, 1939.*

Chicago, IL
September 29, 2001
Place and Date of Issue

Richard Sheaff
Designer, Art Director

Eid

Eid mubarak!

This Arabic phrase, which means "blessed festival" or "May your religious holiday be blessed," is the happy greeting of Muslims during the two most important festivals—or eids—in the Islamic calendar: Eid al-Fitr and Eid al-Adha. This year the phrase *Eid mubarak* also appears on this stamp that commemorates these holidays and the blessings they bring. For an estimated six to seven million Muslims in the United States, this stamp is sure to add a colorful and festive touch to cards and letters. For non-Muslims, it represents an opportunity to learn more about the beliefs and traditions of their Muslim friends, neighbors, and coworkers.

The first day of the Muslim lunar month of Shawwal, Eid al-Fitr signifies "The Feast of Breaking the Fast" because it marks the end of Ramadan, the month of fasting. As prescribed in the Qur'an, the holy book of Islam, fasting during Ramadan begins from just before first light until sunset, when Muslims must abstain not only from food and drink, but also from evil thoughts, sexual activity, and smoking. Eid al-Fitr is observed by offering special alms with prayers, feasting, exchanging gifts, and visiting family and friends.

Signifying "The Feast of the Sacrifice," Eid al-Adha occurs approximately two months and ten days after Eid al-Fitr. Eid al-Adha comes at the end of the hajj—the annual period of pilgrimage to the holy city of Mecca—and commemorates

Ibrahim's willingness to sacrifice his son Ismail. Eid al-Adha is celebrated with prayers and social gatherings and traditionally includes the sacrifice of a lamb, or another animal permitted for food in Islam, as an act of thanksgiving for Allah's mercy. The sacrificial animal is distributed among family, friends, and the poor.

Tradition played an important role in the development of this beautiful stamp. Calligrapher Mohamed Zakariya chose a script known in Arabic as *thuluth* and in Turkish as *sulus*, describing it as "the choice script for a complex composition due to its open proportions and sense of balance." He used homemade black ink, and his pens were crafted from seasoned reeds from the Near East and Japanese bamboo from Hawaii. For the original artwork, Zakariya used paper that was specially prepared with a coating of starch and three coats of alum and egg-white varnish, then burnished with an agate stone and aged for more than a

year. He and art director Phil Jordan then employed modern technology, colorizing the artwork by computer to create a blue-and-gold design reminiscent of great works of Islamic calligraphy. The end result is a graceful stamp design that can be enjoyed by all Americans for its elegant expression of holiday greetings.

FACING PAGE: *The Islamic Center of Washington, D.C.* ABOVE: *A prayer rug from 18th-century Turkey.* BELOW: *The sun sets behind the Sultan Ahmet Mosque, also known as the Blue Mosque, in Istanbul.*

Chicago, IL
September 1, 2001
Place and Date of Issue

Mohamed Zakariya
Calligrapher, Designer

Phil Jordan
Art Director

23

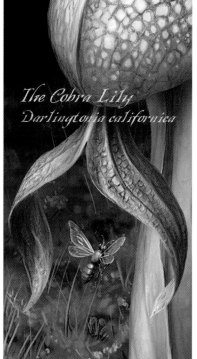

The Cobra Lily
Darlingtonia californica

Carnivorous Plants

Cartoonish depictions of carnivorous plants as voracious, bloodthirsty killers have long lingered in the popular imagination, with further inaccurate myths created by overblown scenes of hapless jungle explorers wandering into the cruel clutches of "man-eating plants." In actuality, these plants are not the aggressive monsters of fantasy, but graceful botanical wonders that demonstrate one of nature's most bizarre role reversals.

Native to North America, the four strangely beautiful plants featured on these stamps have evolved to thrive in mineral-poor soil by feeding on nutrients from the unfortunate prey that chance to land on them. These fascinating plants are a living testimony to nature's remarkable powers of adaptation, and they capture the imagination of anyone fortunate enough to discover them.

The Venus flytrap (*Dionaea muscipula*) is shown with a little metalmark—a kind of butterfly—caught in one of its leaves.

Chicago, IL
August 23, 2001
Place and Date of Issue

Steve Buchanan
Illustrator, Designer

Phil Jordan
Art Director

These small plants have traps ranging from one to two inches long. From Myrtle Beach, South Carolina, to central North Carolina, the Venus flytrap is found in moist, sandy areas near the coast.

Meanwhile, a fly perches on the lip of the yellow trumpet (*Sarracenia flava*), also known as the trumpet or yellow pitcherplant. If the fly enters the tube of the plant, the yellow trumpet's stiff, downward-pointing hairs help prevent the insect from escaping. Once caught in the trap, the insect drowns and is digested in a pool of water and enzymes in the bottom of the plant. Found in the southeastern United States, mature yellow trumpets grow to be 30 to 35 inches (and occasionally up to 48 inches) tall.

An unwary wasp is drawn toward the mouth of the cobra lily (*Darlingtonia californica*), a plant native to the West Coast. Sometimes called California pitcher plant or cobra plant, the cobra lily's colorations and fragrant nectar lure insects into its tubular leaves. Once inside, insects are prevented from escaping by a collar around the entrance.

The Yellow Trumpet
Sarracenia flava

The English Sundew
Drosera anglica

The English sundew (*Drosera anglica*) is a small plant that uses its sticky leaves to trap insects such as the unlucky syrphid fly caught by the sundew on the stamp. These plants are found in mossy bogs across the northern latitudes of the United States and along the West Coast as far south as California.

The Venus Flytrap
Dionaea muscipula

Baseball's Legendary Playing Fields

They have been called "green cathedrals," the beloved ballparks where young and old have thrilled to some of the finest moments in Major League Baseball. Unlike professional basketball courts and football fields, which are measured with exacting precision, baseball fields have varied greatly in size for more than a century. Since they were often integrated into the preexisting grids of city streets, many of these playing fields were also asymmetrical, giving rise to quirks and irregularities that endeared each park to fans and players alike. The individual character of each field has made for some of the game's most memorable and unexpected plays. Although only four of these fields still exist, for baseball fans everywhere they are shrines to America's national pastime, places where history, tradition, and legend all intersect in chalk lines on the grass.

Crosley Field in Cincinnati was the scene of a pivotal moment in baseball history. On May 24, 1935, President Franklin D. Roosevelt switched on the lights at Crosley Field from the White House, inaugurating the first Major League night game. Crosley Field is remembered not only for its intimacy, but also for a notorious four-foot incline in left field that often vexed outfielders.

With its angled right field wall and a sign that won batters a new suit when they hit it, Ebbets Field in Brooklyn was a quirky stadium indeed—but it was also a place where history was made. On August 26, 1939, the Major League Baseball television debut occurred there; and on April 15, 1947, Jackie Robinson took his position as first baseman for the Dodgers at Ebbets Field and forever broke baseball's color barrier.

RIGHT: *Fans at a World Series game in October 1945.*

Major League Baseball trademarks and copyrights are used with permission of Major League Baseball Properties, Inc.

Memorable for its graceful arched windows, Comiskey Park in Chicago was a symmetrical playing field that favored pitchers with an unusually long distance between the backstop and home plate. The first All-Star Game was held there in 1933, with a home run and a single by Babe Ruth leading the American League to a 4–2 victory.

Forbes Field in Pittsburgh also favored pitchers with its expansive foul territory and deep outfield dimensions. Ironically, in the 61 years that the Pittsburgh Pirates called the field home, no one ever pitched a no-hitter there.

Razed in 1964, the Polo Grounds in New York City was one of the more storied Major League Baseball playing fields. Onetime home to the Giants, the Yankees, and, briefly, the Mets, this horseshoe-shaped field was the site of the entire 1921 and 1922 World Series. It also hosted one of the most famous home runs in baseball: the 1951 "Shot Heard 'Round the World," a three-run homer by Giants third baseman Bobby Thomson.

The first concrete-and-steel Major League Baseball stadium, Shibe Park in Philadelphia featured a 34-foot-high right field wall. The park's facade was especially striking, with its stately columns and a French Renaissance cupola. Badly damaged by fire in 1971, Shibe Park was razed in 1976.

Sportsman's Park in St. Louis was demolished in 1966, but for 33 years it had joint occupants: the Browns and the Cardinals. This field is remembered for hosting a number of entertaining spectacles: in the 1930s, fans enjoyed the antics of the Cardinals' Gas House Gang, and in

LEFT: *Dreaming of baseball glory in 1948.*

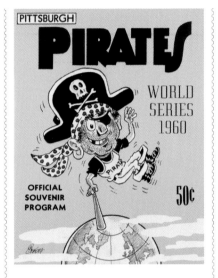

"*They had their faults, no doubt, but they had magic as well, magic that will live for years in the memories of those who were lucky enough to have passed through their turnstiles.*"

— LAWRENCE S. RITTER, LOST BALLPARKS

Detroit, MI
Boston, MA
Chicago, IL
New York, NY
June 27, 2001
Places and Date of Issue

Phil Jordan
Designer, Art Director

1951 the Browns' flamboyant owner put a 65-pound, 3-foot-7-inch player up to bat as a promotional stunt.

Yankee Stadium has hosted more World Series games than any other ballpark. Don Larsen pitched a perfect World Series game there on October 8, 1956; and during Game Six of the 1977 Series, Reggie Jackson hit three consecutive home runs to lead the Yankees to victory. Nostalgia can overwhelm visitors to this historic stadium, where monuments and plaques behind the left-center field fence honor Yankee greats.

Wrigley Field, with its ivy-covered walls, a hand-operated scoreboard, and more day than night games, is still a beloved Chicago landmark. The wind at Wrigley Field is legendary: When it blows out of the park, scores can enter double digits; when it blows in, the field is a pitcher's delight.

Boston's Fenway Park, one of the more intimate baseball stadiums, is the home of the Green Monster, a 37-foot-high left field wall. Red Sox fielders who mastered its unpredictable caroms became legends. Fenway hosted what is considered one of the most memorable baseball games of all time. During the sixth game of the 1975 World Series, a hit by Carlton Fisk in the twelfth inning bounced off the left foul pole for a home run that won the game and tied the Series.

The fate of Tiger Stadium, home to the Detroit Tigers for 88 seasons, remains uncertain. Opened in 1912 as Navin Field, this beloved ballpark put fans very close to the field, and later featured a right field upper deck that jutted out ten feet farther than the lower deck.

Frida Kahlo

"I paint self-portraits because I am so often alone,"

she explained, "because I am the person I know best."

In the intensely autobiographical paintings of Frida Kahlo, one recurring subject appears in many guises: the image of Kahlo herself, painted with an iconic directness that has stunned and moved admirers of her artwork for decades.

Born Magdalena Carmen Frida Kahlo y Calderón in Coyoacán, Mexico, in 1907, Frida Kahlo was stricken by polio as a child. The disease was only the beginning of her ailments: At the age of 18, the bus she was riding collided with a trolley. She suffered horrific injuries that haunted her, physically and emotionally, for the rest of her life—but her convalescence from this traumatic accident also prompted her career as an artist. To pass time, the young, bedridden Kahlo painted lying down using a special easel, beginning the long process of baring her soul in her artwork.

Her physical suffering, her inability to bear children, her tumultuous marriage to Mexican muralist Diego Rivera—Kahlo reworked all of these experiences into blunt and sometimes disturbing paintings that challenge the viewer with their candor and honesty. Her most common subject was herself, and her numerous self-portraits reveal acutely personal details about her thoughts and obsessions. But she was unapologetic about the intensity with which she examined her own heart and mind, seeing self-portraiture as a natural extension of the conditions of her life. "I paint self-portraits because I am so often alone," she explained, "because I am the person I know best."

Plagued by health problems until her death in 1954, Kahlo acknowledged her pain and sadness while nurturing, in one of her last works of art, a remarkable sense of hope. Completed shortly before she died, the painting of cut watermelons against a cloudy blue sky includes the slogan VIVA LA VIDA, "Long live life"—an inspiring testament to her enduring strength and passion.

Since the mid-1970s, Kahlo has been a role model for women in the Mexican-American and feminist communities, and her work has significantly influenced Chicana artists in the United States. For Kahlo's many fans and admirers, her home in Coyoacán serves as both a vibrant memorial and a museum that celebrates her art and life. Like her home, this stamp is a reminder of the persistence of her artistic vision.

FACING PAGE: *A late 1930s photograph by renowned portrait photographer Nickolas Muray.* ABOVE: *Kahlo with a portrait of Jean Wright, the wife of one of Diego Rivera's assistants, in 1931.* LEFT: *Kahlo in 1944.*

Phoenix, AZ
June 21, 2001
Place and Date of Issue

Richard Sheaff
Designer, Art Director

Porky Pig

Never one to hog all the attention, Porky Pig is joined on the final Looney Tunes souvenir sheet by the other characters who appeared in this stamp series.

Porky Pig, diligent mail carrier: It's just one of the many roles this veteran of more than 160 cartoons has played—and appropriately enough, it's his trademark farewell, "That's all Folks!," that concludes the popular Looney Tunes series of stamps.

Porky Pig was the first bona fide star of the Looney Tunes cast. He made his debut in "I Haven't Got a Hat," an animated short in which he performed in a musical and stammered his way through a poetry recital. Porky Pig has popped up in a number of humorous and unexpected roles, especially in his early years when he appeared variously as a young suitor, a father, and even a child. Later he became a more consistent personality with a gentle stammer, wide-eyed appearance, and boyish nature—the popular porcine performer we know and love today.

But Porky Pig didn't always work alone: He and Daffy Duck formed an unforgettable comic team, whether he was hunting the uncatchable Daffy Duck or serving as his affable sidekick. Porky Pig played a roly-poly Friar Tuck to Daffy Duck's Robin Hood, he was a sensible "Watkins" to Daffy Duck's "Dorlock Holmes," and, playing the role of a space cadet, he even followed the egomaniacal Daffy Duck to the stars. Whatever the situation, Porky Pig was never inclined to ham it up, offsetting Daffy Duck's lunacy with innocence and likeable simplicity.

Never one to hog all the attention, Porky Pig is joined on the final Looney Tunes souvenir sheet by the other characters who appeared in this stamp series: Bugs Bunny, Sylvester and Tweety, Daffy Duck, and Wile E. Coyote and Road Runner. Porky Pig may be saying "That's all Folks!" but as these stamps appear on letters and cards, they're sure to be enjoyed again and again—just like the Looney Tunes cartoons themselves.

**Burbank, CA
October 1, 2001**
Place and Date of Issue

Ed Wleczyk
Illustrator, Designer

Frank Espinosa
Character Art

Brenda Guttman
Concept

Terrence W. McCaffrey
Art Director

"*That's all Folks!*"

Honoring Veterans

"Our servicemen and women shoulder the burden of defense as one of the responsibilities of citizenship in this free country. Having participated in protecting our rights and having met opposition on the battlegrounds of the world, they are able to appreciate and savor the blessings of citizenship in the country they serve."

— *The Honorable Melvin Laird, Former Secretary of Defense, 1972*

They have served in times of peace and in times of war. They have answered the call overseas without hesitation, traveling over land and ocean without rest. But once their active duty is complete, our nation's estimated 25 million veterans don't stand idly by; many of them join veterans service organizations, where they continue to serve the country, their fellow veterans, and their communities.

These organizations provide invaluable aid to veterans and their families. For example, completing benefit applications for educational programs or medical care can be a confusing task, but volunteers are there to offer a helping hand with paperwork. They're also there to lend a ride by providing transportation to VA medical facilities, and they brighten the days of hospitalized veterans with their friendly, understanding visits.

America's veterans are also at work in our communities, directing youth sports activities and other programs designed

ABOVE: *Members of VFW Post 10556 in Boca Raton, Florida, visit with a patient at the West Palm Beach VA Medical Center.*

to promote civic pride. The scholarship programs of some veterans service organizations help to send deserving young men and women to college, while other organizations provide support for children in need. They can change, or even save, many young lives with their important drug-abuse prevention programs and immunization services.

At the same time, veterans service organizations are also active in Washington, D.C. Speaking on behalf of millions of veterans, they lobby Congress on a variety of issues and fight for the rights of the men and women who have served the nation.

Featuring the American flag, one of the most recognized symbols of freedom in the world, this stamp is a reminder of our veterans, who lead by example with their patriotism and service.

Washington, DC
May 23, 2001
Place and Date of Issue

Harold M. Lambert Studios, Inc.
Photographer

Carl Herrman
Designer, Art Director

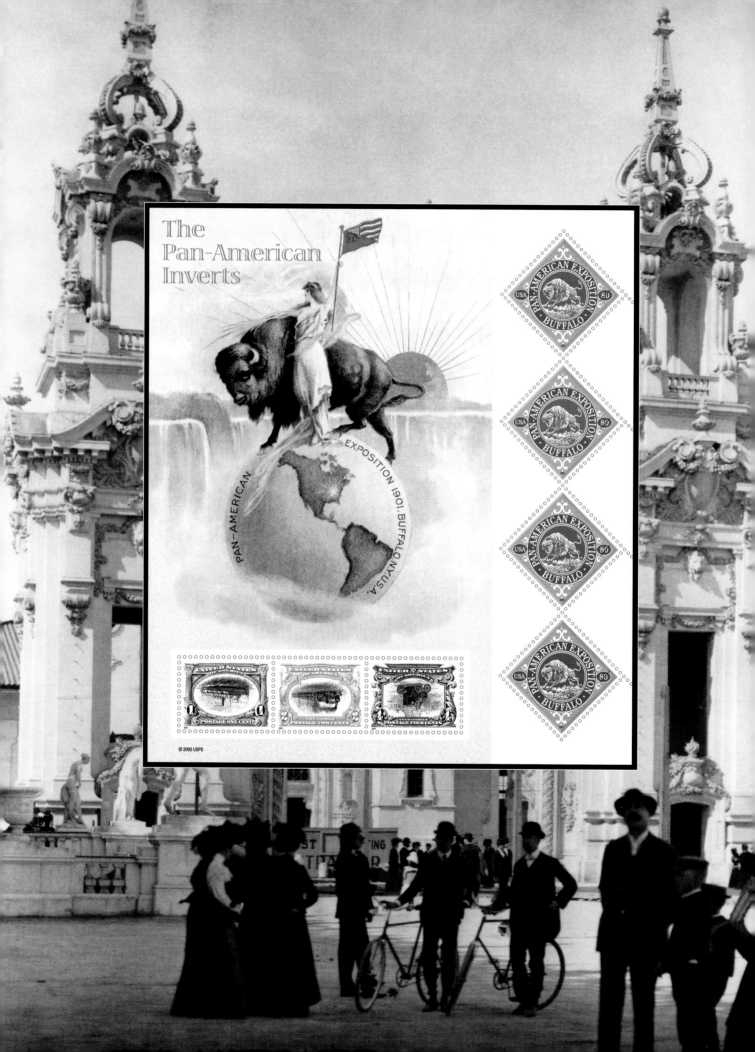

Pan-American Inverts

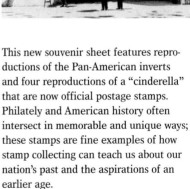

In 1901, an almost unreal city rose on nearly 350 acres of land outside downtown Buffalo, New York, an ornate confection of multicolored pavilions, regal statues, and graceful minarets. Although this wonderland existed for only a few months, visitors marveled at the bright facades of Spanish Renaissance buildings and the impressive Electric Tower looming nearly 400 feet overhead. From international exhibitions to a courtyard of fountains, the many attractions combined to create a grand and exciting spectacle: the Pan-American Exposition.

Designed to celebrate the accomplishments of the 19th century, the Pan-American Exposition highlighted achievements in industry, transportation, manufacturing, and the arts. Held from May 1 through November 2, 1901, the exposition was sponsored by the state of New York, the federal government, and the Buffalo business community. Visitors

New York, NY
March 29, 2001
Place and Date of Issue

Richard Sheaff
Designer, Art Director

wandered among the colorful displays, enjoying such attractions as a mirror maze, a reproduction of an ancient Greek stadium, and a simulated journey to the moon. For stamp collectors, however, the Pan-American Exposition is best remembered as an event that contributed to philatelic history.

On opening day of the exposition, the U.S. Post Office Department issued a series of six bicolored stamps commemorating the exposition. The stamps celebrated the theme of transportation and were on sale from May 1 through October 31, 1901. A limited number of the stamp sheets were accidentally printed with inverted stamp centers: the one-cent stamp depicting the steamship *City of Alpena*, the two-cent stamp depicting the train *Empire State Express*, and the four-cent stamp depicting an early electric automobile. The rare inverts quickly became collectibles.

This new souvenir sheet features reproductions of the Pan-American inverts and four reproductions of a "cinderella" that are now official postage stamps. Philately and American history often intersect in memorable and unique ways; these stamps are fine examples of how stamp collecting can teach us about our nation's past and the aspirations of an earlier age.

FACING PAGE: *Outside a gate at the Pan-American Exposition.* ABOVE LEFT: *Visitors stroll along a promenade within sight of the Electric Tower.* ABOVE CENTER: *Souvenirs from the exposition included this tin beer tray.* ABOVE RIGHT: *The entrance to the exposition's Dreamland ride.*

Lucille Ball

The *I Love Lucy* writers called it her "spider voice," the unmistakable sound that Lucy Ricardo made when her crazy schemes finally caught up with her. Unfortunately for her, she had reason to make that sound again and again. But audiences loved her, just as they adored the ingenious comedienne who played her: Lucille Ball.

To friends and fans alike she was known simply as Lucy, a regular fixture on American television for nearly three decades. She starred in *The Lucille Ball-Desi Arnaz Show* (1957–1960), *The Lucy Show* (1962–1968), *Here's Lucy* (1968–1974), and *Life with Lucy* (1986). But it was *I Love Lucy*, which ran from 1951 to 1957, that made her a television superstar.

The show, which teamed Ball with her real-life husband Desi Arnaz, chronicled the unlikely adventures of a wacky, red-headed housewife and her husband, Cuban bandleader Ricky Ricardo. *I Love Lucy* showcased Lucille Ball's extraordinary gift for physical comedy. Lucy getting increasingly tipsy while filming a "Vitameatavegamin" commercial, Lucy overwhelmed by the speed of a conveyor belt in a candy factory—audiences never knew what sort of fix she would get herself into each week, but they couldn't wait to find out.

Ball was a versatile performer whose talents extended well beyond the small screen. She acted alongside Richard Denning in *My Favorite Husband*, a CBS radio comedy that ran from 1948 to 1951 and served as a precursor to *I Love Lucy*. She also appeared in more than 70 movies opposite leading men such as Eddie Cantor, Bob Hope, Henry Fonda—and, of course, Desi Arnaz.

Behind the scenes, America's "queen of comedy" also ruled the boardroom. When Desi Arnaz retired as president of Desilu Studios in 1962, Ball purchased his entire holdings and became the first woman president of a major Hollywood production company. She later sold it and formed her own company, Lucille Ball Productions.

Lucille Ball won four Emmy Awards, was one of the first inductees into the Academy of Television Arts & Sciences Hall of Fame in 1984, and received the Kennedy Center Honors in 1986. She was posthumously awarded the Presidential Medal of Freedom in 1989 by George H. W. Bush, who hailed her as "a national treasure who brought laughter to us all."

This seventh stamp in the Legends of Hollywood series serves as a reminder of her wit, her charm, her willingness to climb into a vat of grapes simply to make us laugh—all the reasons everyone still loves Lucy.

TOP: *En route to California with Ricky and the Mertzes in a 1955 episode of* I Love Lucy. ABOVE: *Ball with Red Skelton in the 1943 film* Du Barry Was a Lady. LEFT: *An elegant studio portrait of Ball from the 1950s.* RIGHT: *Ball at the makeup mirror during the filming of* Kid Millions, *1934.*

Los Angeles, CA
August 6, 2001
Place and Date of Issue

Drew Struzan
Illustrator

Derry Noyes
Designer, Art Director

GREAT PLAINS PRAIRIE

THIRD IN A SERIES

N A T U R E   O F   A M E R I C A

Great Plains Prairie

In the 19th century, the prairie overwhelmed the senses. Billowing grasses extended for miles in every direction, receding to the distant horizon where the earth joins the sky. On these windy plains, a visitor standing among the purple prairie clover and wild roses could be met by the sounds of far-off bison—or by the suspicious eyes of a thousand watchful prairie dogs.

Stretching from the edge of the eastern woodlands and oak savannas to the foothills of the Rocky Mountains, the prairie is an important part of the landscape. Many people often underestimate the American prairie's complexity and significance as an ecosystem; in fact, it is one of the largest grasslands in the world.

The varied tapestry of the tallgrass, mixed-grass, and short-grass prairies provides habitats for many animals— including humans. The fertile soils of the American prairie have supported farmers and ranchers in the midwestern states for more than a century. The cultivation of crops and grazing of cattle have altered the prairie, but patches of native vegetation remain, largely because of careful management and diligent preservation efforts. Grass and wildflowers make good use of limited rainfall, and fire helps sustain the ecosystem, clearing the prairie of dead vegetation, rejuvenating overgrazed portions of the landscape, and prompting new shoots to rise from the warmed soil.

ABOVE: *Black-tailed prairie dogs.*

The grasslands teem with life. Prairie dogs are a familiar sight, with thousands of them living in labyrinthine burrows. Research indicates that they use a sophisticated system of communication to warn each other about approaching predators. Their large and complex "towns" provide shelter for a number of other prairie-dwelling animals—even rattlesnakes.

Many prairie animals are extremely adept at burrowing. The plains spadefoot, a toad, spends summers in tiny burrows dug with its hind legs, and the plains pocket gopher burrows to protect itself from predators, extreme weather, or fire. Even the burrowing owl has adapted to the nearly treeless terrain of the prairie in a particularly fascinating way: It nests underground in deserted prairie dog chambers and badger holes. This constant digging by so many prairie animals loosens and aerates the soil, offsetting the effect of large grazing animals such as bison that compact it with their hooves.

Great speed is also an important prairie adaptation. With its oversized lungs and windpipe, as well as a very large heart, the pronghorn—North America's fastest land animal—is well prepared to bound across the prairie. Even some snakes and lizards are exceptionally fast—a trait that allows them to be both easy predators or difficult prey.

ABOVE: *A painted lady butterfly.* RIGHT: *A pronghorn, North America's fastest land animal.* OPPOSITE ABOVE: *Swainson's hawk.* OPPOSITE BELOW: *A prairie rattlesnake.*

Bison, the iconic animal of the plains, are also fast for their size. Although some bulls weigh more than a ton, they can sometimes reach speeds of up to 35 miles an hour. They also play an important role in the ecosystem: During rutting season, bison release some of their aggression on ponderosa pines that threaten to invade the grasslands, and the waste that the animals leave behind adds valuable nutrients to the soil. Bison once roamed the prairie by the millions; today they survive in carefully managed herds on parklands and reservations, with cattle replacing them as the dominant grazing animal.

"These are the gardens of the desert," wrote poet William Cullen Bryant of the prairie, "these / The unshorn fields, boundless and beautiful, / For which the speech of England has no name." The prairie may have changed a great deal since Bryant was moved to write these lines in the 19th century, but the defining characteristics of the land live on. This stamp pane, illustrated by John D. Dawson, allows us all to learn more about the prairie—a fascinating part of the nature of America.

Lincoln, NE
April 19, 2001
Place and Date of Issue

John D. Dawson
Illustrator

Ethel Kessler
Designer, Art Director

Amish Quilts

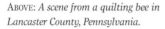

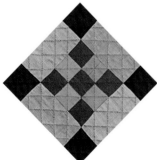

ABOVE: *A scene from a quilting bee in Lancaster County, Pennsylvania.*

With their gorgeous, hypnotic patterns, Amish quilts have become more than simply utilitarian objects. They are both records of the skill of the women who created them—the wives and daughters of farmers—as well as quietly beautiful works of art that are clearly American treasures.

Distinct in their simplicity and symmetry, Amish quilts are a uniquely American folk art form, as well as one of the most expressive traditions in American design. Their deft needlework and broad fields of deep color combine to create works of striking beauty. Robert Hughes, art critic for *Time* magazine, has commented that a fine Amish quilt is notable for "a spare-ness of design just pulled back from dogmatic rigor by its inventive quirks, a magnificent sobriety of color, a balanced amplitude of conception, a truly human sense of scale." Although strongly influenced by family and community traditions that determine specific patterns and designs, each quilt is a unique work representing the deeply personal touch of its creators.

Amish quilting traditions vary from region to region, but they are all influenced by the religious and social values of Amish daily life: humility, simplicity, modesty, and serviceability. The four quilts featured on these stamps display the saturated colors, bold geometric patterns, and central design motifs characteristic of quilts made in Lancaster County, Pennsylvania, during the first half of the 20th century.

Nappanee, IN
August 9, 2001
Place and Date of Issue

Derry Noyes
Designer, Art Director

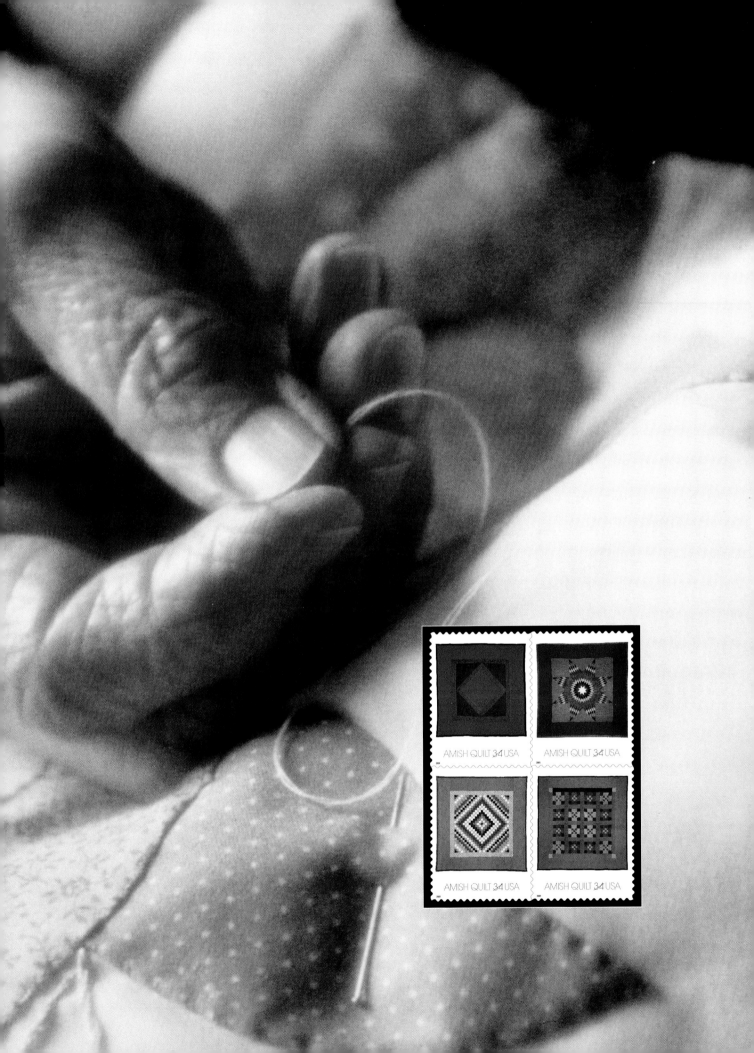

Diabetes

It was the seventh leading cause of death in the United States in 1996 and 1997—but about one-third of all Americans with diabetes don't even know they have it. With the issuance of the Diabetes stamp, the U.S. Postal Service continues a tradition of raising public awareness of health and social issues by highlighting a disease that affects 16 million people in the United States. Diabetes is a serious matter—but knowing more about it could save your life or the life of someone you love.

Most people have heard of diabetes, but not nearly enough people understand its dangers. Diabetes is a chronic disease that prevents the body from making enough insulin or prevents it from using insulin effectively. Insulin is a hormone that helps cells take in glucose, or sugar. By interfering with the production or use of insulin, diabetes deprives cells of energy and causes a buildup of glucose in the blood.

There are different types of diabetes, and nearly anyone you see on the street could potentially have the disease. However, diabetes is more prevalent among African Americans, Hispanic Americans, American Indians and Alaska Natives, and Asian Americans and Pacific Islanders. Among the risk factors are age, obesity, a sedentary lifestyle, and a family history of diabetes. Complications from diabetes include blindness, heart disease, stroke, nervous system damage, amputation, kidney disease, and gum disease.

There is still no cure for diabetes; however, the disease can be managed with proper diet, weight control, exercise, blood glucose testing, and—depending on the type of diabetes—oral medication or insulin injections. Researchers are currently focusing on discovering the causes of diabetes, finding ways to prevent and cure the disease, and learning how to prevent and treat its complications.

The design of this new stamp, featuring an acrylic-and-gouache painting by artist James Steinberg, conveys the importance of diabetes awareness and early detection.

LEFT: *Proponents of increased funding for diabetes research during the American Diabetes Association Rally for a Cure.* ABOVE: *Using a glucose test strip to check blood sugar level.*

Boston, MA
March 16, 2001
Place and Date of Issue

James Steinberg
Illustrator

Richard Sheaff
Designer, Art Director

Leonard Bernstein

With his phenomenal gifts as a conductor, composer, pianist, teacher, and author, Leonard Bernstein brought worldwide recognition to American composers and musicians. Whether composing music in a vast range of genres, conducting the world's great orchestras, or appearing on television to explain Beethoven's Fifth Symphony with clarity and wit, Bernstein awed the nation and the world with his genius, sharing with grateful audiences his unbridled love of the universal power of music.

Born August 25, 1918, in Lawrence, Massachusetts, Bernstein began piano lessons as a boy, graduating from Harvard University in 1939 with a degree in music. The young musician continued his studies at the Curtis Institute of Music in Philadelphia, earning a diploma in conducting in 1941. He also received training at the Berkshire Music Center at Tanglewood in Massachusetts.

In August 1943, Bernstein was named assistant conductor of the New York Philharmonic, and within a few months he soon found himself thrust into the spotlight. On November 14, he was asked

to substitute for guest conductor Bruno Walter, who was ill. Without time to rehearse, the 25-year-old Bernstein took the podium at Carnegie Hall and led the orchestra through its entire program in a nationally broadcast concert that included complex works by Schumann, Rózsa, Strauss, and Wagner. *The New York Times* raved about the performance, and soon orchestras worldwide were inviting him to serve as guest conductor.

From 1945 to 1947, Bernstein was the musical director of the New York City Symphony orchestra. In 1958 he was appointed music director of the New York Philharmonic, the first U.S.-born and trained conductor to hold that position. He retired in 1969 to become laureate conductor, and on December 15, 1971, he conducted his 1,000th concert with the Philharmonic—an unprecedented achievement in the history of the orchestra.

Bernstein's own compositions were breathtakingly versatile. He wrote symphonies, chamber music, and vocal music, as well as works for ballet, opera, film, and the Broadway musical stage. Several of his compositions, including the symphonies *Jeremiah* and *Kaddish*, also celebrate his Jewish heritage. His many contributions to musical theater include scores for *On the Town*, *Wonderful Town*, the comic operetta *Candide*, and *West Side Story*, which was made into an Academy Award–winning film. He received an Academy Award nomination for his score for the film *On the Waterfront*, as well as many Emmy and Grammy Awards.

Bernstein set an example for American musicians with a sublime and accomplished life that was, in his own words, "dedicated to communication, to sharing the wonder of experience with other people."

FACING PAGE: *Bernstein conducts a rehearsal of the New York Philharmonic, c.1960.* LEFT: *Bernstein and the New York Philharmonic rehearse in Hamburg, Germany, in 1959.* ABOVE: *Bernstein conducting Brahms, c.1986.*

New York, NY
July 10, 2001
Place and Date of Issue

Don Hunstein
Photographer

Howard Paine
Designer, Art Director

Thanksgiving

"The year that is drawing toward its close," proclaimed Abraham Lincoln, "has been filled with the blessings of fruitful fields and healthful skies. To these bounties, which are so constantly enjoyed that we are prone to forget the source from which they come, others have been added, which are of so extraordinary a nature, that they cannot fail to penetrate and soften even the

heart which is habitually insensible to the ever watchful providence of Almighty God." The 16th President issued this proclamation in 1863, marking the beginning of national recognition of an annual Thanksgiving holiday in the United States.

The timing of this proclamation was especially important: The nation was in the midst of the Civil War. The President nonetheless enumerated reasons to give thanks: "order has been maintained, the laws have been respected and obeyed, and harmony has prevailed everywhere except in the theatre of military conflict." Lincoln also stressed the nation's prosperity: "Needful diversions of wealth and of strength from the fields of peaceful industry to the national defence, have not arrested the plough, the shuttle, or the ship." Lincoln was suggesting that even in the face of hardship, there is always something to be thankful for.

The Thanksgiving stamp serves as a reminder of the rich history of traditions underlying our modern celebration.

Award-winning artist Margaret Cusack designed and created the machine-appliquéd needlework depicting a cornucopia overflowing with fruits and vegetables. The needlework, which is partially quilted and made of old and new fabrics, is reminiscent of American folk art stitchery. This stamp's image of abundance reminds us to give thanks for the blessings of prosperity—a hopeful thought that unites Americans as they gather on the fourth Thursday of every November to celebrate among family and friends.

Other works by Thanksgiving stamp artist Margaret Cusack include "Country Celebration" (above) and "Mom with Turkey" (facing page).

Dallas, TX
October 2001
Place and Date of Issue

Margaret Cusack
Illustrator

Richard Sheaff
Designer, Art Director

Peanuts
Fifty years? Good grief!

For nearly five decades, newspaper readers enjoyed new installments in the adventures of the "Peanuts" gang: Snoopy, Lucy, Linus, Schroeder, Sally—and a boy named Charlie Brown. When the last original "Peanuts" comic strip appeared on February 13, 2000, its creator, Charles M. Schulz, had drawn more than 18,000 strips, prompting a commentator on PBS to suggest that "Peanuts" was "arguably the longest story told by a single artist in human history."

"Peanuts" has found a permanent place not only in the hearts of fans everywhere, but also in American culture, and the language of this beloved comic strip has become a part of our national vocabulary. The term "security blanket" now appears in dictionaries, and the phrase "Happiness is a warm puppy" can be found in *Bartlett's Familiar Quotations*. Call someone "Pig-Pen" and the reference is clear; and when someone mentions a "Charlie Brown Christmas tree" that just needs a little love, we know exactly what that means.

The success of "Peanuts" was clearly based upon its characters—at times loveable, difficult, frustrating, imaginative, or philosophical. Schulz drew the comic

Santa Rosa, CA
May 17, 2001
Place and Date of Issue

Paige Braddock,
Charles M. Schulz Creative Associates
Designer

Carl Herrman
Art Director

ABOVE: *Charles M. Schulz in 1968.* RIGHT: *A photo of Schulz taken in the 1990s.*

strip from a kid's-eye view, and adults, though alluded to, never appeared. Instead, the world of "Peanuts" was populated with an ensemble cast of children who often seemed wise beyond their years. Once, when Charlie Brown lamented another wildly unsuccessful baseball game, he was joined on the pitcher's mound by his entire team as they cited scripture and pondered the nature of human suffering. "I don't have a ball team," he concluded wryly, "I have a theological seminary!"

Offsetting the quietly profound commentary and gentle philosophy was the irrepressible Snoopy. When Snoopy first stood on his hind legs in 1958, he became a star, and his imaginative adventures became the stuff of comic-strip legends. Like a canine Walter Mitty, Snoopy could be nearly anyone or anything: unflappable college student Joe Cool; a foreign legionnaire; a world-famous attorney; or an ominous, looming vulture. Perhaps his best-known exploits were as a World War I flying ace, locked in aerial dogfights with his eternal nemesis, the Red Baron, or crawling along the frontline trenches of wartime France in search of root beer

and a quiet table in a café. Charlie Brown may have lamented, "Why can't I have a normal dog like everyone else?"— but even those of us who sympathized with his exasperation eagerly waited to see what Snoopy would do next.

Remembered by Lee Mendelson, producer of the "Peanuts" television specials, as "an artist, a philosopher, a humorist, and most of all, a true gentleman," Charles M. Schulz used his wit and wisdom to bring the pint-size world of "Peanuts" to life. Born in Minneapolis, Minnesota, in 1922, Schulz began his fascination with comic strips early, reading the Sunday comics from four different newspapers with his father each week. With encouragement from his parents, Schulz enrolled in a correspondence course in cartooning. His first break came when he sold a cartoon feature called "Li'l Folks" to the *St. Paul Pioneer Press,* and from 1948 to 1950 he sold 15 cartoon panels to *The Saturday Evening Post.* "Peanuts" debuted in syndication on October 2, 1950, and continued to grow in popularity, eventually inspiring a Broadway musical as well as numerous animated television specials and feature films.

Schulz drew every comic strip without the assistance of an art staff. He received countless honors, among them two Reuben Awards from the National Cartoonists Society, and he was inducted into the International Museum of Cartoon Art Hall of Fame. The year 2001 marks the intended date of completion of the Charles M. Schulz Museum and Research Center in Santa Rosa, California—a site that will celebrate Schulz's life and art and the wonderful legacy of "Peanuts."

In his final message to his fans, Schulz offered a touching tribute to the characters he had created and how important they had become to him: "Charlie Brown, Snoopy, Linus, Lucy . . . how can I ever forget them. . . ." Millions of readers share his sentiments. Although Schulz died on February 12, 2000, only hours before his last original "Peanuts" strip appeared in Sunday papers, classic installments of the comic strip continue to appear in some 2,600 newspapers in 75 countries. "Peanuts" is an American treasure that continues to delight the world.

Virgin and Child
by Lorenzo Costa

Some solemn and austere, others sensitive and highly moving, depictions of the Virgin and Child represent fascinating variations on a familiar theme. Rendered with care and devotion, these works encompass the full range of human emotion, offering diverse interpretations of a truly profound subject. Each year, the beauty and grace of traditional religious imagery reminds us of the spiritual bonds that connect us during the holiday season—a time for hope, reflection, and family.

Coinciding with the 125th anniversary of the Philadelphia Museum of Art, this latest offering in the Holiday Traditional series features a detail of Italian Renaissance painter Lorenzo Costa's oil-on-panel *Virgin and Child*, circa 1490. The painting is a part of the John G. Johnson Collection at the Philadelphia Museum of Art. Lorenzo Costa's work is well represented in major European galleries; this painting is a rare example of Costa's work in an American museum.

Lorenzo Costa (circa 1460–1535) was born in the northern Italian town of Ferrara. In the 1480s he moved to Bologna, where he received the patronage of the ruling Bentivoglio family. Costa's work includes altarpieces, frescoes, portraits, and allegories, and his major commissions for Bolognese churches are considered among his best. In 1506, Costa succeeded Andrea Mantegna as the court painter to the ruling Gonzaga family in Mantua, where he remained until his death in 1535.

FACING PAGE: *A painting of the Nativity by Georges de La Tour, c.1645.* LEFT: *A sculpture attributed to Lorenzo Maitani, probably from the early 14th century.* TOP: *A painting by Raffaello Sanzio, better known as Raphael, from the early 16th century.* ABOVE: Adoration of the Magi *by Lorenzo Costa, c.1499.*

Philadelphia, PA
October 10, 2001
Place and Date of Issue

Richard Sheaff
Designer, Art Director

Santas

"His droll little mouth was drawn up like a bow,

And the beard of his chin was as white as the snow . . ."

— *Clement Moore, "A Visit from St. Nicholas," 1822*

Beloved by children and adults alike, Santa Claus wasn't always the familiar character we now see every Christmas. His distinctive appearance developed over the course of several centuries, and his legend has a long and complicated history. The chromolithographs featured on these Holiday Contemporary stamps remind us of the ways in which numerous cultures have contributed to the creation of a figure so rich in folklore and tradition.

Santa Claus began life as St. Nicholas, a fourth-century bishop in Asia Minor who was considered a generous gift giver and protector of children. Over time his reputation flourished throughout Europe, and eventually his legend became intertwined with the Christmas holiday. When the Dutch landed in the New World in 1624, they named St. Nicholas (Sinterklaas in Dutch) as their patron. In America the Dutch legend of

Santa Claus, IN
October 10, 2001
Place and Date of Issue

Richard Sheaff
Designer, Art Director

Sinterklaas merged with the English tradition of Father Christmas, creating the character that we know today as Santa Claus.

Chromolithography, a color printing process developed in the early 19th century, became more efficient and very popular as the century progressed. Chromolithographed die-cuts, also known as scrap pictures, were printed on paper and used for many different purposes. Christmas scrap pictures were used as decorations for holiday cookies and cakes, collected in scrapbooks, and hung as tree ornaments. Today such images are considered collectibles.

The Santas pictured on the upper left and lower right stamps probably date from the 1880s. They may have been designed in England and printed in Germany, and people may have purchased them and placed them in keepsake scrapbooks. The Santas appearing on the upper right and lower left stamps were printed in Germany and probably date

from between 1915 and 1920. Santas such as these may have been used to decorate *lebküchen*, a traditional German cookie.

LEFT: *This Santa promoted a boot and shoe company in the early 20th century.* BELOW: *A late 19th-century flour advertisement and holiday decoration.* FACING PAGE *A late 19th-century chromolithograph printed in Germany for a coffee company.*

We the People of the United States, in order to form a more perfect Union, establish Justice, insure domestic Tranquility, provide for the common defence, promote the general Welfare, and secure the Blessings of Liberty to ourselves and our Posterity, do ordain and establish this Constitution for the United States of America.

James Madison

Remembered for his political and intellectual accomplishments,

James Madison played a key role in developing the U.S. Constitution.

"My life has been so much of a public one," wrote James Madison in 1831, "that any review of it must mainly consist of the agency which was my lot in public transactions." On the 250th anniversary of his birth, Madison is remembered for his formative role in American government and politics— and as a man whose keen interest in ancient republics had a profound influence on the U.S. Constitution.

Born March 16, 1751, in Port Conway, Virginia, James Madison graduated from the College of New Jersey (later to become Princeton University) in 1771. Although an excellent student, Madison was a frail and often sickly young man, and his early correspondence indicates despondence regarding his health and career prospects.

"I am too dull and infirm now to look out for any extraordinary things in this world," he wrote to a friend in 1772, "for I think my sensations for many months past have intimated to me not to expect a long and healthy life." The young student of history and government could not

have known that he would be called the "father of the U.S. Constitution" and would serve as fourth President of the United States. But Madison soon found his vocation: In 1776, only four years after his pessimistic prediction, Madison was elected to the Virginia Constitutional Convention; in December 1779 he was elected to the Continental Congress.

Madison was instrumental in organizing the body of delegates that wrote the U.S. Constitution in 1787. He was also an important figure in its ratification, as his commentaries helped convince the citizens of New York to accept the new government. Later, while a member of the U.S. House of Representatives, Madison played a leading role in the creation and passage of the Bill of Rights.

After serving as President Thomas Jefferson's secretary of state for eight years, Madison was elected President in 1808. In June 1812, near the end of his first term, Madison asked Congress to declare war on Britain; he was reelected later that year. When the treaty to end the war was signed in 1814, his popularity surged.

Madison remained active even in retirement. He served as rector of the University of Virginia, and he advised President James Monroe on foreign policy. When he died at Montpelier, his Virginia home, on June 28, 1836, Madison left behind a note in which his final thoughts on the growing states' rights movement were clear and unequivocal. "The advice nearest to my heart and deepest in my convictions," he wrote, "is that the Union of the States be cherished and perpetuated."

New York, NY
October 18, 2001
Place and Date of Issue

John Thompson
Illustrator

Carl Herrman
Designer, Art Director

FACING PAGE: *Detail of an 1804 portrait of Madison by Gilbert Stuart, with the U.S. Constitution in the background.* ABOVE LEFT: *An 1884 print of Montpelier, Madison's Virginia home.* ABOVE: *A recent photograph of Montpelier.*

Photo Credits

Acknowledgments

These stamps and this stamp collecting book were produced by Public Affairs and Communications, Stamp Services, United States Postal Service.

John E. Potter
Postmaster General,
Chief Executive Officer

Deborah K. Willhite
Senior Vice President,
Government Relations and Public Policy

Azeezaly S. Jaffer
Vice President,
Public Affairs and Communications

Catherine Caggiano
Executive Director,
Stamp Services

Special thanks are extended to the following individuals for their contributions to the production of this book:

UNITED STATES POSTAL SERVICE

Terrence W. McCaffrey
Manager, Stamp Development

Kelly L. Spinks
Project Manager

HARPERCOLLINS PUBLISHERS

Megan Newman
Editorial Director,
HarperResource

Greg Chaput
Associate Editor,
HarperResource

Lucy Albanese
Design Director,
General Books Group

NIGHT & DAY DESIGN

Timothy Shaner
Art Director, Designer

PHOTOASSIST, INC.

Jeff Sypeck
Copywriter

Anne Pietromica
Text Research

Mike Owens
Photo Editor

Nell Whiting
Photo Researcher

Erin Ryan
Jeni Sheaffer
Rights and Permissions

THE CITIZENS' STAMP ADVISORY COMMITTEE

Dr. Virginia M. Noelke
Dr. C. Douglas Lewis
Ronald A. Robinson
Michael R. Brock
Meredith J. Davis
David Lewis Eynon
I. Michael Heyman
John M. Hotchner
Larry King
Karl Malden
Philip B. Meggs
Richard F. Phelps
John Sawyer III

20
OIL PAINTERS
AND HOW THEY WORK

20
OIL PAINTERS
AND HOW THEY WORK

FROM THE PAGES OF *AMERICAN ARTIST* **EDITED BY SUSAN E. MEYER**

WATSON-GUPTILL PUBLICATIONS/NEW YORK
PITMAN PUBLISHING/LONDON

First published 1978 in the United States and Canada
by Watson-Guptill Publications,
a division of Billboard Publications, Inc.,
1515 Broadway, New York, N.Y. 10036

Published in Great Britain by Pitman Publishing Ltd.,
39 Parker Street, London WC2B 5PB
ISBN 0-273-01282-7

Library of Congress Cataloging In Publication Data
Main entry under title:
20 oil painters and how they work.
  Includes index.
  1. Painting—Technique. 2. Painters—Psychology.
I. Meyer, Susan E. II. American artist.
ND1500.T86   1978   751.'5   78-9612
ISBN 0-8230-5491-8

Manufactured in Japan

First Printing, 1978

INTRODUCTION

In selecting these articles from *American Artist* magazine, I was struck again by the overwhelming differences that exist among painters. Their approach to oils is as individual as the qualities that distinguish their personalities. Therein, of course, lies the appeal of oil as a medium for the artist: it is what you make of it. For the painstaking, intellectual personality—one that tends to proceed from A to B with specific goals in mind—the medium is ideal: layer upon layer can be applied in the most determined sequence. On the other hand, for the artist whose disposition is changeable, oil is equally desirable: in each session, the artist can virtually start from scratch, changing direction in a single painting without penalty. Oil is no less attractive to the spontaneous but decisive personality who prefers to start and finish in one sitting, retaining the exuberance of an immediate inspiration.

But the differences only begin here. Given the basic distinctions in temperament that underlie the creative process, the specific methods an artist selects to attain an individual goal vary as greatly as the artistic temperament. However, these variations only enhance the rich potential of oil as a painting medium. Some artists represented here prefer a rich buildup of pigments, applying juicy dabs of paint with a palette knife. Others prefer the texture of the canvas to that of the pigmented surface, barely covering the surface with thin transparent layers. The colorist sees in oil the potential for juxtaposing areas of pigment, taking joy in the color subtleties obtainable in the medium. Others regard oil as a vehicle for good drawing, controlling the medium to obtain astonishing effects of realism.

Each of the artists whose work is reproduced in this book has been inspired in one way or another by artists of an earlier generation, and contemporary results reflect that inspiration. In the artists represented here, we see influences that range from seventeenth-century still-life painting to twentieth century Abstract Expressionism; yet no single influence dominates the American scene.

In fact, if this collection of personalities has any unifying theme, it's this: the creative process is a unique combination of temperament and medium ideally (but not always) working in harmony to achieve a highly personal vision. To that end, oil still remains the most popular medium for the contemporary painter.

Susan E. Meyer

CONTENTS

20
OIL PAINTERS
AND HOW THEY WORK

DOUGLAS ALLEN

BY BONNIE SILVERSTEIN

SOME PEOPLE ARE FORTUNATE enough to know very early in life what they want. Under the gentle guidance of loving, knowledgeable parents, they are introduced as children to a rich artistic heritage to which, instinctively and emotionally, they feel deep ties. They are special people, for they cannot only see the beauty in the art of the past, but they have that remarkable ability to incorporate what is best in it into their own art, building and transforming it for the pleasure of future generations. Douglas Allen is one of these fortunate few.

Allen's father, Douglas Allen Sr., a printing engineer for ESSO, was an avid collector and admirer of Frederic Remington. He even authored two books on the great painter of the West. By the time young Douglas was old enough to accompany his father Saturday mornings browsing in old bookshops on Book-

seller's Row in lower Manhattan, he knew he had already developed a natural interest in collecting old books.

Saturday mornings posed an exciting adventure. The bookstores they wandered through were musty, even in those days. But there were places such as Biblo & Tannen's where back shelves overflowed with children's books illustrated by such talents as Howard Pyle, A. B. Frost, Walter Crane, Arthur Rackham, Edmund Dulac, Maxfield Parrish, E. A. Wilson, Jessie Wilcox Smith, Frank E. Schoonover, and N. C. Wyeth. It was exciting for a collector then, when so many treasures were still available—and affordable.

Of all the artists who fascinated Allen, those from the Brandywine were the most compelling. The so-called Brandywine School of Illustration was actually the name given to the tradition first established

Left: *Solitary Moon* (American Bison), oil on canvas, 28 x 36. Courtesy Kennedy Galleries. Allen begins a painting such as this with abstract paper shapes, subject elements which he moves around until he's satisfied with their placement.

Right: *Mountain Lion,* oil on board, 22½ x 17½. Courtesy Outdoor Life Book Division. Illustration for *Game Animals of North America.* Allen places the mountain lion to emphasize the drama of his psychological position: trees, silhouetted against the sky above, and almost in the lap of the viewer.

At 14 Allen could proudly point to the first painting he ever owned. It was painted in 1887 by Howard Pyle, a black-and-white oil of pirates entitled *The Sacking of Panama.*

Besides his fascination with Pyle, N. C. Wyeth, and the other Brandywine artists, Allen was drawn to the early painters of the American West. His father's interest in Remington had led to a strong friendship with E. Walter Latendorf, the proprietor of Mannado's Bookshop and a pioneer in promoting Western art. Young Allen would sit entranced as the men talked of artists that could fill a *Who's Who:* George Catlin, Thomas Moran, Albert Bierstadt, Henry Farney, William R. Leigh, and others.

Serious, imaginative, and quiet on the surface, Allen's inner world grew bolder and broader. Now all he needed was a means for expressing it.

It was only natural that, from age ten to 14 he took Saturday art classes at the Jersey City YMCA under the gentle guidance of Mr. and Mrs. Leonard Ford. Even then he was attracted to animals. His paintings sported titles like *Cat's Paradise* and *March of the Night Herd.* A local newspaper clipping shows him at the impressionable age of eleven at work on a painting of a Siberian mammoth dubbed *Hairy Elephant.*

By the time he was a teenager, Allen was regularly entering school poster contests—and winning, too. Again they were of animals: herds of longhorns running with the Sante Fe Railroad, chimps joking about ESSO, and an oil of a bull moose that took first prize (the best of 791 entries from 41 states) from the National Wildlife Association.

As a senior in high school Allen received his first commission: the 3 x 14 foot mural in the school library. Illustrating three of James Fenimore Cooper's *Leatherstocking Tales,* the mural shows his una-

by Howard Pyle, an artist from Wilmington, Delaware, who established a school in the nearby Brandywine River Valley of Chadds Ford, Pennsylvania. In his instruction, Pyle stressed the importance of imagination, of the artist's total immersion into the picture, rather than the routine development of technical skills. He urged the students to depict their scenes with such intense conviction that the imaginary world would seem real. The artists emerging from his school, with such now-familiar names as N. C. Wyeth, Frank Schoonover, and Maxfield Parrish, were characterized by their rich imagery, dramatic composition, and arresting palette of colors. Their subject matter included just about everything a youngster could desire: swashbuckling pirates, knights in shining armor, princesses in distress, blind beggars, secret passages illuminated only by candlelight, desperate duels at sword's edge—enough to make a boy's head swim!

Allen's collection officially began on his tenth birthday with a present from his parents: a copy of Lanier's *The Boy's King Arthur,* illustrated by N. C. Wyeth. For Allen, who until then had only collected stamps, odd stones, fossils, moths, and butterflies, it was an awakening. "Wyeth's illustrations cast their spell," he reminisces, "and I've been hooked ever since."

His overwhelming interest in Wyeth led in 1972 to the publication of his book, *N. C. Wyeth: The Collected Paintings, Illustrations, and Murals* (Crown Publishers). While his father wrote the accompanying text on Wyeth's life, Allen gathered what is considered the definitive bibliography of Wyeth's work. Even now, people like gallery owner Nicholas Wyeth—N.C.'s grandson—call on him to identify N. C. Wyeth material.

Right: *Great Horned Owl,* tempera on board, 10½ x 7¼. Courtesy the artist. Capturing the effect of light on an animal's coat and its environment is a major aim of Allen's work. Here he creates the illusion of moonlight.

Far right: *Bobwhite Quail,* tempera on board, 10½ x 7¼. Courtesy the artist. Allen's tight detail and placement almost bring the bird to life.

bashed admiration of N. C. Wyeth, even to the background of puffy, white clouds behind the figure of The Pathfinder. Like most of Allen's early work, it is surprisingly mature and ambitious both in concept and technique.

The following year Allen began classes at the Newark School of Fine and Industrial Art. One of his teachers there was W. J. Aylward, a former Pyle student. It was no accident. "I feel a tie with Pyle and Aylward," Allen explains, "a sort of continuum." There was also an annual class trip with instructor and friend Charles Waterhouse to see Pyle's art at the Delaware Art Center. The trip included a stop at Frank E. Schoonover's nearby studio where Allen heard stories of early Brandywine days.

Paul Bransom was another influential teacher. Allen had first met the noted wildlife artist at Mannado's Bookshop when he was 15. But it wasn't until years later that he managed to spend part of a summer at Bransom's studio in Jackson Hole, Wyoming.

Allen's career as an illustrator began officially with illustrations for Weider Publications' wildlife magazines: "You know, hunting, blood and guts, that type of thing." From there he gradually moved into the book area.

Today considered one of the nation's foremost painters of wildlife, Allen has illustrated 25 books for major publishers. His work has also been featured in such magazines as *Outdoor Life, National Wildlife,* and *The Reader's Digest.*

He has completed the Outdoor Life Series book *Game Animals of North America* which, like its earlier companion, *Game Birds of North America,* contains 20 paintings and 100 wash drawings. Allen's work is shown in the Southwest at the Settlers West Galleries, Inc., Tucson, Arizona, and in New York at Kennedy Galleries.

Although he doesn't always get to select the animals he paints, Allen does, of course, choose the background landscapes. As a matter of fact, he often thinks of his paintings as landscapes with animals in them: "You can get as much of a thrill out of capturing a mood and feeling with the animals' habitat as you can in getting the essence and character of the animal itself," he explains.

From his hikes into northern Maine, the Adirondacks, the West, and into Canada, he has come to know the wilderness first-hand. Favorite spots are the Teton and Wind River ranges in Wyoming, Glacier National Park in Montana, and Jasper Park in Alberta. "The colors are rich and varied there," he says, "and snow stays on the ground until midsummer. The snow on the mountains makes interesting shapes and patterns."

The best time to see animals is early morning or late afternoon, since they prefer to feed during the cooler hours of the day. You may get a glimpse of them near Yellowstone Lake in Yellowstone National Park, by the backwaters of the Snake River in Wyoming, or from horseback in the high country. For some reason, he says, animals are less wary of travelers on horseback.

Once Allen actually got to meet a moose face-to-face in, of all places, Moose, Wyoming. He was walking alone through an aspen wood late one afternoon when he heard what seemed to be distant grunts. It was hard to see through the deadfall of trees and dense brush, so he came upon the bedded-down moose quite suddenly. The bull moose rose in alarm to a height of seven feet. Fortunately, the feeling was mutual. "He and I both ran—in opposite directions."

As for hunting animals, Allen says, "I understand a hunter's point of view, but I'm not a hunter." So, armed only with canvas boards, sketch pad, portable easel, a small box of Winsor & Newton oils, and a 15-year-old Leica M3 camera, complete with assorted lenses, Allen goes in search of material for his paintings. He looks especially for interesting shapes and images, dead trees, foliage, rocks, mountain vistas, and ways to express such intangibles as the coolness of early morning or the oppressive heat of midday. He's not interested in a finished product at this point; he can always refer to photographs later for details.

However, Allen is firmly set against painting animals from photos. "They're just a crutch," he warns. "Anyone who honestly knows his subject can detect when photos have been used. The camera's eye is not always perfect, and lots of detail can never cover up for lack of sound drawing. The best way to know animals is from studying them at the zoo or, better yet, in the wild." So, until he was well into his 20s, Allen would sketch at the Bronx Zoo at least once a week. He was also a regular visitor to William R. Leigh's crowded Saturday lectures at the American Museum of Natural History. Leigh, who painted the magnificent dioramas in the Akeley African Hall, had made his fame and fortune painting the West.

Allen also used to copy Remington's paintings and pen drawings in order to study the movements of horses. His advice: "Anyone who wants to paint animals should study the work of great wildlife artists." And he himself has studied Carl Rungius, Henrich von Zugel, Bruno Liljefors, Wilhelm Kuhnert, Richard Friese, Louis Azassiz Fuertes, Charles Livingston Bull, Paul Bransom, and he admires eminent contemporaries Bob Kuhn, Robert Verity Clem, and Fenwick Lansdowne.

Allen works in a five-room studio in Bridgewater, New Jersey, that is filled with props. There's a pair of elk antlers he'll shift into various positions to solve foreshortening problems, a few mounted skulls that once belonged to Carl Rungius, a moose rack with a five-foot spread, deer antlers plus bighorn sheep and mountain goat horns, and assorted animal skins for study. Remington sketches and paintings by N. C. Wyeth, Pyle, Schoonover, Rackham, Bransom, Bull, Rungius, and others line the walls. Another room contains a photo file stuffed with old issues of *National Geographic, Natural History Magazine, Nature,* and *Audubon.*

When he works on a big assignment—like the *Outdoor Life* book—Allen paints day and night, seven days a week. A typical painting, say 20 x 30, may take

American Wapiti or Elk (Colorado Rockies), oil on panel, 24½ x 18½. Painted for *Game Animals of North America.* Courtesy Outdoor Life Book Division. The elk is bugling, calling to the other elk below. Allen can get as much thrill out of capturing the mood and lighting of the animals' habitat as in getting the essence and character of the animal.

Canada Moose (New Brunswick), oil on panel, 25 x 18½. Courtesy Outdoor Life Book Division. Allen uses zinc white for glazing on atmospheric effects like fog or mist because, "it thins out nicely and is relatively transparent."

The Drifter, oil on canvas, 24 x 35. Courtesy Kennedy Galleries. Here Allen wanted a cold effect, which he achieved by a cool underpainting of cobalt blue and viridian green.

anywhere from a month to six weeks to complete. For paintings that require fine detail, such as those of birds, he works on board in Winsor & Newton watercolors or designers colors. But because of its great flexibility, his favorite medium is oil. He also draws in pen and ink.

In the field he works with palette knife, bristle brushes, and even his fingers. But in the studio, on a large canvas, he uses bristle brushes and switches later to sables for details. On a smaller painting he works on Masonite with sables. Unless the canvas is of fine linen, he tries to cover as much of its weave as possible. He used Masonite for the *Outdoor Life* series for a practical reason: it's much too easy to poke a hole in canvas!

His medium is generally linseed oil alone or in combination with Taubes painting medium. For variety he may turn to a Ralph Mayer recipe that combines damar varnish, stand oil, toluol, and turpentine. He uses a big wooden palette, though he sometimes switches to a sheet of glass, its underside painted white.

His colors are Winsor & Newton: earths, siennas, umbers, yellow ochre, cadmium yellow, rose madder, cerulean blue, permanent or ultramarine blue, and occasionally cobalt blue and viridian green. He rarely uses black. Instead, for a good dark, he mixes rose madder and viridian or combines burnt sienna and ultramarine. "Black is deadening unless mixed with another color," he warns. He uses zinc white, particularly for glazing on atmospheric effects like fog or mist, because it thins out nicely and is relatively transparent; but he turns to titanium white when greater coverage is needed. He rarely uses the "phthalos," which he finds too strong, and has occasional use for cobalt yellow, Indian yellow and brown, and red ochre.

Allen starts his paintings as broadly and loosely as possible, keeping the image of the finished painting in mind. "It's important to keep it loose," he explains. "If it's too tight in the early stages, it will come out too rigid." First he designs the shapes, which sometimes just means moving little black squares around. When he has trouble figuring out the light and shadow patterns, he sculpts little clay forms and throws a light on them to see what happens. But mostly he works from preliminary sketches—as many as 20 or 30 if he's having trouble with a particular concept—and later from oil studies. He may only need a few studies to paint images (like the bison) he's had in his head for years; other concepts may require more work. For an especially large painting, say 40 x 50, he blows up a preliminary sketch with a ballopticon and traces it directly onto canvas. But he often sketches in smaller paintings freely, working directly on the canvas with a brush.

He tries to set the tone and mood of the painting right away through the color of the underpainting. For example, for a moonlit scene, he'll use a cool underpainting of raw umber, blues, and greens. "Even if it's covered up, you get a glow coming through," he says. He especially likes to build color through a series of glazes, such as those on the bison's winter coat. Of all the animals he paints, Allen finds mountain sheep, antlered big game, and bears the most fun. Of bears, he says, "Few painters can paint them without making them appear cuddly and comic. They have a certain character and gait. They're very powerful, but if you're not careful, they can become cartoons."

Although Allen's style is realistic, he finds his work gradually becoming looser and less noodled. He characterizes himself as "sort of a scared Impressionist." He'd like to paint as freely as they did, but tends to cover it up when he does. "You get locked into a certain way of painting," he confesses. "People who follow my work don't want my paintings that loose."

Right now he's at work depicting an Alaskan brown bear on a rocky bar on the Katmai River: "It's a simple, strong painting. There's a haze over everything, but through the mist you can see distant peaks in a pale sunlight." His eyes are glowing now. "Anyone can paint details," he explains. "It's capturing a certain fleeting light, a particular moment of a changing day and night that interests me so much."

The West, Alaska, and Canada hold a particular lure to Douglas Allen. For there lie the last traces of a rapidly fading wilderness and the final retreat of so much of the magnificent wildlife Allen loves to paint.

AARON BOHROD

BY MARLENE SCHILLER

"EVEN AS A VERY YOUNG BOY I found it pleasurable to take a pencil and draw things," recalls Aaron Bohrod. "Later on, when I discovered that there was a class of people called artists who spent their entire lives making pictures . . . well, I thought that was the most wonderful discovery, because that was what I enjoyed doing (apart from temporary deviations for baseball and other social things, of course). Drawing and painting were things I looked forward to being a way to spend a life."

And, indeed, it has been a nice way, for Bohrod began winning national art awards at 22 and hasn't stopped yet.

Bohrod was born in Chicago in 1907. His parents had emigrated there from Bessarabia. His father ran a small grocery store, and as a young boy Aaron and his brother ran errands and did the window displays—his first still-life setups—to help out.

"In Chicago I got a fairly good allover taste of things," Bohrod remembers: "Design, lettering, watercolor. This gave me the advantage of partially knowing what kind of artist I wanted to be."

After two years at the Chicago Art Institute (the second on scholarship), young Bohrod switched to The Art Students League in New York. "The League had excellent teachers," states Bohrod. "But the teacher I learned the most from was John Sloan. The principles he enunciated carried over. Oh, he was a fanatic about drawing: 'Draw,' he told us. 'Draw everything you see or imagine or dream of, and draw in every conceivable way and with every conceivable tool.' And so we did: from memory; with the left hand, both hands; pretended we were Renoir, Picasso, Matisse. Always consciously, as an exercise, with an effort to fathom the artist's thought processes, never with the idea of acquiring style cheaply. For he was a harsh critic. He hated any kind of glibness and decried the smart, the fashionable painting. But what influenced me most was his insistence on a student's own desire to find a personal path and then his encouragement to amplify your powers in that way—to find a direction apart from all others.

"Perhaps too I was influenced by his satisfaction with using humble material: 'Anything that has char-

acter is material for the artist.'"

After these studies at The League, Bohrod returned to Chicago. Inspired by Sloan, he determined "to do for Chicago what Sloan had done for New York." While his wife, whom he had married in New York, taught school to support them, Bohrod spent his days, sketchbook in hand, haunting the outer perimeters of the city, taking down visual notes. On other days, when he wasn't sketching, it was nothing for him to toss off two watercolors or gouaches in the morning and complete a full-scale oil in the afternoon. Twelve-hour days were not uncommon, but they were fruitful.

The first and most outstanding of the artist-in-residence programs was established by the College of Agriculture at the University of Wisconsin for John Steuart Curry in 1936. The success of this experiment interested other colleges and universities, which developed similar programs within the framework of grants from the Carnegie Foundation. Southern Illinois University at Carbondale, under the direction of an enterprising art department director and a progressive president, created a residence for Bohrod. He would probably have remained there for some time if World War II had not intervened.

In 1942 the War Department (U.S. Army Engineers) interrupted his peaceful sojourn by assigning him to the Pacific Front as artist war correspondent. Next he was sent to the Soloman Islands and finally, this time for *Life* magazine, he traveled with Patton's Third Army at the Battle of Normandy. Returning to Chicago in early 1945, he embarked on a series of paintings made from his war sketches (now in the Pentagon).

In 1948 John Steuart Curry died, and Grant Wood recommended Bohrod for the post of artist in residence at the University of Wisconsin. Bohrod was loathe to leave Chicago: he could work in a bathrobe and neglect his beard for days without fear of inter-

Right: *The Cupboard,* 1971, oil, 40 x 30. Collection Dr. and Mrs. George E. Becker. In this, Bohrod's largest painting, he employs his "nothing" background to contrast with and to feature the complex arrangement of highly detailed objects.

ruption, and his children had been born there. But Wisconsin offered a modest approach to financial support, a beautiful studio, and a certain prestige. Bohrod accepted.

The program had started with the dean of the Agriculture School, who envisioned it as a part of just his school at the University. He was a socially minded dean and felt that, apart from telling the people of the state when to plant their corn, he could have someone around who could encourage them to study the arts, adding fulfillment to their lives. The program included regional art exhibits sparked by one-day art schools where criticism and demonstrations were offered. Together with the annual competition, the exhibitions created a unique though nonprofessional art movement in Wisconsin.

By most standards Bohrod, in the prime of his life at this time, was a success. He had international recognition and a lovely family, his job was secure, and he had freedom to pursue his painting with a minimum of demands. Why, then, should he risk his career by embarking on a totally new style of painting?

Bohrod describes it this way: "The summer of 1953 I was hired by North Michigan University at Marquette to teach a five-week summer session and took the family along. I was intrigued with the rugged Lake Superior shore, with its dramatic boulders emerging from the cold blue waters. In the fall, when I returned to Madison with a few finished gouaches and sketches, the first problem I undertook was to translate them into encaustic, a medium I had been working with. But the textural beauty and broad forms usually so desirable to me were found wanting. Instead, looking at the blurred, indistinct depiction, I felt I had missed the quality of incisiveness the sketch had suggested. I decided to refer again to my drawing and produce a smaller work in oil that would more nearly express the intricacies of the craggy landscape. To aid me in this endeavor, I picked up little pebbles and stones, which served as models to stand for the large boulders and rocks. Delving into the stones' character, examining their pits and depressions and subtle color nuances, I experienced a way of seeing that had never occurred to me before. This time I almost rebuilt the rock in order to create the essence and feel of it on a two-dimensional surface."

The rock painting was followed by still-life compositions prearranged, which he used to complement the rocky landscape as an alternative in all-out form investigation. He used the *trompe l'oeil* device of a frontal plane with shallow depth, but it wasn't until

Above: *Three Graces,* 1971, oil, 18 x 24. Collection Ms. Carole Toigo. Photo courtesy Everett Oehlschlaeger. Here Bohrod alludes to Rubens, and the kitsch sculpture echoes a classic pose. Symbols of irony and humor, the fragility of dreams, provide the core of meaning in many Bohrod works.

Left: *A Lincoln Portrait,* 1954, oil, 20 x 16. Collection Elvehjem Art Center. The first of Bohrod's paintings done in what he calls the ''hard-boiled, still-life way,'' where he concentrated on the substance and surface of the objects.

Opposite page: *Rendova Rendezvous,* 1943, oil, 18 x 24. Courtesy of the U.S. Army Center of Military History. Descriptive brush strokes accentuate the horror.

Of Form and Color, 1962, oil, 20 x 16. Collection Dr. and Mrs. Otto H. Salsbery. Bohrod was inspired by the broad spectrum of colors in a bag of onions: they spanned the entire palette.

the Lincoln painting (shown here) that he established the idea of painting all elements in almost exactly the same scale as the objects themselves.

In 1954 Bohrod embarked on what he thought would be a short series of severely executed still-life paintings that would make an interesting diversion from the kind of painting he had considered his life's work. But for more than 20 years he has not been able to tear himself away from the new form of expression. Countless subjects are possible, and he continues to find this form of still life entrancing.

And just what constitutes a Bohrod still life? Bohrod's ideas come from everywhere: "When I look at any part of the visual world, I think, 'Maybe it's a possibility.' Actually, not just the visual world suggests ideas. I may read something and think, 'Isn't that a nice phrase, mentioning a couple of odd objects that could be combined into the making of a still life.'"

Bohrod surrounds himself with objects: knick-knacks, curios, and ordinary objects: odd pieces donated by friends, others from dumps or junkyards, dolls, old magazines, smooth objects and craggy ones. Although he feels intrinsic beauty is a handicap—"After all, what can an artist really say about a beautiful sunset that would improve on nature, unlike those things affectionately or mercilessly touched by time"—he occasionally includes an object with intrinsic beauty. His sketchbook is filled with thumbnail-size sketches—many of which he will never use—that combine literary ideas, a phrase with objects.

"I read an article about the dollar bill. There's the phrase in Latin, which means something like 'He looketh upon us with favor,' and I thought of translating the pyramid with the eye on top into a pyramid of beer cans with a doll's eye on top and somehow alluding to the phrase. Of course, no one will understand," chuckles Bohrod, "but it will give me a good reason for utilizing such things as scrambled beer cans and dolls' eyes and rubber stockings.

Bohrod has still-life stages in various degrees of completion throughout his studio. But it isn't until he feels, "Now is the time to do this thing!" that he starts doing some solid thinking about exactly what objects he should use. The original setups are his roughs, but secondary notes occur when he begins to concentrate. Sometimes the principal object doesn't translate too well, and a substitute must be found; sometimes the acquisition of an object, such as an ugly drinking mug set, sets off a train of thought. (If he hadn't glanced at the mugs or acquired them, the ideas might not have occurred to him.) Ideas generally come from having access to the physical objects; other times an idea comes to mind, and Bohrod must scout around to find the object. Sometimes, for variety, Bohrod may even start with the frame and then design a still-life composition to fit inside. Sometimes two textures are enough to begin casting.

Until recently, Bohrod insisted on preparing his own panels: "I require a surface as smooth as glass, and preparing my own panels was the only way to get it." Generally it would take a week to do 15 or 20 panels, beginning with an 8 x 14 foot panel that was cut down into a variety of favorite or standard sizes: 8 x 10, 9 x 12, 12 x 16, 16 x 20, and so on. Then came the long, drawn-out process of sizing and priming. The panel had to be scratched up and sized with glue, then eight or nine coats of gesso were applied. The first coat was applied in a stipple fashion for successive layers to hold onto. Each subsequent layer was allowed to dry and sanded before the next was applied. Layers were brushed on broadly in alternating directions: horizontal, then vertical, then horizontal. From the fourth coat on, the gesso was brushed on, then spaded down with a wide putty knife to fill the crevices of earlier rough coats, then sanded: "There's a tremendous amount of sanding at the end, because the panel must be devoid of texture."

Bohrod begins painting pretty loosely. No tight drawing is done beforehand. A sort of shorthand diagram of brushmarks tells him where a form begins and where it stops. This permits the fun of gradual development and refinements Bohrod loves.

His work area is set up with north light coming in over his left shoulder. To the right is a rolling taboret that holds his palette, a slab of glass covered with mounds of pigment, a can of turps, another of his medium, an array of red sable watercolor brushes, a tray, plenty of paint rags, and a paper palette on which he does his mixing. ("Working against white," he says, "gives me some idea of where I'm at.")

Bohrod's type of exquisite detail requires a steady hand. "It's impossible to make your hand perform the kind of detail I need when there's no place to rest it," he claims. "It can't hover in space." So he has devised a place to rest it. Placing his canvas behind a thin, outsized picture frame, he stands at his easel and supports his wrist with a mahlstick, which rests along the outer edges of the frame.

Bohrod starts with a broad, lean brush but very quickly jumps down to a small brush to give the required detail. His "nothing" backgrounds are painted all in one piece and in as short a time as possible: several days. "If the background is a piece of rough wood, it doesn't matter very much where you stop or where you start—a day or a week later—but here, because I want the pigment to sort of blend into itself, I require that the final painting of the background be done in one sitting," he explains.

Bohrod works on two or three paintings at a time, alternating between them until he finds himself most interested in one, and then he finishes it. "You can't push in the beginning," he says. "You put things down, let it rest, and start another." This procedure allows time for drying and gives the artist time for a second look.

A small painting takes about ten days; a sizable one—24 x 30—takes seven or eight weeks. Being reconciled to a long-term process from the start, Bohrod finds it "delightful rewarding work; it's play."

The Declaration of Independence, 1975, oil, 30 x 24. Copyright© 1975, Jack O'Grady Galleries, Inc., Chicago, Illinois. All rights reserved. Commissioned by O'Grady as part of a Bicentennial collection by contemporary American artists. Bohrod was given the subject title only; subject matter was up to him.

He builds up his paintings in the traditional manner: fat over lean. His medium, essentially one part linseed oil to about three and a half parts turps, is thinned down even further in the early stages of a painting. In earlier paintings, Bohrod used varnish as a kind of glaze and then didn't varnish after the painting was dry, but now he has switched the procedure around and only varnishes after the painting is finished and dry.

"I start by scrabbling around the way most people do," he says, "making tentative indications, blocking in tonal areas." Generally, the major decisions about placement of objects are made ahead of time or in the early stages of the painting. Once the pattern is set, it becomes a matter of expressing the forms. The whites, which lose body pigment over the years, are built up slightly to protect them from becoming transparent. But not enough to call attention to them as a focal point or catch the light. Bohrod feels that would be "cheating," for although his work is heavily textured in interest, he insists the texture be created by drawing his forms.

Today Bohrod has more time to follow his inclinations. In 1973, after 25 years, he retired from his position as artist in residence, but continues to live in Madison, Wisconsin. "Instead of riding 20 miles to the studio," he explains, "I now only have to walk 20 feet." Bohrod's studio, built above his garage, is laden with interesting and mysterious items.

Bohrod is mellow now. He still feels painting should always reflect and comment on life, but in his work he does it in an indirect way. "I'm not an evangelist," he says. "In a quiet way, I perhaps suggest things to ponder. But I have no solutions. And I'm just as happy seeing what I can do with a red object against another red object."

But Bohrod has always demanded from himself a core of meaning. And if his still lifes have changed over the years at all, they have gotten more meaningful—perhaps more humorous or more ironic. He once wrote about one level of his painting that he "demanded expression within a realistic framework, with the reality carried to so intense a degree that it becomes almost fantasy and a subject painted with such unashamed skill that a conviction of truth evokes beauty."

And he once credited the persistence of his efforts in meticulously worked still life to a desire "to demonstrate aesthetic worth in a form opposite to abstraction, the official art of the mid-20th century." But protests along this line have long since evaporated. And if Bohrod had any advice to give a young art student today, it might be somewhat along the lines of the advice given to him: Experiment. Don't narrow your focus too closely in the beginning. But draw. First master, if possible, the ability to draw expressively. From that, everything stems. And look at the Old Masters. They painted for the ages and as well and as perfectly as possible. But look at the work of other artists too; try to analyze it, and learn from fellow students.

You can learn painting processes, about the properties of the materials—about the surfaces you will work on and the possibilities of the imagery that you are going to contend with. But these are just the technical aspects. What you do with your talent you must decide for yourself.

Pen and ink drawing from *Wisconsin Sketches,* a sketchbook collection of Bohrod's impressions of Wisconsin.

ANTONIO CIRINO

BY CHARLES MOVALLI

Idle Sails, oil, 25 x 30. The artist wanted to catch the mood of the situation: it's the end of a day's work; the sails are slack, resting.

ANTONIO CIRINO lives on a hill outside Providence, Rhode Island, in a house whose big windows let in lots of air and sunshine. The low, flat-roofed building is as much a workshop as a home, and the original Spartan lines of the place—created for him by a student at the Rhode Island School of Design—are obscured by piles of magazines, books, and paintings. Boxes full of typewritten essays and aphorisms lie near a window that overlooks his front garden. Cirino proudly admits to being an addict. Not only was he "incubated in a paint pot," but he is in love with the joys of "wordsmithing." He points to the two dictionaries that rest on his desk; they should be read, he says, with reverence—as you'd read the Bible.

One of the books that weigh on Cirino's overloaded bookshelves is his own *Jewelry Making and Design,* a classic volume that he and Augustus F. Rose wrote in 1917. At that time he was an instructor at the Rhode Island School of Design; later he became head of its Division of Art-Teacher Education. The book shows Cirino's respect for craftsmanship and design, a respect that made him demand loving care from his students even when working on what might have seemed trivial assignments.

An amusing example of his own handicraft rests against his kitchen window: a wrought-iron nameplate from his former studio-home in Rockport, Massachusetts. Above the name on the plate is the silhouette of a painter, seated before an easel smoking a pipe and working on his canvas. A goose looks on. The goose reminds you of the outdoors, and you naturally assume that it symbolizes nature. But you're wrong. "The goose," the artist says, waving his hands, "represents the person who comes up and asks you silly questions while you're trying to work: 'Are you painting, sir?' 'No, I'm playing golf!' " He continues to swing his hands in wide arcs, as if laying paint on an imaginary canvas.

Cirino is a short man with gray hair and a firm, square jaw. His eyes and mouth change expression as easily and frequently as reflections on water, moving from innocence to sadness to world-weariness to a flash of enthusiasm that makes every inch of his face, from his hairline down, crackle with amused aston-

Scintillating Sun, oil, 25 x 30. Cirino didn't blend his colors in this work. He wanted the vivacity of an active sun to be apparent. The painting is not subtle. He chose colors that play against each other to blend.

Above: *Rurality,* oil on canvas, 20 x 24.
Cirino felt challenged by the need to
make the house dark against the light
sky while still having it look white.

Right: *The Village Bridge,* oil, 20 x 24.
Looking into the sun, Cirino captures
the scintillating effect of dark objects
silhouetted against the luminous afternoon sky.

ishment. He prods you when he talks, gripping your elbow and drawing you toward him as if physically trying to make you look more closely at his purposes and convictions. He's the kind of man who sees with his fingers and feels with his eyes.

Thumbing through a copy of *Jewelry Making and Design*, Cirino lovingly runs his finger over the page; he looks intently at the illustrations, as if seeing them for the first time. "I had my students take nature's forms—flowers, buds, seed pods, butterflies, fish—and extract from them motifs for a wide range of jewelry designs," he explains. "They gained knowledge by looking at these natural forms *minutely*." He lingers over the final word, as if weighing it in his hand. "It's much the same in painting," he continues. "Study nature diligently—minutely—and you'll slowly come to know her secrets." He thinks about the idea, wondering if he's stated it in the clearest, most definitive way.

Then he begins to talk of the luck of the artist, as one who is always using his knowledge rather than accumulating it for its own sake: "In art—as elsewhere—the best educated man is the one who can make the most contacts between knowledge and life. I remember a laborer who summed up the idea perfectly: 'Education is knowing what you want, where to get it, and what to do with it once you have it.' That says it all!" Cirino smiles as he thinks about the definition.

He puts his fingers to his lips and looks inside himself for a second; his lips move slightly as he begins to give shape to a thought. "Careful study is good for the student—and good for the professional, too. It teaches a love and respect for objects. I'm reminded of the old-time American illustrators—people like Howard Pyle. Pyle would become an expert on whatever subject he happened to be illustrating. He was faithful to the facts and artifacts of life. That was the way his integrity and sincerity expressed themselves. If there's a Persian carpet in a Pyle illustration, you could have someone weave you a copy of it. He's that faithful to the identity of the rug."

Cirino touches your arm and winks. "The layman looks at the autumn foliage from a car going 55 miles an hour," he says. "Do you get the point? The painter settles on the spot and investigates it. The layman is interested in what he sees; the painter in what he thinks about what he sees." He smiles broadly. "The painter issues a report; he doesn't make a record. He's interested in showing you his personal interpretation of the subject. The final work is never descriptive, never definitive. It's temperamental—it leaves something to the imagination."

The artist's face goes through another of its rapid changes, suddenly clouding. "That's why I keep insisting on the difference between the words 'design' and 'composition.' The designer creates something that's never existed before; you design a brooch, for example, or a house, or an abstract painting. But the impressionist composes; he takes what he sees and reorganizes it, making it representative of what he feels." He again touches his lip with a finger, talking hesitantly, welding his idea together. The artist's subject, he notes, is only the starting point. Otherwise the painter could be replaced by a camera. Nor is there any need to search the world for material: "You can stand on the bank of Rhode Island's Moshassuck River and find paintings everywhere you look." He jerks slightly, as if provoked by a new idea: "I can remember Lester Stevens's basing a fine picture on a few seconds glimpsed out the back door of his Rockport home. Would you divorce your wife on the grounds that you've seen too much of her?" He smiles shrewdly, and his eyes light up. "Near here, there's a group of houses and a church that I must have painted over 200 times. I've done it under dark, dramatic skies, on clear days, and on gray, silvery days. I've painted it in the morning, at noon, in the afternoon, and at night. I've done it as it is—and, at times, as I wished it to be." He pauses again.

"Remember that when you paint outdoors, you're using both imagination and memory." He looks to see if the idea is understood. "Each painting I do, no matter how small, has a series of trials behind it, going back almost to the day of my birth. That's why I weep when I have to part with them." His eyes suddenly droop. "My paintings are the children I never had—I love, caress, admire, and take pride in them. I can never pick a favorite—just as a mother never has a favored child." He looks sad for a few seconds, as if thinking about paintings that he's had to part with. Then he suddenly perks up: "A painter always owns a picture anyway—yes, even after it's sold." The thought seems to comfort him, and, after musing on it for a second, he slowly returns to his subject.

"Outdoors," he repeats, "an artist uses both imagination and memory. I remember being struck one day by the relation between a lobster boat and the blue-green water that surrounded it. I was reminded of colors I'd seen in Europe. This is the same water that's in the Mediterranean, and this is the same sun. Why, I wondered, can't I see the same effects here? So I took the artist's privilege; I improvised. I yearned for something in the landscape; and, seeing it a little so, I made it a lot more so. Nature became amenable to me. You must dominate nature, after all, or it will enslave you." A great firmness enters his voice for a second, and his eyes become dark spots, searching and gauging the quality of your comprehension.

"Your sense of composition shows in what you exaggerate and how you exaggerate it," he says, the intensity of his gaze lessening. "Compositional skill can be acquired. You learn the fundamentals, and then you slowly work out your own concepts. The only real rule in composition is to have just one center of interest. Let all the other parts gyrate around that center." He caresses the word "gyrate." "Think of a banquet table with the guest of honor in the center and the lesser lights to the right and left. I can remember a portrait by a friend, Maurice Compris, in which the hands and face of the subject are painted in different tones. The hands are beautiful, but since

The Grandeur of Rurality, oil, 18 x 20. Cirino always subordinates his methods to his message. Here the lush paint and blended brushwork present the viewer with a sensuous treat.

they're not as bright as the face, they obligingly keep their place. You look at the head first."

Cirino goes to a bookshelf and pulls out a volume on Cape Ann. It's illustrated with pencil drawings by another of his old-time friends, Lester Hornby. He pages through the book, stopping at a sketch of Motif No. 1, the famous fishing shack in Rockport harbor. "Hornby named Motif No. 1, you know," Cirino says, lamenting that no one remembers the fact. "See how he makes you look at the Motif first, despite all the boats clustered around it. They're a conglomeration: no one boat stands out. They're just busy and active enough to set off the large, simple mass of the building." He accidently skips over a few illustrations, then quickly returns to them. "Look at this street scene," he says, smiling at the mastery of his friend's pencil. "He's handled the street just as Compris handled that portrait. The main side of the street is also the most strongly drawn. The other side isn't so important—and so it's done lightly, sparingly. Again, you know where the artist wants you to look."

Cirino puts one book away and pulls out another. It's a scrapbook filled with black and white photos of his work. As he turns the pages, he discusses his painting methods. "Painting is really easy," he notes. "George Elmer Browne said it was just a matter of mixing the right colors and putting them in the right place!" He smiles and proceeds to dismiss all the nostrums and rules about the painter's palette: "I've always used the expedient colors—the colors that I need. People say that you should avoid black and should mix your own greens. Yet I use black; in fact, once you've seen how it can gray a color, you'll never be without it. I've also seen the palette of J. Francis Murphy, the famous landscape painter. It's encrusted with piles of green—all out of the tube! So where does that leave your rules?" He pauses triumphantly.

Pointing to a few of his 8 x 10 inch panels—a size whose potential, he says, was first seen by Childe Hassam—he quickly explains that they're not sketches for larger paintings. On the contrary, they're complete works in themselves: "I don't keep rough pictures. I try to make what was good better, and the better perfect. Besides," he continues, "when you do large pictures from small sketches, you're in danger of copying and exaggerating your own faults." He looks at one 8 x 10 panel and speaks, half to himself and half to his listener, "Oh, this is a sweetheart, a real sweetheart." It's as if he's looking at a work by someone else. "Art chose me," he adds parenthetically; "I didn't choose it. And so I've never played at painting. Everything I've done, I've done with loving care." He continues to look at the picture; then he returns to practicalities.

Rose Majesty, oil, 20 x 18. This is one of Cirino's favorite paintings. It is the first thing he looks at in the morning and the last he sees at night. "The flowers are still alive and vivacious," he says. "It's active life, not still life, which is dead."

"Outdoors, I work for about two hours on a canvas, whether it's an 8 x 10 or a 25 x 30. The light remains constant for only a few hours. And the only real difference between canvas sizes is that you use larger brushes and more paint on the bigger ones. The thinking remains the same. When you paint small, you have to think big." He emphasizes the sentence.

"I usually work all over the canvas, applying the paint as if I were doing a mosaic. I spread the color wherever necessity dictates. Always start roughly—even New England had its rough origins in the era of the glacial moraine. It's this initial roughness that lures you to the betterment, refinement, and perfection of the painting." He raises his eyes from the scrapbook. "When I've come to the end of my knowledge, I stop working. My art is evolutionary, not revolutionary—and I may work over the canvas later, improving it as my understanding of nature and art increases. I never stop because the picture is 'good enough.' I like to do more than is necessary. It's like a commission; you always do it for yourself first rather than the client. You should not only give him what he wants—you should also give him what is good for him."

He stops for a second and begins to look for his book on jewelry making. He stands in the center of the room, not knowing whether to be furious or fatalistic. "This always happens," he says. "I can never find something when I want it. I have to put my affairs in order—but," he continues in a voice filled with plaintiveness, "it will take so long!" The despair passes, and he soon finds the book. Opening it to a page that illustrates decorative Japanese swords, he notes that "these swordguards are works of art—yet they're a part of the sword that doesn't *need* to be decorated. The Japanese never cut corners. I've seen Japanese garments where the work inside the sleeve is as handsome as that on the outer, visible side of the sleeve." His eyes shine with the wonder of such craftsmanship. "Nothing is good till it's done right."

The artist goes to the kitchen and returns with a huge cup of coffee: it looks like a cereal bowl with a handle. It's filled to the brim. He offers some, and then gets more for himself. "I often start to work directly with the brush," he says. "But it's good practice to make a pencil sketch first. The sketch clarifies your thoughts and makes you adhere to your original conception." He asks solicitously if you have enough sugar or cream. "In my paintings," he continues, "the original conception is usually based on a quality of light. Light, after all, is the living substance of life. It's our first commodity. I see something that speaks to my subconscious—to the storehouse of my largest and my most minute observations. Fifty years of accumulated knowledge then help me to get behind the physical facts of the scene, to look on, beyond, and around the immediate."

He looks to see if you can feel the solidity of what might, at first, seem to be an extremely abstract idea. He grabs your elbow, making sure you don't drift off into metaphysics. "The world is alive," he exclaims, clarifying his point. "Doesn't the violinist suspect that his violin is possessed of life? Don't you feel that there's a life in everything, even the inanimate object? Look at the water in a harbor. It's alive; it's moving, undulating. The waves on the bobbing surface each seems to be saying 'See me! Now see me!' Yet people make boats in a harbor look as if they're resting on frozen ice. The masts are all perfectly vertical." He is astonished by such "artistic myopia."

"Every outdoor painting and every still life should have motion and movement in it." He touches his chin lightly with his forefinger. "Look at that still life," he says, pointing to the wall. "Those flowers are in motion. There are no two roses exactly alike in color, size, or importance. Even the background has life in it. It's a picture of flowers with a background—not flowers and a background!" He moves to a portrait on an opposite wall. "Here's a painting by a departed friend. He didn't say to his sitter, 'Sit still, please! Don't move!' Portraits should never be posed. Don't paint things at rest. Leonardo da Vinci had music in his studio when he painted the Mona Lisa; the songs made her animated and alive. Umberto Romano always engages his sitters in conversation. He doesn't paint the person; he paints his or her spirit. It's the soul of a subject that lures you to it. That's what excites you. And that excitement should appear in your work. I've seen lots of landscapes where nature looked as if it had been run over by a steamroller. All the life was squelched out of it. Never paint from complacence! Never paint from apathy!"

Cirino again touches his lips, his eyes widening as if in sight of an especially interesting and provocative thought: "Don't paint inventories. Think of the environment that animates your subject. Nature naturally pulls things together by color and light. But some insist on separating them. They don't see a landscape with a sky; they mistakenly paint a landscape and a sky. Atmosphere pervades everything and gives each hour its own charm. There's beauty in the brilliant colors of a sunny day, and beauty in the sober colors of a gray day." He runs his finger over an 8 x 10 inch panel. "Learn to appreciate the pearl-like grays of an overcast day. Note how each gray differs from another and how even within a mass there's great variation in color and value. Madame de Stael, Napoleon's arch-enemy, always talked about the necessity of seeing 'the differences in similarities and the similarities in differences.' That's a large part of the painter's art." He pauses and repeats the phrase. "See the differences in similarities and the similarities in differences." He savors the words with a gourmand's relish. "Harmony in a picture is like the bird and its nest. Simplicity is a matter of not too much and not too little."

Cirino continues to scrutinize his own ideas, almost as if he could see them as they come from his mouth. "A good teacher," he notes, "can be a real help in developing a student's susceptibilities. He tries to get at the student's basic culture—the 'part of the student that's left after he's forgotten everything he set out to learn.' But it's a rare teacher who can show you how to do a thing better—*in your own way*. Most teachers want you to do it their way. And most students cooperate, because it's the convenient thing to do. Do you remember Whistler at West Point? He'd been working on a drawing for some time and then yielded his seat, as was the custom, to his instructor, Robert Weir. Just as the instructor started to work on the drawing, Whistler exclaimed, 'Please, sir, don't touch it. You'll spoil it!' That kind of talent is rare in the student."

Cirino again smiles, as if he's accidentally bumped into a particularly luminous idea. "There's a difference, you know, between being knowledgeable and being sophisticated. The knowledgeable person knows the difference between good and bad. That's a useful beginning. The sophisticated person, on the other hand, is someone who only knows the popular affectation. He doesn't like being what he is and enjoys being what he is not." He watches the words as they fall into place. "It's a great temptation to follow the crowd. And originality is always a severe taskmaster. It places a high priority on honesty and sincerity. I remember a line from Shakespeare: 'Self-love . . . is not so vile a sin as self-neglecting.' Followship never gets ahead."

As the painter talks, the sky darkens outside his picture windows. A storm, coming from the South, shakes the tops of the nearby firs. Looking at them, you naturally think of the life and movement that pervade Antonio Cirino's world. He fumbles for a minute at an elaborately decorated lamp, set near more of his typewritten notes. The light falls across the man as he leans back in his chair. "I'm tired, son," he says, each of his mobile features drooping. "I hope I've said something worthwhile. I've learned to talk by being silent." The light illuminates the edge of the scrapbook and casts a faint glow over a room filled with memorabilia—framed tributes from various art organizations, and a plaque with the various awards he's won over his career. There have been 59 awards since 1926, the latest only in the late '70s. He mentions it proudly and says that, "As the Germans say, I'm still not *ausgespielt*—played out!"

To one side there's a photo of him painting outdoors in the early '20s, dressed stylishly in knickers and a golf cap. Behind the desk, his easel is now permanently installed in the middle of his living room. As he tries to rest in his chair ("I can't rest," he says, moving back and forth) the light from the lamp falls on a line in "A Prayer," a prose poem he wrote and published a few years ago. The impeccable layout and lettering reflect his belief that a "sense of orderliness" is inherent in the painter's nature. The words echo the fact that, as he admits, "Art has been the sinew of my life." After praying for many things, Antonio Cirino finally asks for strength—for the mental and physical stamina necessary "to continue to work in the spirit of the artist, joyously and conscientiously, fashioning with loving care those things which dignify man and glorify God."

Photo William E. Sharer.

MARK DAILY

BY MARY CARROLL NELSON

"... a man's work is nothing but this slow trek to discover, through the detours of art, those two or three great and simple images in whose presence his heart first opened."

MARK DAILY RECOGNIZES in that quote from Albert Camus an echo of his own response to art. He explains, "I'd like my paintings to be the detour Camus mentions. That's what I aspire to but can't calculate in advance. If a painting is an artistic success, it has a life of its own and can be a medium of discovery for others. There are a hundred things a person might react to. It could be a sense of color, the subject, or a feeling of nostalgia—all, perhaps, quite separate from my personal response to something that was vital to me."

In the last few years Daily has begun accruing honors. He won a John F. and Anna Lee Stacey grant in 1972, chosen from a national juried exhibition. In 1975 he submitted a painting for consideration to the Elizabeth T. Greenshield Foundation of Canada and was awarded a grant to paint and study in France for six months in 1976. His work was accepted by the Allied Artists of America after winning the David Humphrey's Memorial Award for figure painting in their annual juried competition.

In spring of 1975 Mark Daily had a sellout solo show at Sandra Wilson Galleries, Denver, which drew superlatives from James Mills of *The Denver Post:* "In small paintings of the New Mexico and Colorado mountain landscape, Daily manages to evoke a grandeur that other artists might rely more on canvas size to convey." Mills also referred to "lively freshness of brushwork" and "luminous warmth" from Daily's subtle use of color.

Oil painting is Daily's preferred medium, although he does an occasional pastel. And within his oils, he attempts a wide variety of subjects in an effort to be well rounded. "I try to be equally fluent in all types of subject matter," he comments. "It's very typical to run across an artist who does one type of thing only. I'd like to be able to sit down in front of anything and paint it."

Daily has had fluency as a goal for a long time, and

its impact on his art is obvious. He has avoided a glibness that often results from overworking a forté to the point of becoming a production artist. Success in a specialty has rung a deathknell to creativity in too many cases, and for an artist of Daily's caliber, rapid commercial success and glibness are traps to be wary of and to avoid. Nonetheless, since his first venture into the marketplace, Daily's work has found buyers who are attracted by the emotional and aesthetic response of the artist to his subject. It is his direct posture of eye and hand before nature that gives Daily's painted interpretations their traditional cast and their sense of immediacy. Whenever possible he paints directly from his subject. The human figure, the landscape, even his still lifes have a zing to them as a result of his intense looking.

It's always interesting to recapitulate how a person has arrived where he is. Mark Daily is from Chicago, where he was born in 1944. Daily has always known what he wanted. "I was directive from quite an early age," he says. Art had begun to shape his life during grade school years when he attended two summer sessions at the Chicago Art Institute. Recalling his childhood in a family of five children, Daily comments, "My parents did what they could, and that was a lot." They were not only perceptive, but also encouraging, and, with their help, Daily began life drawing classes under William H. Mosby at the American Academy of Art and was apprenticed to professional artist Merlin Enabnit while still in high school. Through these arrangements Daily familiarized himself with an artist's procedures. A combination of stimulating talk, excellent teaching, and examples of admired work by such former students at the American Academy as Bill Sharer and Richard Schmid (Daily began corresponding with Schmid after his school days) formed his roots as a traditionalist.

He was anxious to begin serious art studies as soon as possible and, when he won the school's scholarship competition, he enrolled full time at the Academy. This small commercial school had a student body of only 250 students and a fine reputation. Daily continued his studies under Mosby, who always re-

Summer Still Life, oil, 24 x 30. Collection Clarence McGrath. In this work, large by Daily's usual standards, loose brushwork and warm, rich colors capture the feeling of a summer's day.

sponded to the student who tried hard—and Daily was one who did. His big interest was in learning to draw and paint well. Mosby rode herd on the young artist, demanding his best, and Daily applied himself with zeal for three years, until 1965 when Mosby died.

After that, Daily left the school and painted on his own for the next few years. An interest in the work of Nicolai Fechin prompted a brief trip to Taos. Through the kindness of Jane Hyatt, a prominent art dealer of Taos, he was introduced to Mrs. Fechin, who courteously allowed him to see her collection of her late husband's work.

When asked what he admires in Fechin's work, Daily answers readily: "Two things: his extremely powerful impact, made in the most artistic way. And the painting itself is just 100% quality from edge to edge. It takes in everything: edges, color, flair. He was a superb painter."

Though Daily was not yet in Taos to stay, he was inspired by what he saw and planned to return. In contrast to Chicago, with its urban environment, this landscape of open vistas appealed to him as a place to paint. The brilliant, clear light was a further attrac-

tion. He had made a friend of another former student of Mosby's, Bill Sharer who was living there at the time. Sharer graciously introduced Daily to the art life of the village and told him to keep in touch.

Within a few months after his return to Chicago, Daily was on active duty with the Army as part of his Reserve obligation in New Jersey, near enough to visit with Richard Schmid when he could manage a weekend pass. Schmid advised him to contact Jody Kirberger, owner of the Talisman Gallery, Bartlesville, Oklahoma, with a view toward marketing his work.

When Daily followed this advice, Kirberger accepted his work and gave him his first professional promotion and a start on his career. Because his work was selling, Daily could afford to make his hoped-for move to Taos. He rented a studio in the historic Ernest L. Blumenschein house, originally built for Blumenschein's daughter, Helen. Blessed with north light, high ceilings, and modest space, the studio was work room and home to Daily. He holed up in the place for two years, painting hard, but isolated.

In a pattern Daily has continued throughout his career, he first tried to isolate and solve a problem: how

Above: *St. James Church,* oil, 8 x 16. Collection Mr. and Mrs. James Fisher. Daily's vigorous brushwork captures the flavor of the Taos countryside: bright open vistas, adobe buildings, dark mountains.

Right: *Green Glass,* oil, 18 x 14. Collection Mr. and Mrs. John B. Daily. Daily prefers higher key paintings, as he finds the colors more stimulating.

to understand and paint the north light as it reflected from still-life objects, the subjects he could best afford. He had never had a studio with such light before, and the solution seemed essential to him. Light and its varied manifestations form one of his deepest interests as a painter. Occasionally, with the help of Bill Sharer, he would make a foray to the countryside, dropped off by Sharer and picked up again later in the day. On one notably cold day he painted out in the snow for hours, only to slip and fall in a mountain stream, painting and all, on his way back to the road. This incident impelled him to buy his own car, which finally led him out of his isolation.

His emergence from his studio was timely. He was introduced to his future wife, Jan, when she was visiting in Taos. They were married in 1970, and he deepened his friendships with those artists properly called peers. He and his wife have moved to Denver, and friendship with other artists he admires continues to be vital to Daily.

The neo-traditionalists he associates with—Bill Sharer, Buffalo Kaplinski, and Ned Jacob, among others—are a part of an unheralded phenomenon. There is much to document in the creative vigor shared by Denver-based artists and those connected with them: it's a developing chapter in current American art history. These artists respect traditional precepts and have an expertise in technical control, although each has his own distinct approach. They tend to revere some of the same artists of the near and distant past or present, and they often give encouragement and severe judgment to one another that is to the advantage of all. Generally, their viewpoint is that of the realist. The human form, ethnic portraits, and landscape are their chief subjects, with an occasional still life. They are mostly young men capable of creating convincing illusions, characterized by skillful draftsmanship, design, and modeling.

Surprisingly frequent interactions from artist to artist, place-to-place—i.e., Denver, Taos, Santa Fe, even Guatemala—extend the field of creative energy a good bit farther than simply Denver. Daily is an intellectual, aesthetic, and fraternal·part of this ambience, which includes a large number of other painters and sculptors. A central figure for many of them is Sandra Wilson, whom Daily met on his first brief trip to Taos. She has been a vigorous supporter of and friend to Daily and a select stable in her gallery, which was originally opened in Santa Fe and is now relocated in Denver. Daily has been included in this stable from the beginning.

"The most important thing I've had here that I don't think a lot of young painters have had is peer group support. Each of these artists is important to me in a special way. Each one is an individual with his own outlook and a unique style. The results are positive, new ideas; positive, new input," says Daily.

"Seeing their work over the years and painting with them has made me see things differently. If you're by yourself, as I was—I lived like a hermit for two years—what you have inside will come out with

Taos Blue Blanket, oil, 14 x 11. Courtesy Sandra Wilson Galleries. Daily contrasts a tighter buildup of form in the face with broad treatment of the blanket.

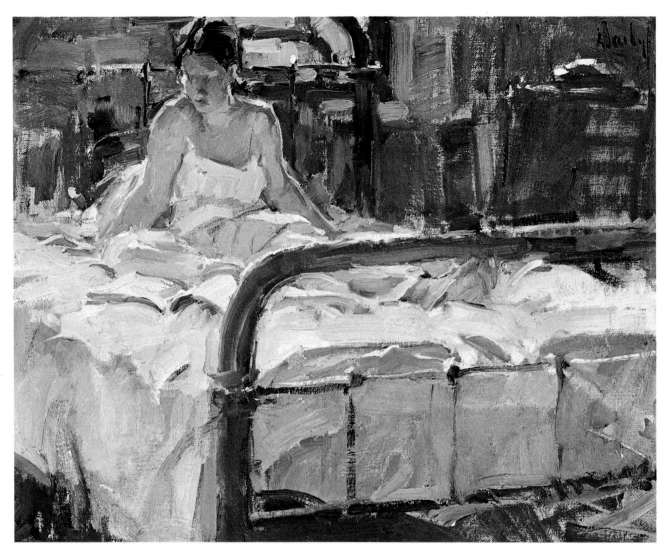

Above: *Studio Light,* oil, 14 x 18. Collection Dr. and Mrs. Thomas Fry. To capture the quality of backlighting as well as the flood of studio light from other sources, Daily used a cool palette with a complexity of whites.

Opposite page: *Brooks Street Peonies,* oil, 20 x 16. Collection Sandra Wilson. Painting outdoors, where ''even the darker areas are colors,'' Daily captures a multiplicity of reflections.

or without stimulation, but there's no way of recognizing it without some form of reference. Cutting myself off was the least stimulating thing I could have done. You must see as much art as you can.

"These fine friends and many others have made my work stronger. By trying to understand what they are doing, to study their quality, there's been a slow process of osmosis, forming a nurturing environment. All of them adhere to universal principles of art—and it's exciting.

"My goal is to fulfill whatever potential I have," says Daily. "In any profession you have to find your weak points, work on them. You must develop the discipline to do this."

Technical matters had become almost second nature to Daily early in his life, and a carryover is felt in the man today. The minutiae of a painter's craft isn't what he dwells upon: which brush to use for which stroke, how to prepare canvas, what medium or varnish to use, and how to frame a painting are not questions for him. One feels that Daily considers their answers an utterly basic component of an artist's professional knowledge. He practices an accepted technique with permanent materials in ways that have been proven sound. If he has an occasional need for information he relies on Ralph Mayer's *The Art-*

ist's Handbook of Materials and Techniques. He does have preferences; for example, he paints small, intimately scaled paintings; he prefers the spring of canvas as a ground; and his only modifier is turpentine. But there are no idiosyncracies about his work methods or studio equipment.

Daily's oils have a lushness of paint surface and beauty of color associated with such words as romantic or lyrical, but the words don't capture the man himself. He is a far remove from the Bohemian in appearance and lifestyle. He seems basically a man of judgment and selectivity. He is thorough in his work as he puts himself through his paces to solve a problem of light or color harmony, to filter a painting through a mental process. The dazzling brushwork in his oils gives the viewer a sensation of rapid, easily created painting. He acknowledges that he paints rapidly, but disavows that he paints easily. "You have to take chances. Sometimes they succeed, sometimes not," he says.

For the concerns Daily has are those difficult problems he continues to set for himself in an effort to be fluent at any subject he desires to paint. He attempted a solution to one of his self-made problems in the painting *Studio Light*. The model was an interesting subject posed on an old iron bed with her back to the

Chinese Silk, oil, 24 x 20. Collection Robert Moore. Entranced by the personality of his model, Daily posed her so that the viewer must look up at her.

north window. He suddenly grasped that the essential interest of the painting to him would be to capture the quality of backlighting as well as the flood of studio light from other sources, which prevented silhouetting his model. A subtle coloration developed: cool with a multiplicity of whites. The painting came off very well and is the one he submitted for consideration to the Greenshields Foundation.

This compulsion to study light has prompted Daily to place nudes, heads, or even a still life outdoors. In *Peonies* he composed a silver teapot and silver plate with his luxurious flowers, but the challenge was capturing reflections of light that came from all directions rather than the single light source in his studio. Many lights, and the play of oranges, roses, and whites give the painting a high-key brilliance. "Outdoors," Daily says, "even the darker areas are colors. I prefer higher key paintings, as I find the colors more stimulating."

A key attraction of the Taos setting for Daily was the warm, clear weather that allows outdoor painting so often in the year. "One of my goals," he states, "is to put it down and not *over*-put it down; a direct response—to compose it on the spot and make a statement. It's a dying art. Not one painter in a hundred can do it. But that's where you learn how to see—by learning to see and to analyze color and form in the immediate painting, from life, whether outdoors or indoors."

The act of painting is paramount with Daily, and his work can accurately be described as painterly. Daily draws as he paints, not with line, but with color. Graphics haven't yet captivated him. He doesn't habitually fill sketchbooks as another artist might; if he goes out on location in search of new material, he'll return with color sketches and a few photographs. What pencil sketching he does is incidental, preliminary and unfinished.

The realist tradition encompasses many styles. A Daily oil is remote from *trompe l'oeil*. It's not a frozen tableau, but a glimpse of form bathed in a light that seems temporary, suggesting an imminent change, as in nature itself. Should the light grow brighter or a cloud pass overhead, it might require another painting to capture the new effect. Yet, Daily is not an Impressionist; his work is too solid and three-dimensional to fit such an evanescent term. What Daily seeks is essential form in color as it is affected by light.

Extraneous detail is eliminated. Less is often more with Daily. He is apt to fill an area with a thinned turpentine wash enhanced by a few random strokes and make that abstract area fit into the total picture in a way that is cohesive, adding color and textural variety but not detracting from the central figure. In other areas a denser network of wet, creamy paint has a

look of fresh application in a delicious melange of harmonious strokes in which edges are allowed to fuse and modeling seems to occur with casual ease. He combines a variation of stroke and an impasto with washed or filmy passages for an effect of total spontaneity, but to achieve it he abandons as many as three-fourths of his paintings because they do not equal his harsh self-monitoring.

Daily explains that his style results from his rapid painting, but where another artist might work four times as long on a single painting, Daily might paint four paintings and only select one that comes up to his standard. Something of his intense effort and constant practice might account for the dexterity and beauty of his brushwork.

"I've worked hard to get an understanding, a grasp of the foundations of art," he says. "I've been trying to apply it with as much integrity as I possibly can."

Daily's work has had its rewards in personal satisfaction. He describes well that nirvana of creative delight that happens often enough in the life of a painter to drive him on: "At a certain point a painting begins to tell you what it needs. You're in that magic realm where you allow creativity its expression without intellectualizing or processing it. You have to be discriminating and alert, but you are so intent on giving the painting what it needs and what you want it to have that you no longer rely on your technical competence. You're beyond such a consideration. This is the high that comes occasionally and keeps you going."

Looking backwards at where he has come from, Daily views these past years as a learning period in which he's sought to master the most difficult of painterly problems. Now he has a new, restless feeling of outreach and a desire to travel. He wants to see the Third World countries, China, and the people of all the world's races. His art heritage is essentially international rather than purely American, although he fits into that strong, ongoing, American tradition of realism and its appreciation for the beauty of our own landscape and peoples. Now he wants to offer to himself a more distant challenge and take his talent to subjects not yet seen or tried. He wistfully explains: "By looking and experiencing as much as I can, I want to broaden my references—those guideposts by which I can evaluate my work—and I want to find new inspiration. Unless I experience many other things—not just the Middle America I know, but areas completely foreign to me—how can I feel confident about the content of my work? How can I test it or renew it? It's time to go and look. It's just starting. I don't know where it's going to take me."

Having already spent his six months in France—the first leg, one suspects, of many trips—he seems eminently ready to go as far as he wishes.

EDWARD FITZGERALD

BY NEAL ASHBY

IF NOTHING ELSE set Edward Fitzgerald's paintings apart, his subjects would. He's staked out a creative universe all his own across the upper floors of hardy high-rise apartment buildings on New York's Upper West Side. In his own 15th-floor pad, Fitzgerald paints skylines and, more frequently, human vignettes that he sees from his windows or the roof of his building. A jogger bending to lace his sneakers before going out. A girl sitting nude on a daybed. A man rolling paint onto a wall. All rendered with a soft, but not photographic, fidelity. Artists' colonies by the seaside or in inner-city Bohemian quarters have no allure for Edward Fitzgerald: Upper West Side Manhattan is his special world.

The painter is in his narrow kitchen helping some neighbor children color eggs when you arrive to get to know him. He looks Irish; his brown hair is not really long; he's of medium height and trim. The four-room apartment is cosy and thoroughly taken over by painterly paraphernalia.

With the children gone to try some eggs in their own kitchens, Fitzgerald guides you to a stool at a long table in what might be called Work Room No. 1. A palette of paints lies there, and works-in-progress are propped before you. Among them are some of the miniatures at which he's so good—little 4 x 5-inch city still lifes: a hat; a window with light streaming in; flowers, of course. These are his mainstays, he admits; they buy the groceries while he labors to capture larger scenes spied from his windows. He can finish a miniature in six to eight hours.

Most of the bigger canvases are in Work Room No. 2, to the rear, and you've seen several more at the FAR Gallery on Madison Avenue in New York: the top halves of out-of-style apartment houses, water tanks or smokestacks atop them, seagulls perched on a TV antenna, someone in a room seen through a lighted window.

Fitzgerald also finds mute scenes that fascinate him *inside* the apartments of his neighborhood and in his own rooms. In *Folding Laundry* (17 x 27 inches), a bag of freshly washed towels rests temporarily abandoned on a floor, next to a bed on which two towels from the bag lie waiting to be folded. A

rotund old woman in a negligee stirring a pot of cereal as the box of Wheatena stands nearby on the stove-top is called *Home Cooking*.

In his creations of this genre, Fitzgerald is like a modern Edward Hopper. Fitzgerald's foot-high, soft leather boots, full of character with their wrinkles and turned-up tips, stand in this picture atop a round, adjustable stool in front of a door. (Doors, doorknobs, and keys turn up frequently on Fitzgerald's canvases.)

The sense of design, of balance, seems sure; the drawing is correct. It's in his selection of colors that Fitzgerald is again distinctive. Grays, blacks, and browns predominate. Yet these recessive tones don't seem brooding but instead have a richness. Fitzgerald's paintings are about the people who live around him and their places, and the somber colors reflect a society whose members don't have much money but are managing and finding some enjoyments in life.

Fitzgerald's understanding of light and his ability to capture its endless variations and effects is formidable. He gives us the light in a room at odd times of day, the blending of night and fog, shafts and halos of brightness.

One critic has written of his work, "Fitzgerald's love of materials and the light they reflect, absorb, and cast in shadows is rendered in detail, and the effect is the transformation of tiny apartments and their cluttered contents into rooms full of what seem to be precious and rare objects—stripped of function, touched and clarified by pure light."

But it's time Edward Fitzgerald did some talking for himself:

"I grew up in the Bay Ridge section of Brooklyn; my father has a textile advertising business. I joined the Navy in 1945, when I was 17. I spent five years in the Navy, mostly as a radio operator, and that's when I started to paint. You may not believe this, but I picked up a copy of *American Artist,* and after that bought a watercolor kit in Norfolk, Virginia.

"After the Navy I went to art school in New York City. Then, on the G.I. Bill, I went through Europe, painting and studying. I was in Perugia for a while,

Black Boots, 1971, oil, 48 x 36. Courtesy FAR Gallery. The artist has a love of materials and achieves a richness of color despite the muted simplicity of his palette. The sheen of the buttons on the vest, the wrinkled texture of the boots: each object is characterized precisely.

Above left: *Potato and Candy Kiss,* 1972, oil, 2 x 2½. Collection Mrs. Jennie Zacha. Photo courtesy Bay Window Gallery, Mendocino, CA. One of the artist's ''jewels'': objects made precious by being framed in a miniature painting.

Above right: *Kodak,* 1972, oil, 2½ x 2. Photo courtesy Bay Window Gallery, Mendocino, CA. All works on this page are reproduced same size as the actual paintings.

Warm Corner, 1972, oil on panel, 5 x 4. Private Collection. Photo courtesy Bay Window Gallery, Mendocino, CA. The artist uses a warm glow of light and a familiar setting to create a feeling of intimacy.

Above: *The Collector (I),* 1970, oil on canvas panel, 12 x 16. Collection Mr. Leo Levitt. Photo courtesy Gallery 52, South Orange, N.J. Fitzgerald's attention to the distinctive characteristics of objects and their reflective qualities creates the illusion of minute detail.

Left: *Late Edition,* 1970, oil on panel, 5 x 7. Collection Eileen Kuhlik. The artist expresses a mood of late afternoon or evening: a dark room illuminated by the glow of reflected light; a figure physically relaxing, yet mentally active.

The Telephone, 1972, oil, 36 x 30. Collection Robert Del Hillman. Photo courtesy Sneed-Hillman Gallery, Rockford, Ill. Fitzgerald wants the viewer to see tones that normally go unnoticed. ''Green is green,'' he says, ''but a gray may require study to understand what the color really is.''

Rome, Vienna, Madrid. Then I went across to Africa, to Morocco. I got a job as a city planning draftsman in Casablanca.

"It was a wild time there. There was a fight for independence on, and there were tanks in the streets and murders constantly. I came back to New York.

"I starved and painted downtown—long before the SoHo colony got started. Then, around 1960, I organized a cooperative gallery located near Cooper Union in lower Manhattan. The idea was that a bunch of us would act as a jury, judging each other's work, deciding what to show in the gallery. And we would share the work of the business. But I found *myself* doing most of it—hanging paintings, being the accountant, even cleaning out the place. After four years of that, I tried running a conventional Madison Avenue gallery for a year. My own work was suffering badly; I became just a weekend painter, and even then I only worked on miniatures. That's when I returned to full-time painting."

In his life today, Fitzgerald shops along upper Broadway, chats with neighbors he encounters, runs in the park, and drinks in subjects for paintings that his surroundings present.

"So many ideas come to me, I'll never be able to deal with all of them. I've got them tucked around on scraps of paper and even written in journals. I've got 200 toned canvases ready to go. I look out the window to study the architecture, the *scale* of the architecture. Or I can see something in someone's home that in a painting can be an island of music in the dark. From the roof there's a broader perspective. I can stay up there for hours at a time with a mug of wine, studying the way sunset falls on the city. Or sunrise. In one direction I can see all the way down to Wall Street, and west, across the Hudson, to the hills of Jersey."

Fitzgerald follows no schedule for painting itself. "I may goof off for two days and then get so deep in work that nobody can reach me for a week," he says.

He makes no preliminary drawings. "I decide on something I want to do—and it goes!" Then, when uncertainties develop, he pulls back to "brain out" his concept, does sketches of troublesome objects in drawing pencil, erasing a lot, rendering the object in closer and closer detail. He may have as many as 40 pictures in progress at a time, all started with a rush and pursued as long as certainty held. A few times it's held right through to an almost nonstop marathon completion.

He uses the Maroger formula for oils because he feels it produces a well-unified medium: he can work in it quickly; it dries overnight and holds unchanged for years. Work is begun with a bristle brush to mass in color. As refinement progresses, he moves down to softer sable brushes. This can mean all the way down to No. 0 or No. 000 sizes for miniatures.

Fitzgerald does his final mixing of colors on the canvas, not on the palette.

And he's ready to defend his heavy use of grays and other subdued hues. "There are great shades in grays and darks," he maintains. "There are all kinds of grays. It may be tinged with blue or red or yellow. Green is green, but a gray may require study to understand what the color really is. Take a bowl of white carnations in the sun. The *shadows* may have the most interesting color. A lot of thick, bright color means nothing. Night is not just blue paint. I know I hold back on color. But I want you to see the tones that you don't see."

And, in fairness, one does encounter contrasting vivid patches of red or yellow or blue in many of Fitzgerald's pictures.

A whole catalog of nuances in illumination is recorded in Fitzgerald's output, from bright to dim with a thousand levels in between. "Light can change," he notes, "within the space of a few inches."

He finishes a full-sized painting in from 15 to 20 hours' working time.

Since the early '60s, Fitzgerald's canvases have been exhibited in galleries in New York, Long Island, Philadelphia, and Kansas City. He's had solo shows in New York, New Jersey, and California. Individual works are owned by several wealthy art fanciers, by the prominent painter John Koch, and by Broadway playwright Neil Simon, among others. And he's won many awards, including those from the Audubon Artists Annual (1974); Miniature Painters, Sculptors & Engravers Society of Washington, D. C. Award for best oil, National Academy of Design Annual (1973); Miniature Arts Society of New Jersey Award for Artistic Non-Conformity (1972) and their Founders Purchase Award (1971).

Fitzgerald says prominent realist painter John Koch has been a strong influence on his development, particularly in his exploration of light qualities. Others whose styles and techniques he feels he's drawn from include Bernard Childs, Frank Mason, Henry Hensche, and, in Vienna, Edward Baumer.

The true-to-life school of painting has an ardent advocate in Fitzgerald. His early paintings were abstract. Back in the dark corners of his storage closet, a few of these abstracts survive for his personal record. And Fitzgerald hardly denigrates this form. ("The abstract and the realistic stand side by side, as equals.") It's simply that he's cast his lot with the figurative approach.

"Realistic painting is very hard," he says. "You don't have the luxury of free interpretation. You have to recreate it as it is. In abstract, there is balance and form, but no probing of life. Figurative painting must have balance and form, too, but it also *interprets* life. We haven't begun to exhaust the figurative possibilities. We'll never go *beyond* realism.

"I'm trying to lead the viewer to some truth, some reality, essence. I try to build to a crescendo. Dark leads to light, and *there* you find the point I am making, imbedded in the surroundings."

Outside Edward Fitzgerald's windows, through which he has seen and continues to see so much, it is plain that darkness and night have come. Hours have passed. And Fitzgerald is summing up: "I've made a

Peonies, oil, 16 x 12. Fitzgerald draws from material that surrounds him: a still life or a view from his apartment window.

total commitment to what I'm doing. I won't take any commissions or do anything that could be considered commercial. (Though I don't criticize anyone who does.)

"I'm trying in my paintings to show people some things they haven't been aware of. To get across some of the meaning in the scenes around us. What you see as the meaning is up to you. I guess I'm saying, 'there is meaning to be found here.' I'm encouraged to find that I'm able now to achieve more rapidly on canvas what I see as a vision."

Left: *The Prizewinner,* 1963, oil, 43¾ x 42. Collection Mrs. Richard Ullman. Fitzgerald spoofs the over-liberated painter and the establishment that demands a work be abstract in order to be a prize winner.

Below: *Summermoon,* 1971, oil, 14-inch circle. Collection Victor Policar. Shafts of light draw the viewer into the shapes, up to the moon, and then out front to the frame.

TED GÖERSCHNER

BY CHARLES MOVALLI

TED GÖERSCHNER stands in the middle of the room, wearing sky-blue jeans and a plaid shirt to match. He slides into a white wing-backed chair—hooking himself onto it crosswise, dangling his legs over one side, and puffing on a curved calabash pipe. During the conversation he occasionally gets up to give the pipe some genial prodding. Directly behind him, a slash of light cuts through a bay window and hits the room's clean, white wall. It's a bit of the clear Cape Ann light that he loves so much. The warm light, however, belies the nature of the day.

"Different seasons suggest different kinds of work," he says, apropos of the raw December weather. "In the spring and fall, you want to hit the road. But a Rockport winter is quiet and relaxed. You're buttoned up in your studio and feel ripe for still-life and figure work." He shifts a bit in his chair, looking more and more comfortable with each movement.

"Many people don't like to do still lifes," he says. "But they probably had a bad introduction to them. When I was going to school, my teacher made very boring arrangements. I wouldn't do them—and so flunked the course!" He laughs at the memory. "Now my own students groan when I set up a still life—until they see how interesting it can be. But I'm reluctant to start them on something as complicated as a land-scape. In a still life, the form and color are always the same. There's plenty of time to work. And the teacher can control the lighting. All the problems are there: edges, forms, light and dark, warm and cool textures, color." He emphasizes his point by gesturing with his right hand.

"When I finally take my students outdoors," he continues, "I like to start the day with a quick demon-stration—not to give them something to mimic, but to suggest a way to attack the problem. Students *need* direction and guidance." As he talks, Göerschner cradles his pipe in his hand. "We work from nine to three in the summer workshops and do two pictures. Morning and afternoon light are completely different things, and you can't start a picture at ten and finish it at two. By using small canvases—about 12 x 16—the students manage to do two pictures without much trouble."

Göerschner gets up for a minute, cleans his pipe, and again slides back onto his chair. "I don't make stylistic corrections; I simply try to point out general principles. The teacher has to be analytical; he has to explain why he makes a particular suggestion. Students sense when you don't know what you're talking about. Remember," he insists, "that you can't be spontaneous and creative till you've been analytical. I like trees," he says, searching for a concrete illus-tration to his point. "I've always liked them, and I think my years out of doors have taught me some-thing about how they grow. Many painters just do one kind of all-purpose tree. But trees are like people: you can tell who they are at a distance, just by look-ing at their silhouette. When drawing trees, I'm re-minded of the rhythm of figure drawing. The two ac-tivities aren't that different. You have to know your subject, and you have to sense the movement of rounded forms. You're just trading skin for bark." He smiles at the comparison. "So if I see a branch that isn't growing as a branch *should* grow, I don't mind correcting the stroke on the student's canvas. You should know *how* a branch grows—that's fundamen-tal. Then you can paint it any way you want: with a brush or a palette knife, realistically, abstractly, heavily, thinly. You can take liberties with what you see. But start by drawing what's in front of you. Ex-periment, but get a solid foundation first. Render ac-curately; and as you become more proficient, you'll learn what to leave out."

Göerschner ponders his last few words. "The big-gest problem in art is to see things in a simple way. You have to avoid becoming overly involved in a part so that you see and say too much. I remember a fine example of such simplicity in a marine by Frederick Waugh. You know how his pictures almost knock you to the floor! In this case there was a large area of shadowed rock in the foreground. And Waugh had simply washed it onto the canvas. The whole thing was little more than a stain! Then a few heavy high-lights were painted into it." Göerschner straightens in the chair as he thinks about the picture. The stu-dent, he points out, rarely understands the value of simplicity. "The student tends to doodle on part of

Summer Flowers, oil, 20 x 16. This is a demonstration picture done in about two and a half hours at one of Göerschner's summer workshops. Göerschner is concerned with the design rather than the flowers themselves. ''Don't ask me what variety of flowers these are,'' he says; ''I'm no horticulturist.'' Photos Phillip Callahan.

51

the canvas without thinking about the design as a whole. That's when a teacher is really useful. He can take a big brush and pull things together." Göerschner makes a sweep with an imaginary brush.

"When the class does floral subjects," he continues, "I try to get the students to think in abstract terms. I want them to look for color and the pattern of light and dark. Squint at the still life and try to think of it as a jigsaw puzzle—with the background as part of the whole design." He squints in order to emphasize his point.

Göerschner smiles, obviously amused by, yet sympathetic to, the problems of the student. "The student," he says, "has a tendency to overdo the obvious. He wants to do subjects that are beautiful in themselves and are thus very hard to paint. I remember a quote from Plato: 'I seek beauty, not beautiful things.' It's good to remember that the 'pretty' subject isn't always the paintable one. And there's often a thin line between the beautiful and the garish." Göerschner smiles an easy smile and notes that students also have a tendency to work too slowly. There's a difference, he suggests, between being accurate and being over-cautious. "When I do figures, I warm up with very quick poses. Once the adrenalin is pumping, I make more careful drawings. But I try to keep the work spontaneous and unlabored. I tell my students that what they do in the first two minutes—when they capture the *attitude* of the model—is more important than all the work they do from then on. If they only have two minutes, students always do good work! But give them half an hour, and they slow down, fumbling with the contour instead of quickly brushing it in. I tell them to approach a long pose exactly as they would a short one and to apply the same principle to their landscape and still-life work: speed up a little; go right to the heart of the subject."

As Göerschner talks, a small black cat, about as big as a ballet slipper, sneaks silently into the room. Göerschner reaches down and pats her, then returns to the conversation. He notes that he always begins a canvas by drawing directly with the brush. He doesn't use charcoal because he finds it too stiff and confining. "I draw with a small filbert in a neutral tone, taking the paint right out of the tube, without any medium," he explains. "It's easy to rub a line off with turpentine and a cloth. And I think you get a better drawing. I choke up when I have to use a little three-inch piece of charcoal. I end up scratching at the canvas. With a brush, you can stand away from the design and get lively, free-moving lines."

Göerschner also avoids doing a detailed preliminary sketch. "I may put down a few lines," he says, "a suggestion of the relative proportions of the subject, maybe a dot here and there. If the subject has a lot of architecture in it or is a particularly intricate still life, I draw somewhat more carefully." He pauses for a second. "With a still life," he notes, "I have an advantage. I can take time setting up a good composition. I sometimes spend a day just arranging the props! And those extra pains are worth the trouble; they pay off in the end. If you get the design figured out from the start, the picture will almost paint itself."

The treatment of the subject is usually dictated by the subject itself. Some, Göerschner says, are made to be done *alla prima*—at one go. Others require a more elaborate approach. Göerschner's small flower pieces—very abstract in nature—are usually done *alla prima*. The spontaneity of approach matches the liveliness of the subject. "But," he notes, "there are some subjects that just can't be done that way. They need a gradual development, with a lot of underpainting." He points to one of his favorite pictures, an elaborate still life with a glass jar, a pottery vase, pears, a hanging cloth, and a bouquet of milkweed. He stresses the subject's great textural variety. "The different surfaces," he explains, "and my own interest in the subject made me want to say as much as I could. That's what really determines how far you carry a painting: stop when you've said all you want to say." He moves his pipe slowly in his hands. "When you work *alla prima*, you're concentrating on

The New Arrival, pencil on gesso panel, 8 x 6. Collection the artist. Large detail of a drawing with a 2-B pencil on a textured panel. Göerschner purposely left the body of the figure unfinished; he didn't want a subordinate part of the composition to carry excessive weight.

Micque, oil, 10 x 8. Collection the artist. In this *alla prima* painting of his wife, Göerschner was challenged by the problems of back-lighting. He often says that to him the most stimulating thing in art is "the act of painting, the excitement of a new subject and the challenge of mastering it."

September Sail, oil, 20 x 24. When painting clouds over the ocean, Göerschner has to work fast; an effect lasts only a few minutes. Since clouds are abstract in character, he can take great liberties with their shapes.

the surface; you paint wet into wet. But with a more slowly painted picture, you have to think in a completely different way. You work from the bottom out. Every time you make a stroke, you have to think of what will eventually go over it."

Göerschner likes experimentation, but there's always a logic behind the choice of a particular technique. Consider mediums. When working *alla prima*, he uses the paint directly, with only a touch of turpentine. He sometimes sprays the painting with retouch varnish while working to soften the paint and "make it move." If the painting process is going to be continued over several days—or even weeks—he may use a standard medium of turpentine, damar, and raw linseed oil. Applying the age-old fat-over-lean approach, he uses one-third of each ingredient for the "lean" underpainting—and then works over that with a fatter, more concentrated medium. On occasion he also tries more exotic mediums. "I've used the various copal mixtures," he says, "and I've also used boiled linseed oil and powdered lead. That makes a honey-colored medium that dries hard and glossy and that gives great depth to your darks. I've

also tried the Maroger medium, even though it's controversial. It's great for painting wet-in-wet. It's buttery and has a low luster. And when you do nudes, the medium lets you work like a sculptor. The paint stretches and stretches, feels nice—and the medium itself has a wonderful smell!"

Göerschner uses stretched canvas—a fine, single-primed linen—only when painting *alla prima*. Over 90% of his work is done on Masonite panels. "They don't expand or contract, and the paint holds up better," he explains. "I use ¼ inch untempered Masonite, both for my large and small paintings. The more popular ⅛ inch width is too flexible. I like the extra strength."

Göerschner notes that he has the panels cut in all sorts of sizes. Although you can attach canvas to them, he prefers to prime them with rabbit skin glue and white lead. He paints corners, edges, and front and back, thus sealing the panel from moisture. Such panels are very tough: "You could bounce them off a wall and not hurt them!"

Göerschner frequently textures these panels before using them. "I used to work on burlap before I

Reflections, oil, 8 x 10. Private collection. A ''fun'' painting, this small panel was done on an alkyd primed panel. Göerschner glazed color over a wash underpainting.

knew better," he says, describing his early days as an abstract painter. "Or I'd glue tissue paper to the canvas with polymer." Now he may lay the white lead on the panel with a palette knife, as if he were plastering a wall. Sometimes he uses bristle brushes. "Some subjects," he says, "call for a panel with a granular texture. Others need a panel as smooth as the ones I used when I worked in egg tempera. Those panels were polished and looked like porcelain!" He smiles just at the thought of that beautiful surface. "Of course," he adds, "there's always the danger of over-texturing the panel. You don't want a ridge in the wrong place." From the look on his face, you can see he's talking from experience.

"Everything," he insists, "depends on the subject. Sometimes I like to work on a clean white panel. I want light to go through the paint and bounce back from the brilliant ground. When working *alla prima*, I like a surface that takes the paint and isn't too absorbent." On occasion he'll tone the panel with a stain of burnt sienna or terra rosa and let some of the color show through as he works. If he plans a more elaborate picture, he often uses an "alkyd" primer: two or three coats of Benjamin Moore semi-flat house paint. That creates a very absorbent surface, a surface that takes the oil from the paint like a sponge. He can work over the underpainting very quickly and doesn't have to wait days for the first coats to dry.

Göerschner enjoys discussing the technical aspects of his work. And as he talks, it's clear that *oil* painting is what interests him: "Oil fights you a little; you feel like you're painting! Oil is the most flexible medium—and if you haven't tried it, you don't know what you're missing."

As Göerschner praises his medium, the conversation slowly turns to pigments and the colors he uses in his own pictures. Since he believes in experimentation, he has an extensive list of colors. In any one painting, however, he will rarely use more than six or eight colors. The basic reservoir of pigments includes yellow ochre, raw sienna, burnt sienna, raw umber, burnt umber, cadmium yellow pale, cadmium yellow dark, cadmium orange, cadmium red light, alizarin crimson, ultramarine blue, cobalt blue, cerulean blue, Thalo blue, viridian green, sap green, and Mars violet.

He also uses ivory black. "I didn't use black for years," he admits. "You know how you're taught to avoid it in art school. But one day a friend of mine suggested I try it. After all, it was good enough for the Old Masters! It can be very useful, if used properly. Personally, I avoid lamp black and Payne's gray; they're too cold and dead. I like my darks to be transparent and on the warmish side. That gives them more depth; they're richer and have more life to them." He particularly warns against using black "whenever you want to darken something. If you want to darken a color, use the complement. That keeps the color alive. But mix ivory black and burnt sienna, and you get a wonderful warm brown. Mix ivory black and Mars violet, and you get a gorgeous

Morning Flowers, oil, 8 x 6. Using a slightly textured lead-primed panel, Göerschner concentrated on the relationship of one shape to another—the light-dark-light-dark pattern.

violet gray. Let's face it: black is beautiful, if you use it with respect and know its limitations."

Göerschner prefers to use lead white—with little concern for its poisonous reputation. "I use titanium when lead white isn't available. It's colder than lead and doesn't dry as fast. Some swear by zinc white, but it's too juicy and runny for me. I like my white to pull a little as I put it down."

He prods his pipe a little, observing that much of his interest in color came from part-time work as a painting restorer. He had to match colors unlike those we have today—colors that had also undergone 400 years of fading. "After a while you get to the point where you can look at a color and automatically break it down into its parts."

He tries to get his students to duplicate—in part, at least—his own experience. He gives them several color exercises; hopefully, such exercises help break the student's natural inclination to paint a landscape by putting out green, yellow, red, and blue—without giving any thought to what the colors are or how he's going to use them.

After his students begin to understand color, Göerschner shows them how the subject will itself suggest a specific palette. To illustrate his point, he leads you from his living room to his upstairs studio. You go up an L-shaped stairway, the artist ahead of you, taking two steps at a time. The studio is dominated by a metal palette set on a black bureau. An antique studio easel is angled toward the window. Sketches are tacked on the walls, and gold frames and prepared panels are in a corner near a bookcase. Atop one book pile is a catalog on the 19th-century American painter Frank Duveneck. A large volume on John Sargent nestles near another book, in Italian,

about Giovanni Boldini. A postcard reproduction of a Mancini sticks out from between two volumes. On a lower shelf is Göerschner's lap paint box, built by himself and hand rubbed to a beautiful finish. On the cover is a brass plate with the family name. He removed the plate from the work box of his grandfather, a Swiss sculptor and painter.

There's an 8 x 10 inch panel on the easel, a nocturnal water scene done in subtle grays. "I actually based this design on a two-inch square section of another picture," he says. "It reminded me of Whistler. I used eight colors in the picture, plus white. Since the theme is a study in grays, I use complements or near-complements to mix my neutral tones. Viridian and alizarin give me one gray; viridian and Mars violet, a different kind; and Terra rosa and cobalt blue yet another variety. I use cadmium orange with white for my highlights. Cadmium red light warms the Mars violet and tempers my highlights when I want to make them less intense."

Göerschner pulls a black notebook from his bookcase. "When I work with a new set of colors—like this one—I jot down what I learn." The book describes the theme of the picture, the colors and surface used, and the medium. "If you break your back trying to get a particular tone," he says, "it's worth noting how you did it. My notes are like hieroglyphics, but I can understand them." As Göerschner puts the book back on the shelf, he says that "when you experiment, you need a big garbage can—and a big notebook. Ask questions, and you'll soon start finding a lot of answers!"

He looks for a second at an abstract painting hanging in the stairwell. "I've tried a little bit of everything myself," he says, continuing down the stairs.

The Old Crab, oil on panel, 30 x 40. Göerschner says this picture took "eons" to complete. The old tree reminded him of Chinese calligraphy: it was "exciting, menacing, and macabre." He did the large picture from a 16 x 20 sketch, darkening certain areas in order to lose some of the form. Because of the complexity of the subject, he had to subordinate some areas in order to emphasize others.

"I've tried not to live in a closet." As he slips into his chair, he explains that "I started in commercial art, but soon discovered that wasn't the life for me. I went to Florida in the mid '50s when the area was dominated by the work of Karl Zerbe, William Pachner, Eugene Massin, and Syd Solomon. I admired their work and began to paint abstract pictures myself. I learned a lot about design that way." He notes, however, that he soon found abstract painting more restricting than representational painting. "I wanted to say more than just 'design.' So around 1960, my work began to become more realistic. Now I've begun to simplify my material; and I feel myself coming closer and closer to my original heroes: the French Impressionists." Göerschner notes that the more varied the styles he studied, the more alike they seemed. Wyeth's work, for example, is very abstract; he's a great designer and realizes that abstract elements form the basis of all good painting.

"I'm convinced," Göerschner continues, "that the greater the painter, the simpler his work becomes as he grows older. Look at Monet. Compare his relatively detailed early work to his late abstract pieces. He spent his last 25 years purifying one idea."

Göerschner waves his hands in the air, graphically indicating the chaos that he feels all around him. "Universities teach art as if it were science or mathematics, in cold, sterile buildings, with plenty of gimmicks and degrees. They don't mean a thing. The instructors have to spend so many hours teaching that they lose touch with their own work—and with the problems of painting. If you see students making the same mistakes over and over again, you can become cynical. Fortunately, I'm not that far from painting myself. I know I make the very same mistakes!" Göerschner smiles broadly. "That's why the best art schools have practicing artists on their faculties—like The Art Students League. There, at least, you're getting closer to the best system of all: the old apprentice system. A one-to-one relation of a young painter to a Master." Göerschner's enthusiasm for the apprentice system is more than theoretical. In fact, he's already joined with friend and fellow artist John Terelak in an experimental apprentice workshop, a workshop that takes a limited number of talented students and exposes them to as many of the technical and practical aspects of art as possible.

Göerschner continues, "The painter shouldn't teach more than two or three days a week," he says. "You need time to think. A full-time painter may not spend much time in front of the easel—but he's always preparing himself to paint, thinking about what he's going to do. Teaching is demanding; it wrings you out. When I taught four days a week, I could see my art going downhill."

As you move into a short, close corridor, Göerschner continues to talk about the relationship between teaching and painting. "The great Robert Henri might spend only a day or two with his students," he says, nearing the kitchen his wife—herself a painter—has piled a platter high with sandwiches. The hallway is dark, and the kitchen looks particularly inviting. Göerschner swings open the door, letting the light tumble into the foyer. "Henri might spend a day or two with his students," he continues, "but he combined teaching and painting. And four hours spent with him were worth four days spent with anyone else!"

Autumn Trees, oil on panel, 14 x 18. Painted on an alkyd-primed panel, this picture was developed in the studio from several outdoor sketches. Göerschner took liberties with the trees, emphasizing their rhythmic movement.

JAY HANNAH

BY DOREEN MANGAN

JAY HANNAH is an artist who has spent 30 years learning to see. "I think that nobody sees the way I do," he says frankly and without a trace of self-aggrandizement.

What is his secret? To begin with, he takes keen delight in posing problems for himself. "What's learning," he asks, "if you work with a supply of answers already worked out?"

Hannah seeks answers to such questions as: Where is the light? What is the exact color? How is the subject behaving? What is he or she saying? To find the answers, says the artist, "I must suspend judgment until I can find the truth. If I make a judgment too soon, I limit myself. I must first get in all the evidence."

The answers flow most freely, Hannah feels, if he lets the subjects tell their own stories. In his own way, the artist conducts an encounter with each subject. His quiet, hazy still lifes, landscapes, and figure paintings are subtle essays in oil, "written" by the subjects themselves.

When you let the subject speak for itself, Hannah finds, "you discover what its capacity is, and you let it go as far as it can without losing its identity. "What I'm saying," he goes on, "is that when you allow natural rules to prevail, the subject will impose its own rules, and the result will be a painting that truly represents that subject."

In allowing his subjects self-expression, then, Hannah applies his paint in broad, generous strokes, blithely overlooking small details, textures, even faces. An emotional painter, the artist's concern is for the overall feeling—the impact—of the subject. As in a true encounter, Hannah gives of himself to his subject. If he is painting a person, for instance, he tries to be frank and open so that the subject will respond with equal candor and the artist will be able to catch the essence of the personality, rather than produce a portrait that merely flatters. "What I dislike about conventional portraiture," he says, "is it forces you to see people the way they want to be seen."

The story behind *Portrait of Peter* illustrates Hannah's modus operandi. Peter, a nephew of the artist, was interested in studying art. Hannah was asked to teach him something about the subject. Instead of giving formal instruction, however, he preferred to discuss his ideas and insights on art while Peter sat for a portrait. Hannah even set up a mirror behind himself so Peter could watch what was going on at the easel. At each setting or "encounter" the two talked at length about art and life, getting to know each other, revealing themselves to each other. Hannah did not suggest a pose to Peter. He never does. "If I pose a model, placing the arm in such a position and tilting the head a certain way, I am in control and nothing of the subject reaches me." Instead he lets the person tell him how he or she is to be painted, "not by words, but by actions, by how they present themselves. Each time Peter came to the studio he sat in whatever position felt comfortable, and I painted him that way." The two versions of the portrait reproduced here in black and white reflect, Hannah feels, not only a time difference of four or five weeks but something more vital in terms of growth or self-discovery for Peter. The completed version, he points out, "has more assurance. In the earlier one he hasn't found out yet how he wants to show himself to me."

Hannah does not dwell at length on faces in his paintings of people. Sometimes he skips them altogether. "I think the body is more significant. A face is often a mask that allows us to play a particular role," he says, "and can hinder communication. It is not the whole person by any means."

In his handling of still lifes and landscapes Hannah also relies on encounter. He leaves himself open to experience his subject totally, to let it take him where it will: "Even fruit has something to say to me; it's undignified to approach it with a set of rules." But his encounter sometimes reaches battle proportions as he struggles to remain objective—to keep "hands off," in a sense: "One of the most difficult things is to let the thing talk to you without trying to impose yourself on the painting." To grasp the impact of a still life, therefore, he paints the subject from several different angles, trying to incorporate these several points of view into a natural whole. In a way this is a process similar, though reversed, to that of having his figures change their poses to suit their feelings.

Round Table and Apples, oil, 36 x 48. By combining different angles of view into one painting, Hannah presents ''a more natural way of seeing.''

The Tiffany Vase, oil, 27½ x 26. Hannah develops the formal tonalities of the surroundings first, then paints the flowers within the value relationships already established.

Morning and Afternoon Light, 1972, oil, 45 x 24. The artist utilizes shadow effects from both morning and afternoon light to create an illusion of atmosphere.

Studio Light with Flowers, 1972, oil, 34 x 28½. Similar in setting to his portraits of Peter. Hannah worked on this painting between sittings to ''keep the portrait warm.''

Right: *New London Harbor,* 1971, oil, 42 x 48. Late afternoon, when this work was painted, is Hannah's favorite time for painting. That time of day has "a sense of quiet; things seem to rest."

Opposite page: *Pemaquid Point Light,* 1971, oil, 24 x 36; painted in one sitting. The vigorous brushwork and limited palette create a strong atmospheric effect.

Hannah learned this drawing concept from Earl Kerkham, a New York painter he met in Paris in the 1950s, and he has been working on it for a number of years. His aim was and is to present a more natural way of seeing. He describes what he was after in *Round Table and Apples,* a painting he considers an important achievement: "I wanted to show the viewer how I see the top and bottom of the table. In other words, I've seen the table from many angles, and I want the viewer to see it that way too, but in a natural way without distortion. A camera would catch only one angle at a time. I wanted to show a composite. Yet I didn't want the viewer to be conscious of these different points of view." Hannah worked on this painting six to eight hours a day, including weekends, for about three months, "taking it in and out; making it sometimes wide, sometimes narrow; making the height of the pitcher work from many angles." The pitcher alone was painted over about 15 times before the artist achieved what he was after.

Light and color are also integral to the artistic encounter—just as important as a person's pose or the roundness of a bowl, "When I paint something," Hannah says, "I am trying to find out what the precise color is for that object and the space surrounding it."

The endless array of premixed colors on the market are not for Hannah; instead, he glories in mixing his own shades: "I just move the paint around, al-

ways driving, shifting, pushing, until I arrive at what is right." He works from a "fairly ordinary" palette of about 12 colors. In his early painting days he used a primary color palette and later added black for a "highly seasoned, rich palette." Now he includes earth colors to neutralize and lend a quiet vibrance: yellow ochre, raw sienna, burnt sienna, raw umber, burnt umber, cerulean blue, Dana red, alizarin crimson, viridian green, cadmium orange, cadmium yellow light, cadmium yellow medium, plus ivory black, and Permalba white. A TV table serves as his palette stand. Its rotating top makes for ease in mixing colors.

The middle range of tonal values Hannah employs—arrived at because of Connecticut's many cloudy days—is further proof of the artist's surrender to his environment. "If you paint a dark area—a shadow on a gray day, for example—it looks like a hole," he explains. "If you make it a little lighter, you must make your lights a little grayer; therefore, you're working with middle values. You strike an average and end up with a painting that looks good in all qualities of light."

Hannah's color study never ceases. He even goes so far as to employ another medium—collage—in his experiments. "It's a logical medium in this case. By simply tearing shapes of color to fit spaces I can take bigger steps, and with more vigor, than in painting." His collages, however, often go beyond the experimental

stage. Three have appeared in a book, *The Technique of Collage*, by Helen Hutton (published by Watson-Guptill).

He also uses colored paper for quick color selection. "It's simpler to hold a piece of paper up to the canvas to check color suitability than to mix a color that might not work. Using the paper can save time and paint," says Hannah. And with a lot of colored paper spread out on the floor the eye can make many, many more color comparisons than when dealing with paint.

The artist's quest for color is matched in intensity by his pursuit of light. It is a constant source of wonder to him as he tries to capture it in oil from morning to evening, from season to season. *Morning and Afternoon Light* was actually painted in both morning and afternoon light and is a combination of the two. In this painting, light is everything. The landscape seen through the window is highly simplified, as is the bowl of flowers. These elements are merely vehicles for the artist's encounter with light. When he worked on *Morning and Afternoon Light*, he often painted from ten in the morning until four in the afternoon, moving with the shadow, "yielding to something," letting the light reveal its different aspects as the day progressed. (Again, a similar process to his encounters with people and still-life objects.) "This is my feeling of the studio," he explains, "both morning and afternoon light."

Hannah painted *Morning and Afternoon Light* and *Studio Light with Flowers* at the same time he did

Portrait of Peter. It is no coincidence the first two paintings share the same settings as the latter. The artist explains, "Peter came here once a week and, because of his involvement with the painting, I worked on it only when he was here. But I wanted to do something to keep that corner of the studio alive; otherwise, I would have had a cold start each time." Hence his studies in light.

After such intense communication with his subject, what is the result? What does a Hannah painting look like? Feeling and form are very much in the fore. Minute details, texture, faces are given scant attention. There is an acute sense of balance, not so much in terms of mechanical symmetry, but in the often-ignored relationship between subject and surroundings.

The spaces surrounding the subjects in a Hannah painting are given as much, if not more, consideration as the subjects themselves—emphasizing his concern for the total look. "The negative areas are like the pauses between musical notes," he explains. "Those spaces between sounds are what hold the tune together. They can make the difference between a dignified funeral march and a gay waltz." Take, for example, Hannah's beautiful formal flower paintings. "The last thing I do is the flowers. First I work on the tonalities of the surroundings." These, he feels, are what make the flowers seem real. "I suspend judgment on what is going to happen to the flowers. But by the time I've dealt with the surroundings, I'm ready for them."

Portrait of Peter, first version, in progress, oil, 45 x 30. Seeing Peter as ill at ease and insecure, the artist paints a broadly defined figure dominated by his surroundings.

Portrait of Peter, final version, 1973, oil, 45 x 30. Here, painted with equal solidity, but more variation and detail, Peter subtly dominates his surroundings.

A similar sort of thinking went into *Portrait of Peter,* as the artist grappled with the task of treating Peter and the studio wall behind him as equal qualities: "I wanted to paint him as I know him here in my studio, not as he is in Boston, not as his parents know him. Now I know this wall a lot better than I know Peter. I've lived 'in' for three years. If I can get them to become absolutely equal, then I've done something." Hannah felt that "the whole thing finally reached a resolution" when Peter became comfortable in his surroundings.

Small details, Hannah finds, slow him up, interfering with his encounter, with the rhythm of his approach: "I'm moving fast; there's a certain rhythm when I'm dealing, say, with the radiator or a chair. Then all of a sudden the rhythm changes if I have to work with tiny details."

The artist's pace varies from painting to painting. *New London Harbor,* for instance, developed at a contemplative pace. Hannah worked on it for a year and a half. He began it when he first moved into his present studio, a former dance studio in the seamier part of downtown New London. He was charmed by the view from his window of the buoy tender that docks regularly at this harbor on the Thames River, an estuary of Long Island Sound. "The painting changed, however, as my vision changed. After a while the view didn't seem so romantic. As the year went on I painted it over and over. It was like moving a piece of furniture until it finds its place. You have to live with it for a little while." Again, the key is movement, letting the subject shift and stir until it settles in, finds its niche in Hannah's world, so to speak.

In vivid contrast to this painting is *Apples,* a "one-shot painting that went together in an hour." Obviously done in a rush of emotion, the paint is thickly swirled onto the canvas, and the texture of the canvas is allowed to show through. "I could see this painting all at once," Hannah says. He compares it to a short story: "It has a sharp focus, rapid pace, and strong impact. A novel, on the other hand, can go more slowly and explore value relationships. It's solid." *Round Tables and Apples* and *New London Harbor* are such paintings.

Although Hannah is deeply involved in feelings, he expresses them with a minimum of technique. He purposely casts technique in a secondary role because it "closes things off. You get involved in a preconditioned idea of what a thing looks like, instead of letting the subject speak to you." In other words, he feels that "you have to invent a new approach for each painting, not relying on formulas that worked well with other paintings." His technique, therefore, amounts to "pushing the paint around" until his subject reveals itself. He rarely does a preliminary study. And only occasionally does he put a sketch on his canvas (raw cotton, stretched by the artist himself). When he does, it's the merest outline—just a few fast, swooping lines, "to tell me roughly what goes where."

Apples, 1972, oil, 12 x 14. Using simplified shapes and sharp focus, Hannah creates a strong impact. The curved base reinforces the basic roundness of the apples.

Round Table from Above, 1972, oil, 43¾ x 33. The artist eliminates superficial detail and literal texture. Instead, he prefers to create spatial balance between his subject and the surrounding area with tonal relationships.

Hannah's medium is oil. "It's sensuous—has a certain earthiness to it," he says. The paint is usually mixed with Grumbacher's oil medium No. 3, but "sometimes, if I'm going fast, I don't use any medium." His brushes are pigbristle, Nos. 8, 9, or 10, round or flat. Often one brush suffices for an entire painting. Occasionally Hannah uses a sable brush for linear effect. His first concern, however, is always for freedom of expression of the subject.

Hannah did not discover art until he was 21 and studying the piano at the San Francisco Conservatory of Music. He studied both music and art for a year, but art won out: "The clock just stopped when I painted." And for the past 30 years painting has been his life, aside from occasional forays into automobile sales, shopkeeping, graphics, design, and commercial art as means of earning a living. He now devotes all his time to painting.

An important early influence was Seldon Gile, a member of a group of California painters known as the Society of Six: "Gile opened up the world of painting to me. He saw things in terms of beauty and harmony. If you looked through his eyes you saw something really lovely."

At one point Hannah went to Paris. There he indulged in a virtual orgy of nonobjective action painting. "That was a loosening up period for me," he says. "I learned to throw a pan of paint at the canvas." In Paris he met Earl Kerkham, who "taught me to take the color and the drawing apart. He taught me to use color as a tool. I learned from him, for example, that a warm color could recede as well as advance, depending on what you use around it. He also gave me a consciousness of painting form."

Hannah, now 50, white-haired, serene, is not easily summed up. Very much a free spirit, he shies away from labels. He admits, though, to being a figurative painter—"for now, anyway." What his style will be five years or even five months from now is an open question. His artistic career has been a series of explorations—in various media: watercolor, acrylics, collage; and other styles: nonobjective, Japanese watercolor—until he arrived at his present style.

To become an artist, however, involves more than knowing "how to." In Hannah's words, "It takes a lot of humility, a full complement of living, and a childlike sense of joy to see the world and live in it as a painter."

HENRY HENSCHE

BY CHARLES MOVALLI

HENRY HENSCHE slouched on the cushioned bench, squeezing himself into the corner of his green-and-yellow study. He wore suede sneakers and a loose, patterned sweater. His head rested against the wall and was covered by shadow. The spring light, coming through the window on his left, fell across his hands. The long fingers were intertwined, motionless at first. But as he talked, they became animated and mobile. To his right, another window opened on the backyard of his Provincetown home. You could see large, lacy trees, colorful clumps of daffodils, and a garden, turned and ready for planting. That's where he spends much of his time, studying and painting with the same intensity that Monet, late in life, devoted to his own gardens and streams.

The painter is loose jointed, and his face records emotion quickly. The shifts come unexpectedly—from a languidness mirrored in his long fingers, to an anger, vented in an intense look and a sharp, charged eloquence. For the moment, he hovers somewhere between these two states, his eyes moving from his hands to the window as he makes his points.

"Painting is the science of seeing," he says, "and the thing to look for when you work is the visual truth of the material before you." He pauses, groping for one of the analogies that pepper his conversation. "Let's say we eat dinner together. What's the most important visual truth about our activity?" The question is rhetorical, but he pauses for a second as if expecting an answer. "It's the fact that the scene is lit by electricity. If you painted the scene and didn't convey a sense of artificial light, then your picture would be a visual lie." He emphasizes the last word of the sentence—and for a second painting and morality come very close together.

"Now, the same thing applies out of doors. Light changes, but artists took a long time to understand the fact. The older painters could distinguish between a gray day and a sunny day, for example. But they didn't do it very well." He thinks for a minute. "Their world looked as if it were made of old parch-

ment. It wasn't the kind of world you'd want to live in." A smile crosses his face, flickering tentatively. "For hundreds of years, this brownish view of nature dominated painting. But by the 19th century, people began to look at nature more closely. Science had a role in this: the Industrial Revolution was part of the new way of looking at things."

As Hensche moves his head out of the corner, the light falls momentarily across his face. "Acute as these painters were," he continues, "they were limited by their materials. Monet, feeling the same things that Turner and Velásquez felt, had two technical advantages. He was able to use the new, brilliant, cadmium colors that had just come on the market. And the new, collapsible, tin paint tubes let him go right into the field, something that was difficult—if not impossible—when painters had to carry their colors around in animal bladders. He could study nature on the spot. Of course, Monet had a great eye; but if Turner or Velásquez had had cadmium colors and a convenient way to work outdoors, either one of them might well have been the founder of Impressionism. Monet created a revolution in seeing, but it was a revolution that *had* to come. It was just like a scientific discovery: if Einstein hadn't developed relativity, someone else would have."

Leaning back into the shadow, Hensche glances out the window. His shock of white hair bristles alertly. "The important thing to remember is that Impressionism is a way of seeing; it isn't a technique. It doesn't mean working with complementary colors or painting with little dots and dashes. Monet showed that there's more to the world than the simple distinctions between a sunny and a gray day. He saw that on a sunny day, morning light was cool and an afternoon light was warm. He saw that every hour of the morning was different: every five minutes, every minute. Our eyes are too dull to see these minute changes; our peanut brains can't comprehend them. But Monet at least made us realize that such changes exist. The crudeness of his early work is a result of the newness

Opposite page: *Self-Portrait,* charcoal sketch, 1976, 20 x 16. Courtesy Grand Central Art Galleries.

Above: *The Slave,* 1972, oil, 24 x 28. Collection Marjorie Sorensen. Here the day was sunny, but the work was painted indoors. Hensche chooses still-life objects that complement each other in the "usual scheme of things" and create a nice local color harmony as well.

Left: *Ada Reading,* 1935, oil, 24 x 20. In this early painting, Hensche "still used black as a darkening agent." His wife, the model, was placed close to the window for the full effect of natural lighting.

of his idea. At the beginning, his eyes could only see rough distinctions. As he grew older, a greater harmony and subtlety entered his work." He pauses for a part of a second. It's hardly a pause at all, for, like most born teachers, Hensche talks effortlessly about his subject. "The painter who takes his cue from Monet—who tries to record the subtleties of light—is an Impressionist, whether he paints roughly or smoothly. His goal is to train his eye to see."

The question of training leads naturally to the function of the teacher. "I was lucky," Hensche says. "I was able to study for ten years with the finest teacher America has ever produced: Charles Hawthorne. I was his assistant during the last three years of his life; and when he died, he left me his school and asked me to carry on his work." The death of Hawthorne clearly marked an era in Hensche's life. "Hawthorne was much more than a teacher. You learned technical points from him, but you learned an attitude, too. He was gentle, extremely honest, and full of reverence for nature—for what was true and beautiful." Hensche's feeling for Hawthorne vibrates in the room, as clear as the light that throws a pattern on the floor.

"I'm going to give you some more history," he says, a quick smile crossing his face. "You may not like history, but I think it's important that a painter have some sense of where he fits into a tradition. And it's necessary background if you want to understand Hawthorne and myself." He pauses. "My friends are always saying: talk less about Hawthorne and more about Hensche." He smiles again, with a combination of shrewdness and modesty that shows he under-

stands his friends' advice—but doesn't feel he has to follow it. "Monet was a painter; he didn't teach. What was needed was a way to put his principles into some kind of teachable form. Now, in the America of that day, William Merritt Chase was the most famous teacher. He taught Hawthorne—and almost everyone else. But he never really came to grips with the Impressionist idea. His paintings were really done in tone—in black and white—with Impressionist colors added. He never developed a clear method; and when he said that you could both draw and color at the same time, he really confused matters more than he clarified them." A wasp bounces against the window and then flies off toward the distant trees.

"Chase was a wonderful painter," Hensche adds. "And he made a real contribution. He was exuberant. He got people to look at things with their own eyes rather than those of the old-time painters. He was bold, wielded a big brush, and hated rules. You know his famous mottoes: 'Queer your compositions,' he always told his students; 'Don't do the expected thing.'" He understood nature, and as a result he loved it; he loved the visual world. But he didn't unravel Impressionism. That was Hawthorne's job; and, as he told me, it took him 15 years to figure out just how Monet's ideas could apply to his own painting."

For a moment, a cloud covers the sun and the room becomes gray. There's a slight breeze in the trees. "Hawthorne discovered that the standard academic art course was all wrong. There, the student drew first and then learned to fill his outlines with color. Hawthorne was the first to say that drawing (*despite* Ingres!) is *not* the basis of art. Color is. Looking at

Dominic in the Winter Light, 1964, oil, 24 x 20. Collection the artist. Painted indoors on a gray day. Hensche's palette was close in values: muted, yet light.

Teddy, 1952, oil, 24 x 20. Collection the artist. In this stylized portrait, Hensche introduced a classic bowl of flowers to complement and reinforce the curved shapes of the sitter's face and figure.

things from what he called 'the painter's point of view,' Hawthorne showed that drawing is really a question of the proportions between color masses. Develop your ability to use color, and you'll gradually improve your sense of proportion. You don't teach students by starting with the hardest subject: the human figure. That's like a man lifting a hundred-pound sack and expecting his five-year-old son to be able to do the same."

Hensche looks around the small, book-crammed study and out the door that leads to his living room, a room filled with colorful pictures by his wife, Ada. It's a fleeting glance, a glance that doesn't seem to have any real object. He continues to illustrate his point by referring to the way his own classes are organized. "When a student comes to me," he says, "I like to think of him as a savage. I don't let him do whatever he wants to do. After one piano lesson, you don't play Rachmaninoff! Instead, I'try to structure his experience. Hawthorne never developed his insights into a logical series of color exercises. That's been one of the goals of my 40 years of teaching." Hensche's voice betrays the pride he takes in the years he's devoted to his students. "As I see it, color isn't a 'gift'—as many people believe. It can be learned, but it takes an analytical ability. When I find a young man or woman with a logical mind, I know I have the makings of a painter." His voice takes on a tone of great firmness and conviction. "I'm not saying that it's easy to learn to paint in color. I've been at it for 60 years and still feel as if I'm just beginning. It's much easier to work 'tonally'—to model your forms in a simple black-and-white way and then add color.

But when you think in color, you discover that every change in the shape of a form isn't just a value change—a change in black and white—it's a *color* change. You have to learn to see the world as a mosaic of color changes." He places a hand on his chest. "I was never a facile painter," he says. "It takes me a long time to analyze a color and paint it. But I've always had a lot of perseverance, and I'm glad of it. There's nothing quite like getting at the truth of nature. As Hawthorne used to say, there's a delight in telling a visual truth—it makes you feel clean inside." The word "clean" resonates; art and morality touch for the second time in the conversation.

"I start students outdoors, on a sunny day, with very simple objects," Hensche explains. "I may have them paint a brick, for example. On a sunny day, the differences in color are obvious. There's clearly a sunlit side and a shadow side." Again, he pauses for a split second. "I've often thought that the ideal school would start in Florida in the winter and follow the sun up the coast, always maintaining a uniform source of light." He smiles at the idea. "The students get close to the object and try to match the color of each side as carefully as they can. They're not after finish or accuracy of proportion. They just put a spot of color down for each plane—and they keep doing that, in small sketch after small sketch, till they begin to hit the color with some accuracy. These first efforts are crude. But that's all right. You don't judge a student by the individual piece of work; you look to see if he's learning and improving."

Hensche leans forward into the light. "This kind of painting isn't based on ego. The egoist paints a white

Nancy in Sunlight, 1948, oil, 24 x 20. Collection the artist. The glimmer of light on the background bushes contrasts with the long, elegant neck of the sitter.

Pamela in Sunlight, 1976, oil, 24 x 20. Collection Pamela Donner. A quick study of a student, done as a demonstration for a class. Hensche's primary concern was to capture subtleties of color relationships to bring the subject alive in color.

Above: *October Glory,* 1970, oil, 20 x
24. Collection Tom Moore. Hensche
feels that the intensity of colors seems
less indoors, and the difference between light and shade planes is not as
great. Here he accentuates the sunny
brilliance of an October day near his
Massachusetts home.

Right: *Blue Still Life in Sunlight,* 1976,
oil, 24 x 28. Courtesy Grand Central Art
Galleries. Like the Impressionists,
Hensche treats the constant changing
of light and its effect on objects as his
primary subject.

house in sunlight and says, 'I've solved that problem'—he paints every white house the same way from then on." He shrugs and compresses his lips. "Stupid! The real painter gets down on his knees before nature. He humbles himself and looks at everything with a fresh eye. For him, every painting is a journey of discovery, with new problems and new challenges." He takes a book from a nearby desk, a desk covered with volumes of art history. He lays the book on the bench, so that its white dust jacket is half in light and half in shadow. "You shouldn't paint just any white," he says, tapping his finger on the area in sunlight. "You paint the particular white in front of you. What makes this white different from every other white?" He raises his eyes from the book. "Let's say you're painting my portrait. But I'm in here and your easel is in the next room. You look at me for a while and then go and paint. I'll grant that you can probably get a generalized idea of what I look like. Just as painters once got a generalized idea of nature. But if you want to capture my personality, to show what makes me different from everybody else, you have to set up in here and really study me."

He again looks down at the book, resting his finger on the sunlit part of the dustjacket. "If a student is painting a white object in sunlight," he continues, "he may paint the part in sunlight pink or orange and the part in shadow blue. The blue may be almost straight out of the tube. Well, in terms of absolute accuracy, he's wrong. But he's gotten a part of the truth. He sees the sunny day's warm and cool contrast—he sees that he's dealing with two different colors. The more he looks and studies, the more he'll see that a white in shadow can be thousands of different shades of blue. And as his eye becomes more sensitive, his paintings will begin to look more like objects in light—and less like just a bunch of discordant colors.

"At first," Hensche continues, "the students' sketches look like posters—they're made up of big, flat areas of color. I don't let the students go any farther than that. They aren't supposed to look for color variations within the mass till they can get the big mass down with authority. The trouble with a lot of students—and professional painters, too—is that they try to register the shifts of color within a mass before they've gotten the mass itself. The shifts don't 'hold,' and all you have is a bunch of spots. The painting looks as if you threw a pile of colored feathers at the canvas and they stuck. Everything falls apart.

"I don't like to recommend a particular palette or technique," he says. "I personally enjoy the clarity of color I get with a palette knife. But if the student knows what he's doing, he can paint with manure and put it on with a pitchfork!"

He thinks for a second. "The only thing I do insist on is that my students keep their materials in good shape. House painters take better care of their equipment than do many artists! Clarity of judgment rarely comes from a dirty palette—it's like trying to play an out-of-tune piano. You could have eaten a dinner off Hawthorne's palette!"

Hensche knits his fingers together and continues to explain his teaching method. "Once the student has begun to master angular and rounded forms in light, the still-life setup becomes more elaborate. As he develops his ability, he may then do part of a hedge; then a hedge and part of a house; then the whole house, with a little background foliage. Eventually he tries a picture that takes in a large area of light and atmosphere.

"This sense of atmosphere is the hardest thing for the student to master. He has to suggest the objects' positions in space. He has to show that there's air around and between the things on the canvas. To take an obvious example, the grass in the foreground of a scene isn't the same green as the grass in the background. Atmosphere affects it. Nor is either of those greens the same as the green in the trees. And a nearby tree won't be the same green as one 50 feet away. You have to get these relations right." He pauses for emphasis. "I've seen outdoor figure paintings in which the figures near to you have highlights identical to those on figures in the background. Now, skin a foot from you can't be the same color as skin ten feet away! The painter obviously used one model for all the figures, made no comparisons, and then stuck the piece together mechanically. The result is a visual lie."

Hensche looks stern. "When the student begins to do landscapes from 'the painter's point of view,' he's become a juggler, handling numerous problems simultaneously. But he always comes back to a simple beginning: color spot next to color spot."

The wind continues to move through the trees. Hensche looks out at the sunlight and the long shadows that lie across his small vegetable garden. Over his head, shelves sag with the weight of heavy art books. The walls of the study are covered with drawings and paintings: charcoal studies, "imaginary" pieces by his wife, a print by one of his dearest painter-friends. A number of paintings are stacked behind a desk, some finished and some waiting to be worked on.

"I don't talk much about composition," he says, wrapping one leg around another. "Of course, there are certain basic compositional ideas. You don't want to divide a canvas in half, for example. But composition is best understood if you think of it in terms of *function*. What's your purpose in the picture? What's your meaning? Your emphasis? Composition is like poetry; it should clarify emotion, not obscure it.

As he talks, his eyes continue to move from his hands to the window. Occasionally he looks at you, as if studying how the light falls on your face. "Well," he continues, frustration pinching his face, "look what's happened to art in the years since Hawthorne's death! For 60,000 years, artists had been striving for a clearer understanding of the visual world. With the Impressionists, logic finally triumphed. Painting began to become the science of seeing. But what happened? A few years after Mo-

Above: *August Garden,* 1971, oil, 24 x 28. Collection Mrs. Glover.
Here Hensche was inspired by the late afternoon shadows, which lent
drama to the area. Compare this painting to the landscape shown earlier. Hensche has painted the same general area at a different time of
year. Notice the difference in the light scheme.

Opposite page: *Lavender Harmony,* 1961, oil, 20 x 24. Collection the
artist. ''Composition is best understood,'' says Hensche, ''if you think
in terms of function. What's your purpose in the picture? It should clarify emotion . . .''

net's discoveries, 'realistic' art was in retreat. And now all we see is one fashion after another, one theory after another—as if a great idea came along every month." His agitation increases. "Monet said that America had a landscape that was the equal of any on earth. So why don't we make America our subject? Why don't we work here rather than going off on 'painting trips' to Mexico and who-knows-where? Great subjects are right under our nose. Armed with the advances made by the Impressionists, we could make art true again. It could once again be both wholesome and honest!"

Hensche's anger passes as suddenly as it came. He again leans back into the shadows. "As I see it," he continues, "a painting should be a poem of visual delight. The painter senses that if he can get the color relationships of nature right, that truth will itself be beautiful—no matter what the subject. He wants to be true to what his eye sees; and by studying more closely than most people, he is able to show others more than they know.

"I'm reminded of a story Robert Frost told me. He and a friend had both set out with grand artistic plans. Frost persevered and, of course, became a poet. His friend didn't. They met late in life and the friend, somewhat shamefaced, told Frost that he'd like to have stuck to their ideals, 'But I had to live.' Frost waited a second. 'Well,' he replied, 'have you?' If you hold to your ideals, you'll never really fail—no one fails when he spends his life in pursuit of the good and beautiful."

Hensche again leans forward, and a smile begins to form at the corners of his mouth. The sunlight illuminates the delicate pattern of his sweater and accents the subtle modeling of his head. His white hair looks very white, and his fingers seem to taper endlessly. "I know one thing," he says. "I've always lived with a single goal in mind: to get into Painter's Heaven. I don't want to be down below, shoveling coal." He pauses. "I want to be with Monet and Hawthorne and Velásquez," he says, smiling broadly. "Even if all I do is clean their brushes!"

GABRIEL LADERMAN

BY DIANE COCHRANE

IF YOU WANT TO GET AHEAD in the world today, you have to specialize. Everybody knows that: doctors, lawyers, even hairdressers. And so do painters. Once an artist has carved out a niche for himself, he frequently sticks with it. A successful abstract painter of grids, for example, may ponder the mathematical possibilities of his specialty year in and year out. Or a landscape painter who knows he has a good thing going at his gallery may spend a lifetime perfecting his subject. Many of these specialists find their work highly satisfying.

Gabriel Laderman would not. His ambition is to conquer a broad range of subject matter—landscapes, cityscapes, portraits, genre painting, still lifes—and expand his boundaries over the whole tradition of painting. Says Laderman, "I want a whole lot of things to be alive in my work."

Laderman's catholic approach to painting stems in part from a rejection of the idea behind that now sacred tradition started by the Impressionists, the one-man show. He doesn't reject the one-man show per se; indeed he has had many. But he thinks they can be detrimental to the development of an artist. Why? Because the purpose is to sell, and in order to sell a gallery full of paintings, the artist must create paintings that are basically the same in quality while varying in size so customers can find a place for them in their houses. If the quality is uneven, only some will sell. So the painter is hesitant to try something new, something he hasn't mastered. The result: paintings with little difference in character, style, or subject matter: "The quality of the individual work becomes subservient to the quality as a whole, causing the artist to work on fewer and fewer ideas."

Laderman's answer to the emptiness and predictability of this kind of thinking is twofold. He works on different subjects so his shows include the whole gamut of painting from landscapes to nudes. And he works at different rates; he may do quick studies or a painting that takes a long, long time. Such a major work accompanied by preliminary studies would be worthy by itself of a one-man show, he thinks. The first solution allows him scope to satisfy his wide-ranging interests; the second lets him treat his subject

on a more contemplative basis. Together they make Laderman an artist for all seasons.

This duality—variety balanced by serious study—is reflected in the way Laderman approaches every subject. So keeping this in mind, let's look at how he works.

Landscapes intrigue Laderman because of the changing light. He paints directly from nature, rarely even putting on a finishing touch in his studio. He does this because he believes direct observation combined with his response to it produces unique work and prevents duplication or turning out paintings that are, in his words, "all cut from the same bolt of cloth."

Painting from nature creates a particular problem for him, however. He organizes his paintings by breaking up form with light and shadow and he wants to see the actual light casting the shadows he wants. But nature, as any landscapist knows, doesn't always cooperate by providing the right combination of light and shade. So he maintains a vigil until the shadows do add up. Take the cityscape *View of Florence*. He painted this picture over a period of four hours, watching the shadows and the shapes they made. Some shadows worked, others didn't. The result was a combination of triangles and other geometric forms created by shadows that appeared at one time or another during the afternoon as the sun moved across the sky, not as they appeared at any other time.

Occasionally the shadows don't add up, or at least not right away. Laderman waited two and a half months for the shadows in *View of North Adams* to jell. The beautiful acid green of the store in the foreground, the perspective-defying building on the left that grows larger as it retreats, the strong vertical of the spire almost at dead center were all just right. But it wasn't until a cloud moved over the mountain, casting a large dark shadow, that the painting made sense. Actually the shadow was in an initial drawing of the scene (while Laderman doesn't work from sketches, he does make preliminary studies), but he lost the shadow as he worked out the bits and pieces of form.

Still Life with Large Ceramic Jug, 1972, oil, 40 x 50. Courtesy Robert Schoelkopf Gallery. The artist made the objects into one basic shape; then he related them to the rectangle of the canvas.

Portrait of Linda, 1971, oil, 35 x 28. The artist used a closed, curved shadow to break up the floor area and to reflect the model's intent attitude.

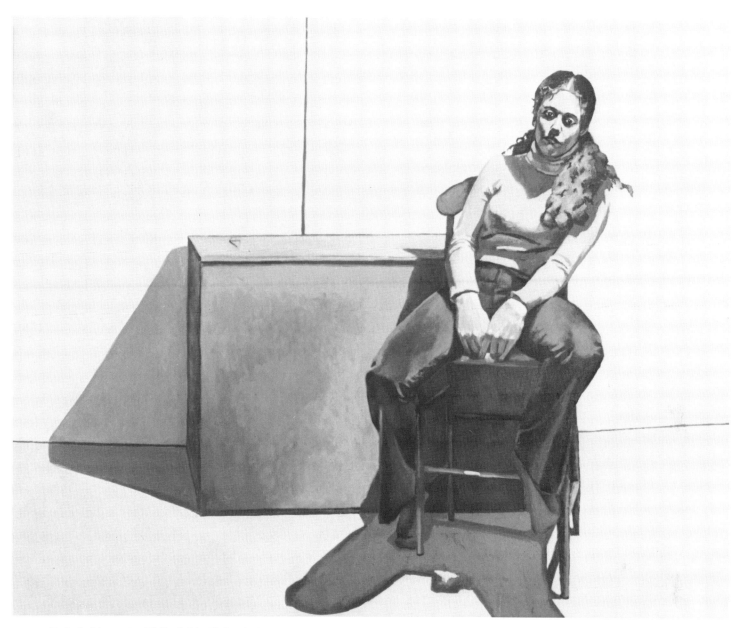

Portrait of Jeannette, 1972, oil, 24 x 30. By placing his model against a bare wall, Laderman focuses attention on her relaxed pose.

Little Falls, 1972, oil on canvas, 38 x 45. Laderman feels that very interesting forms and very ugly forms make for a complex view.

The device of breaking form into light and shade is carried over into figure painting. Like the shadows in the landscapes, they too are a combination of observations. Constructing figures out of light and shade is relatively new with Laderman, however: "When I first started painting the figure I tried to hold the forms together and show the relationship between, say, the hand and the arm and how the arm goes into the shoulder. I still think people should be able to read this. But because I am basically a painter who organizes by light, I realized that I could paint the figure the same way I painted landscapes."

Laderman's figure paintings recently assumed a new dimension. He has already begun to paint genre scenes rather than portraits; the emphasis in genre painting is on people going through the routine motions of life, not the people themselves. In Gabriel Laderman's paintings it is the poses, or non-poses, that earn them the classification as genre. Placing his subjects against bare walls, Laderman focuses on attitudes or postures: a girl slouches tiredly, or a teenager listens intently to someone off-stage in a pose typical of the Pepsi generation. In the past, however, the great masters of genre painting—Vermeer, Chardin, etc.—painted their subjects in their homes amidst the accoutrements of daily living. Laderman, too, plans to locate his figures in environments in future paintings, but not as one might expect. He isn't going to ask his sitters into his living room or kitchen. No, he's going to use a device of 16th century Dutch painters: the dollhouse. Over the past few years he has been acquiring large Victorian dollhouses, and, when he is ready to paint, he will follow this procedure: First he'll set up lights and arrange the dolls and furniture within the dollhouse. Then after he has worked out the composition on canvas from the scene in the dollhouse, he will call on live models to work out the figures.

Laderman frequently uses the ideas of other painters or traditions to come up with an original work of his own. An example of how he puts these ideas to work can be seen in Still Life with Large Ceramic Jug. Here he borrowed the Cubist concept of making objects into one shape before relating them to the rectangle of the canvas. With this concept as the underpinning he then worked the objects against a grid to produce a pleasing geometrical progression. "This device isn't crucial to the painting, of course, but it does add music to it."

Laderman's quest for variety and originality in painting is not a recently acquired philosophy; it began years ago when he was an abstract expressionist. As early as 1953, after several years of study with De Kooning, Hans Hofmann, Mark Rothko, and Alfred Russell ("the only man I don't feel embarrassed about calling a genius"), he began to chafe within the limitations of the style: "I felt that the great abstract painters had chopped up the territory into one type of compositional framework per man. Their followers within each system had to accept a lot of things as absolute, and little room was left for personal search

or development of ideas." So he drummed himself out of the corps of abstract painters.

Back in the real world, Laderman faced an enormous challenge. He had to teach himself to be a figurative painter. His early teachers had provided him with an understanding of space, but he had to learn to paint a picture in relation to nature. He didn't know, for example, how to use atmosphere, how to represent different forms, like trees, at different distances. "I had learned how to paint a picture that came out of the canvas; now I had to discover the kinds of logic I had found on canvas that would be appropriate, or specific, to nature."

Self-education can be self-deluding. Fundamental mistakes can be repeated and solutions arrived at that appear satisfactory but are not. Laderman skirted these potential dangers by investigating art history to see how other painters had solved the problems he faced. The decision to study other painters is firmly rooted in his philosophy that painters, like magicians, learn their craft from their predecessors. "It's hard to find yourself only by looking at nature; you must also look at and work from other painters. In other words, use history as a magic mirror in which you see yourself."

And you don't have to worry about accidentally becoming an imitator, says Laderman: "You can't be Corot or Giorgione, but you can gain a particular insight into how a painting is structured; you can find yourself in their work. There is a fruitful interaction between painting landscapes and painting from the masters. You learn the qualities of their hands, but not their hand."

Laderman's own researches led him to discover many useful ways to organize painting. Seventeenth century painters like Poussin, for example, employed a method of using alternating light and dark horizontal lines. Corot, in the 19th century, created a moving surface by constructing a series of shapes. Other painters devised a pinwheel system that allows an arabesque of light to lead the eye through the painting. No one system, Laderman insists, works for every landscape, but a knowledge of all of them is necessary so that a specific scene can produce a synthesis between a particular system and one's own style.

As might be expected from Laderman's intellectual approach to painting, he is an extraordinary teacher. Students at Cornell, Yale, Pratt, Brooklyn and Queens Colleges, Louisiana State University, and the Art Students League have all benefited from his method of teaching painting through a study of history. His aim is to make available to them many systems. So he asks them, for example, to study 17th-century landscapes by letting their eyes travel through the painting and then to make a diagram showing how space developed from the surface.

Laderman also advises his students to read. The systems used by the old masters may not always be easily discerned by the eye, so written explanations are in order: "Art historians, when they stick to their

Above: *View of Florence*, 1962-63, oil, 48 x 72. The artist selected the shape of his shadows to harmonize with other geometric shapes in the landscape.

Right: *Lake Shore Drive No. 2*, 1966, oil, 40 x 50. Courtesy Robert Schoelkopf Gallery. The artist uses the gradual coming together of largely unbroken areas of sky and water to create atmospheric space.

specialty and are not criticizing contemporaries, can be useful." He himself had been puzzled by certain aspects of the way Giotto organized space until he read John E. White's *The Birth and Rebirth of Pictorial Space*. And he frequently consults and draws insight and inspiration for his landscapes from rare 18th and 19th century volumes in his enormous collection of books.

Laderman has been called the most articulate con-

temporary spokesman for neoclassic ideas. Because he has immense command of the language, he has influenced both students and readers of art journals, for whom he has frequently written. He has successfully demonstrated to a new generation, looking for direction now that abstraction has lost its hold, that all traditional forms of painting are valid. But it is his paintings that give him the authority to speak.

View of North Adams, 1969, oil, 40 x 50. Laderman uses shadow to break up form as well as describe it. Note the shadow areas on the church.

ROBERT LAVIN

BY LORRAINE GILLIGAN

Above: *Cupola and B.O.F.*, 1969, oil, 36 x 48. Collection Allegheny Ludlum Industries. Commissioned by Allegheny on the occasion of opening their new plant where the cupola and basic oxygen furnace (B.O.F.) replaced the open hearth as a means of making steel. Interestingly, the company also had engaged an industrial photographer, expecting Lavin's paintings to be impressionistic and the photographs to be more realistic. The opposite turned out to be true. As Lavin explains, "The picture I painted focuses on the main elements of the process. In the actual setting, there are so many obstructions, it is impossible for a photographer to get a picture showing what this painting shows."

Opposite page: *Okan (No. 1), Oil Field, Nigeria*, 1968, oil, 20 x 30. Private collection. Commissioned by Gulf Oil Co. This painting was part of Lavin's first venture with oil companies. The artist likes to relate a painting to what is characteristic of a particular area. Here the native fishermen add interest and dimension. "What may surprise many people," says Lavin, "is the fact that there are a lot of fish around oil rigs. They are attracted by the mollusks, etc., that form on the platform, as well as the garbage."

ROBERT LAVIN is a one-man business. He is a promoter, solicitor, researcher, writer, traveler, and photographer. All this work culminates in his studio, where he carries out commissions from industries all over the country. For the past 15 years Lavin has devoted himself to the portrayal of American industry, specifically its steel, oil, mining, transportation, construction, and chemical corporations. The artist, working in oil on canvas, depicts working facilities, people at work, products being made, and dreams being built. His work is placed not only in executive offices, but is used for promotional purposes, such as a company commissioning a reproduction suitable for framing as a form of self promotion, and illustrations for annual reports and calendars or for clarifying an industrial process.

Lavin's philosophy is straightforward and indicative of his enthusiasm for his work: "There is great beauty in industry, and it seems to me that nothing is more absurd than those corporate collections which ignore what the company does. A major steel company hangs pictures of clipper ships on its walls; an aerospace company has flying ducks. It is pathetic that these companies cannot see the beauty in the work they do. Interior decorators and art consultants fill each company with identical abstract prints so that, if by accident you got off the elevator at the wrong floor, you might not know it for hours. I believe that art *for* industry ought to be art *of* industry."

The artist, no stranger to the business world, spent many years in the advertising business before deciding to leave Madison Avenue in the early 1960s. It was a critical period in his life. Although he intended to pursue a full-time professorship offered him, his thoughts were occupied by the possibilities of the relatively unexplored areas of art and about corporations.

Meanwhile Lavin found the bureaucracy of an art department frustrating and time consuming and the many rules and regulations stultifying. The more time he devoted to teaching, the less time he had to spend on his own work. He comments, "It simply is not true that you can paint and teach. When I looked at the other artists, I found that little by little they would stop painting. Teaching is really a full-time job if you do it right, and I'm a very intense person when I teach."

As Lavin's disillusionment with teaching increased, the developing idea of exploring corporate art assumed first priority, whereupon he left his teaching post. Lavin's strength was in evaluating his feelings about Madison Avenue and its changing attitudes in the late 1950s combined with foresight regarding a new field for his talents. From the beginning, Lavin envisioned industrial portraits that combined the skills he had developed in advertising with his fine arts background. He approached contacts he had made in advertising with his new idea. In the meantime, he designed a brochure explaining his new work and printed several hundred copies.

Lavin speaks of these early days: "When I first started out, I contacted mostly steel companies, because a lot of my work in advertising art had been with them. Since I also found the subject extremely picturesque and dramatic, this is what I did for the first few years."

With the first response to his brochure came a challenge that Lavin took in his stride. "A man called me and asked if I could paint a steel mill that hadn't been built yet," he recalls. "The company supplied me with hundreds of blueprints, and I had to learn blueprint reading. I built models in clay, because I had no idea what this complex would look like. So I built the models, laid it out on the floor, lit it, took photos of it, and painted the mill. Four years later the mill was finished and it came out looking exactly like my painting."

When he decided to tackle oil companies, Lavin received a commission that was glamorous and exciting. "In 1968 Gulf Oil commissioned twelve paintings," he remembers. "The marvelous thing is that they sent me around the world. My first trip was to Milford Haven in Wales, where I painted the royal family, then to Japan to see the launching of the world's largest tanker, on to Nigeria and Angola, and finally to the Mackenzie Delta. I went to the four corners of the earth."

Lavin is very open about his self-promotion but somewhat disappointed about the time it takes away from his painting. He maintains a clipping file, compiled from trade magazines, of personnel changes, projects, and other information that aids him in approaching corporations. "I always address my brochure to the chief executive officer," he says. "Usually, if it goes to a public relations person or some other personnel, nothing will come of it. It is best to deal directly with the head of the company, because he can tell me what's on his mind. By the end of our meeting I understand what he wants, can suggest things to him, and when I leave I know what I'm going to do." One of Lavin's dissatisfactions with the advertising business was dealing with the generation gap between old timers and new recruits. He decided that he would rather deal with his contemporaries, with people who thought like he did.

Lavin usually likes the people he contacts. He has found that certain industries are headed by people who grew up in the business, know all aspects of production, and have an emotional involvement in the company. "For example," he explains, "a lot of the people who buy my paintings used to be roughnecks in the oil fields, as almost everybody was in Texas at one time or another. It was a great summer job for a kid with brawn, so all over Texas you meet people who used to do this, and they regard the subject with some romanticism."

Many industries are so expansive, combining many specialties, that most workers at headquarters have never seen the operation of their company. Lavin is incredulous about this attitude: "This is one reason why employees rarely have any identity with the company. I did a series of paintings for American

Banana Boat, 1966, oil, 36 x 48. Commissioned by United Fruit Co. Each time a ship is launched, a picture of it is commissioned. Lavin accepts a limited number of commissions of this type.

Zinc Company on how zinc is made. Most of the people who worked in that company had never seen zinc production nor did they have the vaguest idea of how it is done. They didn't feel any rapport with the company." Lavin is also disturbed by what he feels is a lack of self-confidence in industry: "I believe very strongly that one of the reasons corporations have such a bad image with the American people is that they themselves don't believe in corporations. They themselves are embarrassed by what they do."

Workers who are frequently wary of Lavin as he sketches at a site soon become enthusiastic about his work. The artist sees the men as heroic figures. "I find that I have a great rapport with these people," he says. "Sometimes they dislike me because of a class distinction, but after awhile we become comfortable with each other. I was doing a sketch at a coal mine, and a miner walked up to me and said, 'If you put me in the sketch as a beast, I'll knock your block off.' Strength is the only thing the working man has. He gets furious and worried about his ability declining." Lavin admires the rhythm and cooperation needed among workers to complete a task, and he captures this movement in many of his paintings.

Photography is one method Lavin employs to study this flow of action, but he is keenly aware of the me-dium's potential and limitations. A photograph can zero in on a specific scene or aspect of production, but it is difficult to arrive at a panorama. The artist sees his work as going beyond this limitation, because he is able to synthesize many points of view to obtain a single composition. Also, his own vision of the work dictates the utilization of his photographic studies: "One reason I can't take a photo and work from it is because I conceive of the picture being composed in a certain way, and of course nature doesn't compose that way. I'm very influenced by the light and dark and spatial reality of Baroque art, and I conceive of the composition basically as a Baroque composition. God was not a Baroque artist, so I have to arrange the picture to my own way." Recalling earlier days when he first used photographs, he advises, "Even if you take a thousand pictures, one will be so terrific that your impulse will be to copy it. Don't! It would always end up a disaster. It would be a terrible painting. That's not the way photography is to be used. I use photographs extremely well now. When I've made up my mind, I take pictures of all the pieces of the composition."

Often his clients are unaware of the drawbacks photographs have and try to commission Lavin to paint a picture based on photographs taken by a pro-

Above: *Making a Trip,* 1970, oil on panel, 40 x 44. Commissioned by Kewanee Industries. The first time Lavin looks at his subject, he leaves his cameras home. After he's returned to his studio and sketched out his composition, he returns to the scene with cameras to get pictures of the particular information he needs. Here a group of "roughnecks" are engaged in a job that requires absolute synchronization. A string of pipe has been dropped 20,000 feet into a well, and the bit has to be changed, which means the 20,000 feet of pipe has to be brought out and stacked. The job requires great strength and endurance as well as a spirit of teamwork.

Opposite page above: *Open Hearth,* oil, 1972, 20 x 40. Collection Granite City Steel, Division of National Steel. Open hearth, the "old fashioned" method of making steel, is fast disappearing, replaced by the cupola and B.O.F. shown before. Lavin, a romantic at heart, wanted to capture the drama of men of the steel industry working at an open hearth. He conceived a series of paintings, each a composite of events, which he planned to exhibit, and he persuaded Granite City Steel, for whom he had fulfilled many commissions, to let him visit their open-hearth operation. When the painting was finished, they liked it so much that they bought it for their collection.

Opposite page below: *Ocean Victory in the North Sea,* 1975, oil, 48 x 72. Commissioned by ODECO. For Lavin the aesthetic experience is essential. A painting begins with a vision of what he wants to say about a subject, a personal impression. In order to have a view of this rig, Lavin arranged to board the small fishing boats, shown in the foreground, which must circle the rig constantly, just in case someone falls in the ocean. Unfortunately for Lavin, on the day arranged for boarding, which was to be accomplished by dropping him down by a tire from the end of the crane (shown on the left of the rig), there was a severe storm. After an hour of hanging on the end of the rig, trying to make contact with the boat, a cold, drenched, and exhausted Lavin gave up. Instead of the rig, he had gotten an impression of the storm. The following day the sea was calm and he was able to board the boat with ease to get a view of the rig.

Off Shore Rig, 1970, oil on panel, 36 x 20. Private collection. When Lavin fulfills a commission, he generally presents five or six sketches to the client, of which one is selected; the rest go into a drawer. Recently, the artist took time off to develop some of the rejected sketches that he liked. This was one.

fessional. He is amused by this attitude but very earnest about what he has to say. "A man wanted a picture of his oil rig in the North Sea. He showed me pictures of it. The first thing I had to convince him was that I had to go out there and see it. He'd paid a photographer thousands of dollars to take these gorgeous pictures, and he expected me to take one and paint it out. But I have to have an aesthetic experience; I have to feel it. Plus, I think the picture is exciting when there's an anecdote. I just don't want a picture of an oil rig; I want to relate it to what happens there."

Conveying a story is part of Lavin's background as a magazine illustrator as well as part of his academic training and formative years as a painter. He attended City College of New York and the National Academy Art School in the 1930s, when much of the art being produced was Social Realism. He studied the work of Grant Wood and Thomas Hart Benton and others. Then a very simple but important thing happened to Lavin: "I met a fellow at City College, Irv Miller, who had dropped out of school for a year and worked as a sign painter. He wanted to be a commercial artist. I had never heard of such a thing. But in the '30s there was no future for an artist except the WPA project, and even teaching jobs were impossible to come by. I didn't even think in those terms, and when Irv came and implanted the idea of commercial art in my mind, it fit in perfectly well with my political ideas: that art should be art for use. Throughout the history of art, except for the past 150 years, people have always thought of art this way, as having a function in the community."

After college and his return from the war, Lavin realized that he was entering a changing world. He didn't want to leave Social Realism and tried to achieve his own interpretation: "I still liked the theme, and I like it now. In a way, I feel I've devised a method of painting Social Realism and keeping it alive, but not with the same leftist or regional slant that the artists of the '30s gave it. I have a romantic attitude about it that they did not, which expresses itself in a kind of romantic realism."

In some aspects his commercial background has been a mixed blessing. Working at Cooper Studios, he was exposed to the best advertising pros and learned how and why his academic training wasn't always suitable for media solutions. "I found that when I quit doing advertising work and wanted to do these paintings, I would instinctively revert to commercial solutions," he recalls. "Commercial artists can work their way out of a bad picture by just technique. That's all right. A painting in a magazine is quickly read, but if I'm going to put a painting in a person's office that they have to look at year after year, it has to be a slow read. It must be complicated."

Lavin's artistic awareness enabled him to abandon the clean-cut technique that was necessary in advertising but makes little sense in his present work. Usually Lavin presents a number of oil sketches to his client. From these the final, expanded versions are selected, and for this reason the sketches must be accurate conceptions of the finished work. The sketches never have the paintings' careful realization of volumes or the intricate construction of spatial arrangements or design of negative spaces.

Lavin is intensely devoted to his work. He and his wife have been able to live comfortably through their joint efforts, and he believes that any competent artist can make a good living outside of the gallery system. He smiles, saying, "People sometimes ask me what I paint on weekends; the presumption is that I'm prostituting myself all week for commercial reasons. I don't feel that way. The house is filled with these pictures; I believe in these pictures."

Scoffing at the 19th century image of the struggling artist, Lavin says, "Throughout history most artists have made a living. Some of them made better livings because they were better businesspeople. You are in a business, and you have to operate as if you are in a business." Lavin uses this philosophy in promoting his own work. For example, he just had a new brochure printed. He had his written presentation edited by a professional writer and has no qualms in seeking specialized help. The increased competition in his field over the past ten years makes a highly professional brochure and presentation an absolute must.

His tenacious attitude toward learning and correcting problem areas in his own work makes him feel that an artist can develop his potentials and career. "A person who does portraits has learned certain things that are imperative for a portrait, and he or she learns how to do a portrait that sells."

Lavin's suggestion to the fledgling businessperson is to investigate all possible markets. He notes the many art shows at suburban shopping malls and the numerous artists making a living selling paintings there. The message is to see what is selling, who is buying, and for how much; the artist must learn his market. Lavin makes a valid point: "Cowboy paintings are very popular, and people who jump on the bandwagon will never be as good as those people who have made it their life's work. Pick something that you are comfortable doing, stick with it, and be sure it is fulfilling a need."

Reflecting his past training and milieu of development, Lavin is convinced that an artist can flourish in this format: "Every painting in the Renaissance had conditions, but that didn't prevent great artists from developing. Artists have to learn that there is nothing about rules that will prevent them from being great artists. You work within the limits of these rules. It also enables society to give its opinion about works of art."

FRANK METZ

BY DOREEN MANGAN

SCOTLAND'S OUTER HEBRIDES, the West of Ireland, Maine's Penobscot Bay, and Gran Manan in the Bay of Fundy are among the sources of inspiration for Frank Metz's oil paintings.

Each locale has its own attraction. Maine, for example, with its rocky coast, meadows, and evergreens "is a part of the world that I have the most empathy with," Metz says. And the ever-changing weather conditions in Ireland and Scotland illuminate "nuances of landscape" Metz seeks out.

"Ireland, and also England and Scotland, are subject to the weather from the west," he explains. "Sunshine alternates with gentle rainfalls; then more sun, then torrential rain. You see rainbows and, later, huge black cloud banks. In the Outer Hebrides the wind never lets up, and you get incredible cloud formations.

"It is fair to say that I am far more attracted to grayer and more turbulent weather conditions than placid, conventionally pretty summer weather, with blue skies and bright sunlight."

Ireland and Britain are ideal for an artist with such a penchant. Even under wet or overcast conditions, the landscapes never lack color: green, gold, purple,

Opposite page: *Low Tide, Bay Of Fundy,* 1976, oil, 30 x 40. Courtesy Alonzo Gallery. Metz's paintings suggest the brush in such a way that the viewer becomes a part of the painting process.

Above: *Sea Loch,* 1974, oil, 42 x 40. Courtesy Alonzo Gallery. Inspired by literature, Metz uses paint instead of words to evoke the illusion of a landscape so completely that you can almost smell the salt air and feel the wind.

Right: *Salt Marsh,* 1976, oil, 38 x 38. Courtesy Alonzo Gallery. Photo eeva-inkeri, New York. Metz does not paint on location. He develops a painting in his studio using photos and sketches, keeping it loose and quite form-less—building up and shifting shapes until he feels it is through.

Below: A page of studies for *Salt Marsh,* (top), ink, 9½ x 12. While Metz often uses drawing as notetaking for future painting, it is fre-quently a clarification of what's happening. Here the linear quality of the drawing cap-tured the feeling of movement, the rhythmic quality Metz saw in this early morning view. When he began to work on the painting, the color notes (above) and photos comple-mented each other.

blue, and gray. Metz's painting *County Mayo*, shown here, is an excellent example, with its silver-gray sky, dark and brooding mountains, and beige and golden beach. This painting belies the stereotypical emerald Ireland of the travel posters and TV commercials.

The artist added black, a color he rarely uses, to his usual muted color selections to create this painting. The abstract elements in the sky and beach are typical of his style.

Interestingly, many of the areas that reappear again and again in Metz's paintings are islands. He became aware of an unusual fascination with islands when he first began visiting Maine's Monhegan Island in the 1950s. His excursions in serach of subject matter have taken him also to Vinal Haven in Penobscot Bay. "There's a limitless feeling to the Maine Islands," he says. "I get tremendously nostalgic when I think of the lure the islands have for me . . . and the sadness I feel when I leave. It's greater than leaving a place on the mainland."

His most recent paintings explore and interpret the flat, grassy geography of eastern Long Island.

Metz's interest in islands and places of uncertain climate is somewhat explained by his love of literature from and about these regions. The sense of movement and torment found in the literature matches the moody landscapes and unpredictable weather changes. "I have always found the relationship between literature and art to be a support for my work," he observes.

Irish writers such as Sean O'Faolain and Edna O'Brien, therefore, have helped shape Metz's artistic vision of their country. And England's D. H. Lawrence, whose brooding novels investigate the landscape of the country and of the mind, has also captured his imagination; as has Lawrence Durrell, "an incredibly descriptive writer."

In 1960 Metz and his wife stayed for a month in Sussex, in the south of England, where the writer Virginia Woolf had settled early in her marriage. On reading Woolf's second volume of letters, Metz says he experienced a sense of *deja vu* as Woolf referred to the "same geology and weather conditions of the area that were so important to us when we were there."

Henry James, who spent so much time in England, is also a strong literary influence on the artist. His *English Hours*, descriptive pieces on English countryside, cathedrals, towns and villages, are "most evocative," Metz says. "This man could describe a house and its surrounding landscape so completely you can smell the salt and see the marsh."

Metz garners subjects for his paintings by trips to these favorite places. He does not, however, paint on location, preferring to make ink sketches and take photographs. The latter are for use solely as a color reference. The heart of his paintings comes from the drawings. "The eye is selective, but the camera, as I use it, is all-encompassing; everything is in the ground glass. What I am trying to say is that drawing is an absolute necessity to my painting."

The ink drawings, done in sketchbooks whose steadiness offers immediacy and permits close detailing, are "sometimes hasty notations, sometimes highly detailed drawings. They are kept intentionally permanent within a bound book." He also makes occasional watercolor sketches on loose watercolor sheets for the convenience of pinning up on his studio wall for quick reference as he paints. "They are used as a sort of constant filing system," he explains.

One trip can produce many drawings. A 1975 summer vacation on Grand Manan Island, for instance, yielded 30 to 40 drawings of many aspects of the area: beaches, rock formations, vegetations, bird life, tidal ponds, clouds.

Once back in his home, however, Metz does not immediately plunge into paintings based on the latest drawings. He did not, for example, turn to the Grand Manan drawings until the following spring, and a year later he was still producing paintings from that experience. "There's always a delayed reaction," he explains. "To immediately start to paint from the drawings produces false starts." Instead, he lets the drawings sit in his studio while he turns his attention to other paintings, until some inexplicable instinct tells him he's ready to begin the new paintings.

Metz's painting method, as he describes it, has changed somewhat over the years. Formerly, he would apply a fairly detailed charcoal-and-ink sketch to a primed canvas, and then gradually paint over the drawing. His present method is to tone the canvas and, while it is still wet, lightly and quickly sketch in a "loose, amorphous drawing—an idea of shapes and forms, working from one or two drawings made on location."

The subsequent growth of the painting is a "building-up process—a sequence of moving and shifting; a certain amount of overpainting, of closing of large areas. There are heavy areas of paint and very thin areas. Of course, it's a very, very slow, gradual process. I do not work with great sweeping applications of paint in an attempt to cover a canvas in a short period of time. The painting is kept loose and quite formless until I feel it through."

He is constantly working with shapes, testing their relationship to each other in the painting context versus the drawing context. "There is always something to be eliminated, no matter how exquisite it may be, if it simply doesn't fit," he explains.

This ability and determination to exclude interruptive elements have earned Metz critical praise: "Mr. Metz's oils, like his drawings, are as impressive for their selective editing of the scene as for what they include," was the way a critic summed up a Metz show in 1974.

Metz uses a double-primed, finely woven canvas. His palette is "an old piece of butcher glass I've had for about 35 years." The most frequently used colors are muted: earth shades, soft lavenders, earthy greens, gray-blues, off-pinks, muted yellows, for example. He mixes his shades in large sea shells collected from the many beaches his travels have taken

Opposite page, top: *County Mayo,* 1971, oil, 32 x 42. Courtesy Alonzo Gallery. As a painting develops, Metz continuously "works" the shapes, testing their relationship to each other in the painting context, versus the drawing context.

Opposite page, bottom: *Sheltered Cove, (Grand Manon),* 1976, oil, 22 x 36. Courtesy Alonzo Gallery. Each locale has its own attraction for Metz. Using a low-lying shoreline and far horizon along with a muted palette, he suggests a feeling of limitlessness, of quiet and isolation—perhaps melancholy.

Above: Sketch for *County Mayo,* ink, 12½ x 20. Metz feels the heart of his paintings comes from his drawings of an area, although he does use a camera. "The eye is selective," he comments, "the camera all-encompassing."

Sketches of Greenport, 1976, ink, 8 x 10. Photo Studio Nine, New York. Not all of Metz's drawings become paintings. Here are two of several sketches Metz made on a weekend voyage "purely for the pleasure of the moment—of being somewhere and wanting to record it."

him to. His brushes range from very small to fairly wide. "The painting suggests the brush," he says, pointing out that choice of tools is as personal a matter as style of painting.

It's Metz's custom to have three or four paintings in progress at a time. Usually two of them are of the same subject, "so I can interrelate qualities of one into another. I try to find a continuity from one painting to another." For example, the clump of trees seen in the distance in *Sheltered Cove (Grand Manan)* was also part of another painting in progress, in a different perspective, at the time of our interview.

As noted earlier, drawing plays an important role in Metz's painting. Besides using drawing as a sort of notetaking for future paintings, it is frequently a clarification of what's happening on the canvas. "Sometimes there's a need to do a drawing in order to explore something that has been baffling me about a painting," Metz explains. "I might want to find out more about the subject, specific details such as rocks,

weeds, skies. Drawing has always been a way of resolving and seeing the things that I have been working on, also pointing to new directions in my paintings."

But drawing is more than an aid to painting, for Metz is an accomplished draftsman who has successfully exhibited and sold his drawings. In fact, at one time early in his career one critic wrote, "The real Frank Metz is in the drawings."

Today, however, critics praise both the drawings and paintings. Each has an important place in the artist's life. "I have always found drawing to be an unbelievable pleasure," he says. "I interrupt the painting year by doing drawings for their own sake, drawings that have nothing to do with the painting I'm working on. Sometimes I feel, during the course of a year, that the time has come to stop painting; there's a feeling of unresponse to a particular picture, or a need to rest or build up again to a new direction. The drawings are then a necessary interlude."

Metz, who has been painting professionally since the early 1950s, was born in Philadelphia and got his introduction to painting through a high school art course with a teacher who emphasized landscape.

Philadelphia was a good place for a budding landscapist to grow up, Metz says, because of easy access to the country, although metropolitan aspects of the city also pleased him: "It has so many different neighborhoods within neighborhoods. A 45-minute bus ride from my area would bring you to another section of the city which had its own name, architecture, and dialect."

Shortly after finishing high school, Metz was inducted into the army. After that he studied advertising and design at the Philadelphia Museum School. "It was a means to an end," he explains, "the end being to get a job in advertising." Interestingly, he continues, painting was very much emphasized at the Museum School, partly because of the traditions of the school and partly because of the traditions of the city, which has produced a number of artists. "Two painting instructors were very helpful and supportive. They led me and others into directions we might not have ventured into."

This period in the late 1940s and early '50s was one of the most exciting times to be studying art, Metz found. For the first time, Americans were exposed to the great 20th century French painters, such as Braque and Matisse. This was also the coming of age of contemporary American painting. People such as DeKooning were beginning to create excitement.

Metz also traveled to Europe for the first time. There he was confronted by "monumental pictures" he had seen only in reproduction and had regarded with just passing interest, such as those of Giotto and Rembrandt.

All this intensified his desire to paint professionally, and he has done so ever since. He produces about ten or eleven paintings a year, plus several drawings, which is remarkable when one considers that he paints only in the evenings and on weekends in winter.

During the day he pursues a full-time career as Art Director at Simon & Schuster, a large New York publishing company. "I have never seen any competition between my art and my career," he says. "Many artists have to support themselves in ways totally unrelated to their art. Some have tried freelancing in art-related fields, such as design, and then try to pack painting into whatever time is available. To me that would be more distracting than having a schedule in which you know how many hours of the day and how many days of the week you are obliged to set aside for your career and therefore how much time you can work in your own studio. The time I have for painting is my own and does not compete with the world of commerce."

Like all artists, Metz agrees that the urge to create is not always present and cannot always be programmed into the time that is available. "Often the time is there, but the urge to work is not," he comments. But at least that time was set aside by him and did not interfere with his day job.

The whole question of an artist's time and self-discipline is one Metz has given a great deal of thought to and has, over the years, worked out to his own satisfaction. His observations may help young artists who may not yet have resolved this in their own minds.

"I don't really think," he says, "that one can use the excuse that one never had time. You have to observe a discipline no matter what you are doing. That you are destined to create, I think, is something one accepts. There are people who for various reasons simply do not have the drive, the urge, the ability to work in the face of frustration and disappointment.

"I don't see myself as a shining example of someone who has surmounted all sorts of hardships. Yet I felt all along that I am an artist and I must work. It is always amazing and somewhat tiresome to meet an old friend or acquaintance and be asked the inevitable question, 'Are you still painting?' To me that is akin to asking whether you are still breathing."

So the artist continues to work, always seeking self-improvement: "I look back on my work of the last ten years with a mixture of admiration, impatience, and disgust. I want to grow, to excel, to refine the art of landscape."

JOHN MOORE

BY EVE MEDOFF

The Letter, 1975, oil, 75 x 90. Courtesy Fischbach Gallery. Moore flattens out the illusion of space by placing the drape—interrupting it by the edge of the painting—almost completely across the lower half of the picture.

IN THE TWO DECADES before the '70s, figurative painting had all but disappeared from public view. In major museums and galleries, with few exceptions, it was most often relegated to basement storage rooms and exhumed only on special occasions. It was also conspicuously absent from art school curricula, its study considered neither vital nor relevant, and, as a consequence, was largely ignored. An art student could complete a four-year course without ever drawing or painting a still life or living model.

The re-emergence of realism in painting, when it did come, was not without its disquieting effects. Those who expected to see the old, familiar formulations were doomed to disappointment, if not actual shock. New labels found their way daily into the art lexicon. *Super Realism*, the title of a critical anthology by Gregory Battcock, is used as an umbrella term to cover New Realism, Photo Realism, Sharp Focus Realism, Humanist and Existential Realism . . . the list goes on and on.

John Moore's work has been described, analyzed, and appraised in any number of contexts. He has been called a "metaphysical naturalist"; some aspects of his work have invoked comparison with the *trompe l'oeil* of William Harnett. The "careful, premeditated, artful" arrangements of his still lifes have been dubbed "classical," and he is regarded by some art historians as a throwback to Chardin, Fantin-Latour, della Francesca, and Vermeer. Everywhere, however, he is grouped with the New (that is, second generation) Realists.

Many scholars and critics tend to see the panorama of art history as a vast jig-saw puzzle; it is not difficult to picture one such, a piece held between thumb and forefinger, glancing anxiously from it to the tantalizing contours and color cues on the board, seeking to fit it into the mosaic of the whole. Perhaps, after all, the most telling statement about Moore's work was made by John Perrault in a review of an exhibition at the Fischbach Gallery of New York in 1972. "It is almost," he wrote, "as if photography and abstract art had never existed . . . it is almost as if Moore has been trying to re-invent realist art from scratch."

In a sense, he has been doing exactly that.

Basic Days, 1977, oil, 75 x 90. Courtesy Fischbach Gallery. The subject is morning light. Moore developed this painting in his studio from small drawings and color studies done on the spot. Interestingly, Moore found the haze useful: it obscured parts of the cityscape and proved an aid in summarizing forms.

Three L.A. Pinks, 1977, watercolor, 22 x 31. Courtesy Fischbach Gallery. In a current series of watercolors, of which this is an example, Moore contrasts objects he uses for pattern information and objects he uses to illustrate space. The former are muted grays—the tablecloth—and the latter, while somewhat muted, retain the local color of the object.

Except for a brief interval (two summer sessions and his first year of graduate study), Moore has moved steadily in the direction of the style, technique, and subject matter characterizing his work today. Very possibly, when he elected to enroll in the David Ranken, Jr., School of Mechanical Trades instead of college, he had no more than a vague idea of picking up a marketable skill in the shortest possible time. Without doubt, the certificate in drafting he received at the end of the year helped land the job at McDonnell-Douglas Aircraft where he was set to drawing parts of rockets and planes, a stint that led in turn to participation in Project Mercury of the U.S. Space Program.

The value of that experience to his subsequent career is obvious now. First the study and later the practice of geometric principles gave him an understanding of the relationships of lines, angles, surfaces, perspective, arrangements of volumes and their configurations, and exacted the hand-and-eye coordinated skills serving him so phenomenally well today.

There was nothing vague about the impulse that led him to take an evening drawing course at Washington University. A sense of urgency had begun to gnaw at his consciousness even before he realized its exact nature. The feeling persisted and grew; from a part-time extracurricular activity, drawing for its own sake began to assume the proportions of an obsession. By term's end, Moore knew what he had to do and did it. He resigned from his job at the aircraft factory and registered as a full-time student at the university with a special sense of gratitude to his teacher, Barry Schachtman, whose rigorous standards demanded the utmost accuracy of observation and the precise documentation of three-dimensional forms.

It is interesting, in tracing the development of this artist, to see how unerringly his instinct drew him to the mode of painting which has proved so eminently to be his true métier. At the Yale University Summer School of Painting in 1965, during his junior year at Washington University, he was virtually surrounded by practitioners of abstract painting. He was also exposed to the works of outstanding proponents of the movement. Yet even while he was himself experimenting with abstraction, he was at the same time powerfully affected by an exhibition of the realistic still-life paintings of William Bailey.

The following summer in New Hampshire, on a grant from the National Endowment for the Arts, Moore elected to study the mountain landscape directly and intensively, recording the fading light of late afternoon as it changes to dusk. He returned to St. Louis with 110 miniature paintings, none larger than four by six inches, done in acrylics on paper. It is an impressive group, rapidly brushed in without detail, an essay on the departing day, seen "as through a glass, darkly." Several of these small works show the sky lit by the last streaks of light after sundown. In all of them the low-keyed color registers

with amazing fidelity the quiet mystery of the remaining light in the last moments before dark.

By the time he entered Yale that fall to begin working for a master's degree in fine arts, he was, in his own words, "desperate for something concrete to paint." Though not quite ready to abandon abstraction, he began to incorporate figures drawn from life into imaginary landscapes. He was beginning to recognize in himself a growing disposition toward realist painting; the works of Lennart Anderson and Philip Pearlstein may have brought it into sharp focus in that period. In any case, 1967 can be seen as a watershed in his career; it was then he began painting the still lifes and interiors that have occupied him ever since.

After graduating from Yale in '68, Moore joined the faculty of Temple University's Tyler School of Art in Philadelphia. Abstract art continued its smooth course, its majestic calm barely ruffled by the stirrings of Pop, Minimalist, Op, and other currents. New Realism hadn't officially surfaced yet. It was to do so a year later in the Whitney Museum of American Art exhibition titled "22 Realists." Moore's first act at Tyler was to initiate a course in Direct Painting, his own term for drawing and painting from still life and living models.

For many students the course was a new, invigorating experience that channelled their sensibilities into unfamiliar paths of perception. Direct Painting necessitates an almost 180 degree turn from the subjectivity of the abstract painter to the objective view of the realist a challenge for the adventurous student.

Harking back to John Perrault's comment about Moore's approach mentioned earlier, "... to re-invent realist art from scratch," it could be argued that realism in art has no need to be re-invented. Its irrepressible faculty for survival is amply recorded in art history, from Giotto to Caravaggio, from Constable to the Impressionists. However, the significance of the words "from scratch" is undeniable.

Born in St. Louis in 1941, John Moore opened his eyes to a physical environment bearing little resemblance to that of his forebears. North light studios were fast disappearing, the gentle glow of candlelight and oil lamp or flickering gas fixtures long since gone. Artists in our time are usually dependent on fluorescent and incandescent lighting; daylight, when it is available, is filtered through veils of pollution. We grow accustomed to neon signs, shiny automobiles and refrigerators, chrome furniture, and plastics everywhere, to the point of insensibility. Without doubt, technological and cultural change alters our perception of reality, and inevitably the artist will respond to the existing environment in an idiom shaped by it.

His New Hampshire experience convinced Moore that he needed a viable alternative to landscape painting, invented or real. The immensity of the great outdoors, with its infinite visual complexities, overwhelmed the precisionist who could not be satisfied with less than a detailed rendering of every blade of

View of New Haven, 1967-68, oil, 88 x 74. Courtesy Fischbach Gallery. Certain paintings often represent major turning points in an artist's career. This was one of those paintings for Moore. It was the first time he worked directly from a source on this scale. In addition, his previous works had been more abstract, and color was unrestrained. Here he defines the problems he would begin to concern himself with, not only the specific problems concerning form that come about when painting from life, but the use of a more restrained palette and less arbitrary color as well: the challenge of conveying a sense of the place and the time.

Red Snapper Soup, 1975, oil, 90 x 75. Courtesy Fischbach Gallery. This painting followed *The Letter,* which is more restrained. Here the forms are more aggressive and the pattern of the drapery bolder. In both paintings, however, Moore uses the mirror to make the space of the room more visible. He also admits to a certain enjoyment in stepping inside another artist's idea of something, which happened when he painted the painted flowers on the drapery.

grass, every leaf, every twig. He found the answer in his studio among such familiar objects that he had not thought of them as "something concrete to paint." His decision to give up landscape painting for still life and interiors was based on a reasoned estimate of the means available to his purpose: that of studying and recording volumes in space. The objects he employs are neutral in character, virtually anonymous, like the drinking glass and the plastic chair.

Is Moore thus trying to tell us something about the monotony of modern culture, its mediocrity, its lack of drama? Probably not. More likely he is consciously avoiding the clichés of 19th century academicism, "beauty" and "good taste," in order to present reality without associative reference to classicism or romanticism. Moore tells us, "My work has nothing to do with photographs or other second-hand visual information, but rather attempts a precise analysis of forms in space with appropriate considerations of, or concessions to, picture plane and other two-dimensional realities." Not the camera, but the mind's eye, is at work here, registering on canvas or paper a lucid description of observable phenomena, unclouded by illusionary embellishment.

We should not be deceived, however, by what may appear to be a simple, literal statement of fact: a glass tumbler reflected in a mirror, a cast shadow, a draped cloth. The deceptive simplicity of his paintings belies the complex problems that Moore sets himself— problems of light and shadow, transparency and opacity, color and its absence, volume, perspective, and dimensionality.

Another conflict he has resolved concerns the use of watercolor. The idea of making some paintings on paper was tempting, and watercolor offered the advantage of transparency. Traditional techniques somehow did not solve what he was after; once more he began "from scratch" to apply it simply, without striving for virtuosity. With flat, ungraded tones he found he could match the exact value, hue, and degree of transparency of an object's color. The results were surprisingly agreeable. The watercolors, which may have begun as preparatory sketches for large canvases, came into their own as fully realized paintings. They are done on full sheets of 300 lb. Fabriano with Winsor & Newton colors, assisted by several colors from Pelikan.

The glass surfaces (tabletop or shelf) on which he places his arrangements not only reflect the objects but also catch the glare from multiple light sources. These are situated to create crossed shadows. A phenomenon never failing to intrigue him is the tendency of shadows to disappear under fluorescent lighting, as though swallowed up by the light itself. The edge of the clear glass tabletop, possibly no deeper than ⅜ inch, appears greenish as it, too, catches the light. As a counterpoise to the reflections, glare, and cast shadows, he sometimes lays overlapping sheets of colored opaque or transparent paper between object and table surface. In other paintings of the watercolor series, he permits the white paper alone to act as the ground plane.

Moore's canvases run the gamut in size, from 12 x 18 to 93 x 139. The oversize canvases favored by Abstract Expressionists survive in the work of New Realists. In his larger paintings, Moore expands the environmental setting in stages up to nearly life-size interiors.

Perspective is seen from any number of viewpoints. We may be looking down on a round glass table that almost covers the small 12 x 18 canvas and gives no clue to the angle of vision except the depth of its ellipse. In a much larger 1974 canvas, *Still Life with Glass of Tea*, 50 x 60, the same table is seen in its entirety with foreshortened legs and standing so close to the wall that the floor molding cuts diagonally across the picture, seen through the glass in an unbroken line. Tilting the floor plane occurs in a number of paintings that exploit a corner, showing part of the floor joining two walls.

Light and color in Moore's paintings are so completely interdependent as to render them virtually inseparable. A cool ambience sustains the separate color elements in a harmonious relationship. The pervasive light draws color into itself from the objects it illuminates, acquiring a tonality of its own in the way that certain great cities—Paris, Rome, Florence, Athens—exhibit a characteristic tonal light.

Large areas of his canvases are painted in cool, silvery tones of gray, blue, and brown, the latter achieved without the use of earth pigments. Strong accents of black occur. An object might be selected because of its particular shade of color. One example is a small drinking glass, which can be exactly matched by Winsor & Newton's Rose Doré. In many of the paintings color functions as staccato accents against large, neutral areas. It also appears in the pattern of cloth.

While his decisions regarding color are made only after patient study and reflection, his compositions are arrived at almost spontaneously. Placement of objects in the still-life arrangements happen more or less instinctively. So do the choices of shapes, both geometric and natural, such as folds of draped cloth and flowers to offset the uncompromising lines of rectangular windows, cylindrical cups, circular mirrors, and hemispherical bowls.

Recognition came rapidly to John Moore, but quietly, without the usual fanfare of press-agentry. Over a relatively short span of years, a prodigious quantity of critical analysis and evaluation has been expended on his work in art publications. The first exhibition that drew attention to his painting was a group show, held in 1969 at the Fischbach Gallery in New York City, called "Direct Representation." A subsequent review of that exhibition devoted a full paragraph to a discussion of the paintings entered by Moore.

In 1972 Fischbach gave him a solo exhibition and followed with another three years later. Also, in 1973, the Pennsylvania Academy of the Fine Arts held an exhibition of his work at its Peale House Gallery.

Other solo exhibitions occurred in Princeton, Boston, and Rochester.

The group exhibitions in which he participated are too numerous to list here, but the theme titles of several are indicative of the company he finds himself in: "From Life," "New Realism," "The Realist Revival," "Selections in Contemporary Realism," "Figuration in American Painting," "The Figure in Recent American Painting," "Forecasts."

Where does he see himself heading? Moore feels the question is not an easy one to answer: "The trouble with defining my intentions is that it rules out flexibility, and I want to be free to change or modify my ideas as I go along.

"Looking over the slides of my work, certain themes emerge which have held my interest for a number of years, themes I touched on as far back as graduate school. For example, thinking about the still-life paintings, I feel as if I have never really moved away from landscape. You might say they are surrogate landscapes, subject to the tighter control the studio makes possible. The movement of light in the paintings is related to nature; remembrance of landscape phenomena is always present. I think of still life in architectural terms and choose specific objects deliberately, like the tall, slim glasses which suggest smokestacks. Industrial architecture has always interested me and shows up in my paintings, seen through a window. And always, light: the bright outdoor light contrasted with the soft, diffused light indoors.

"In recent paintings, diagonals have become more extreme; one-point perspective gives way to two-point and other perspective systems. Before I have finished one painting, it has given me a new idea to carry into the next. Yet, far from being diverted from my basic concerns—the quality and movement of light, perspectival space, architecture, landscape, and human activity—I hope it comes together in one all-encompassing theme.

"It is difficult enough to know exactly what you are going to do in a single painting, much less where the work will go eventually, but I am excited enough by what has happened in the painting previously to be very hopeful about the way it is going now and how it may continue to go."

FORREST MOSES

BY MARY CARROLL NELSON

Above: *Rio Grande, South of Taos,* 1976, oil, 48 x 50. Courtesy Watson/de Nagy & Co. Moses begins a painting by covering the entire canvas with an earthy, pale yellow about the color of sand, allowing this underpainting to show through successive layers.

Left: *Rio Grande at Taos,* oil, 42 x 60, 1976. Courtesy Watson/de Nagy & Co. Moses's present motif, which, according to his custom, will evolve through numerous paintings of related imagery, is the sanctuary: a place in the desert region favored with water.

Opposite page: *The Rio Chama at Abiquiu,* 1976, oil, 48 x 50. Courtesy Watson/de Nagy & Co. Moses feels he tends to get more involved in a work that has a sense of movement in it, and he accordingly leaves some areas unfinished. "Things in process are more life-giving than work completely resolved," he says.

FORREST MOSES places a large canvas on his easel, one of his *Sanctuary* series: In a yellow, sandy desert Moses has painted a stream flowing in a shallow bed, reflecting an unseen blue sky as it passes some hot cadmium rocks and grasses. Broad gestures and sweeps of paint become a close-up of nature. A fresh, unworried look prevails in the work. Though painted on a grand scale, the scene is a private one, made restful by poising unfilled areas amid the active spaces.

"A sanctuary," Moses believes, "is a place where life, both physical and spiritual, is nurtured." When, in the '60s, he was searching for a nourishing atmosphere in which to paint and to grow personally, he found it in Santa Fe, New Mexico.

An energetic, well-knit man of medium height and slim build, Forrest Moses gives an impression of spruce grooming. His beard is trimmed close. "Trimming close," "paring down"—these words suit the man. There is a leanness about him that affects his person, his art, and his philosophy.

Though Moses is complex, his thoughts, expressed in the soft accents of the South, are cogent and complete. He doesn't leave half-formed sentences dangling as one waits for the predicate. He is hospitable and engages in conversations, rather than monologues. There is an easy give-and-take with him on subjects that range across disciplines, reflecting the ideas he has been pondering. It is clear that he feels he is emerging from that vague period in life when vestiges of hand-me-down philosophies passed on from one's family forebears are finally examined and culled.

Moses describes his heritage as one that is familiarly American: respectable, social, law-abiding, and upright. Chief among the tenets of his childhood, as for most of us, was the dictum to "be good." One senses that Moses has had a recent victory over the whole syndrome and is finding more and more proofs that life (and art) include everything, and an encompassing viewpoint is more sustaining to him than a dogma.

Forrest Moses began expressing himself as a painter at an early age. Born in Danville, Virginia, on May 14, 1934, his obvious talent was encouraged by his parents. From the age of nine he attended art classes at two local junior colleges and went on to Washington and Lee University, where he majored in fine arts (art history). After graduation in 1956 he served his military obligation in the Navy for three years as an Air Intelligence Officer in the Philippine Islands; he was thrifty enough while in the service to support a long tour of Europe in 1960.

From 1960 to 1962 Moses pursued study in interior design at New York's Pratt Institute. He practiced this profession in Dallas and Houston for three years before determining to paint full time. In 1965 he had his first one-man show, and it was a near sellout. Painting and exhibiting have rhythmically filled his life since.

After living in Northern California for three years,

Moses taught at the University of Houston for a term, but he discovered that "Painting is a 24-hour job. I can't work at something else and also be a painter. Even teaching saps the same energy—the creative energy—needed for painting."

The thought occurred to him that he could live in Santa Fe and paint for a summer. Santa Fe had been serving as a way stop for him on trips from California to Houston to deliver paintings to his Texas gallery; it wasn't a new place to him, but it was one where he was almost unknown, and he felt a certain risk in going there. Almost immediately he realized an intense need for the area, and he stayed on.

"I definitely feel that one's habitat affects one's attitude. You are what you eat—well, you are what you live in," Moses says. "Santa Fe is itself a sanctuary—an oasis. Contrasts make the dynamics of living in Santa Fe. There are mountains where water rushes among aspen groves and lush vegetation. Descending toward the west, the landscape quickly changes to badlands of dry arroyos, great eroded mesas. These alternatives are always at hand.

"There is a challenge to pushing to the edge of survival," he feels. In the desert or skiing down the nearby mountains, Moses finds he is conscious of the exhilaration of his own vulnerability in this environment.

But these are not the only aspects of Santa Fe that drew him. "There is a continuity and rightness to it," he explains. Its adobe houses date back to the primitive style of the Pueblo Indians. The buildings evolved naturally and from necessity from the land, and they could, if unattended, return to the earth. "I felt that this was a place where someone could live and grow in basic ways. I could get down to essentials in such a place."

Within one month of his 1969 arrival in Santa Fe, Moses bought a small adobe house, seasoned with age and nestled against a hill on an obscure street. It has grown as he has added rooms, one at a time. Around it he planted a garden with masses of daisies, poppies, and irises among pines and aspen between the protective outer wall and the house itself. There is a strangeness to this moist garden surrounded by arid land, an incongruity of which Forrest Moses is entirely aware. His feeling for the use of space is acute and is central to his aesthetic.

The house Moses lives in is his own sanctuary and one that satisfies him. A large room with a north window cut in it serves as his studio. The corner fireplace, the brick floors, and the exposed, round beams mark it as a Santa Fe room. All other details mark it as Moses's workspace. He doesn't clutter it up. There's a worktable loaded with empty cans, tubes, and brushes. Under it is a trunk of clean rags. A small table, covered by his glass palette, stands next to his easel and the window. There are a few racks on the end wall and a couple of director's chairs.

The rooms of this distinctive house are light. The textures of leather, wood, and clay complement its bare white walls. Rooms flow together functionally.

Desert Water Variation No. 1, 1975, oil, 40 x 50. Courtesy Watson / de Nagy & Co. Spaces around the objects are used to counterpoint the basic flatness of this subject.

Overleaf:
Desert Water, 1976, oil, 42 x 66.
Courtesy Watson / de Nagy & Co.
Water, the life-sustaining element in New Mexico,
relieves the harshness and threat
of rocks and sand, creating a drama of color.

Well within the house is another delightful incongruity: a shadowed retreat whose walls are covered with bromiliads and orchids. A few steps above the tiled floor in this green space is a sunken wooden tub—a whirlpool—under a skylight. A showerhead inconspicuously set in the wall identifies this as a bath—but it is more nearly an environment for meditation. Moses is a maker of spaces and a creator of contrasts.

"I've put a lot of energy into an environment for myself: spare, a background that doesn't scream for attention. Perhaps with my training in design it's natural, but my environment has always been important to me. I'm attracted to an Oriental sense of space, of sparseness. I like monasteries and churches. Sensitivity to these things influences my work," Moses says.

Immediately, Moses makes a link from his home to his art. It is his custom to paint a single motif for a long time, letting it evolve through numerous paintings of related imagery. His present motif is the sanctuary.

Currently the sanctuary is to Moses a place found in the desert region that is favored with water. "In New Mexico," he says, "you find yourself acutely conscious of the sky, the land, and water." Water as the life-sustaining element relieves the harshness and threat of rocks and sand, and it has been a developing theme in his work.

The *Sanctuary* series grew from an earlier one called *Tesuque Watershed*. That group of paintings is based on a fast-moving mountain stream north of Santa Fe. It involves deep greens, wet fall leaves, spring grasses, and rocks. There are reflections and collections of flotsam in pools. Colors are rich and shadows dark in those places.

The *Sanctuary* paintings are set in flatlands where the sun beats down on tenuous, marshy, shallow ripples of water. The colors are hotter and the juxtaposition of desert and water is more dramatic philosophically than in the *Watershed* paintings. Moses deals with these things in his mind and on canvas, taking pleasure in their role as opposites.

Opposition and duality intrigue Forrest Moses. He discusses them not only in his work, but in relationship to life itself, pointing out the positive and negative forces throughout nature. "We're more comfortable when we can perceive these opposites," he believes. In his work he tries to allow positive and negative areas to have equal power. "The spaces around the rocks and trees are just as important as the objects themselves," he concludes. Intuitively, Moses designs in contrasts: as a counterpoint to the basic flatness of his subject, he finds that he has unconsciously added dynamic diagonals that create stress and excitement.

From 9:00 to 2:00, Moses works almost every day, taking advantage of the light when it is at its best. He uses only natural light, so he is not involved in any concern over which fluorescent lamps to use. He stops at 2:00 because the light fades then. When a major show is in the offing—and one always is—he strives to begin two new canvases a week. For each show he presents from 15 to 30 new paintings. With two one-man shows a year, Moses is used to the discipline required to keep to this schedule. He finds he works best under pressure, when everything needs his attention—the garden, social life, and painting. A bachelor, Moses enjoys cooking and hosting parties. Despite a tough schedule, he takes an active part in the cultural life of Santa Fe.

A Forrest Moses oil typically is 48 x 50 inches or 42 x 60 inches but may be as small as 12 inches in one direction, or much larger than the sizes given here. Size depends on subject matter and his response to it. Pre-primed linen canvas is his preference: he stretches it on Craft Cut extra-sturdy stretcher bars that are made in Santa Fe. He orders them by the dozen in a variety of sizes.

His method is simple and direct. Moses is not a theoretician about technique. He speaks more of reaching the psyche of the viewer than he does of technical matters. However, he does have his own modes of operation. Finding that he is allergic to turpentine, he has lately switched to using Texadine. He uses a medium in this proportion: five parts Texadine, one part damar varnish, one part stand oil, and about a teaspoon of Venice turpentine. Texadine is a petroleum-based rather than a resin-based material. A generic name for it is mineral spirits.

His paint palette includes a wide range of natural earth colors by Winsor & Newton and Blockx. He uses raw sienna, raw umber, yellow ochre, cadmium yellows and oranges, alizarin crimson, French ultramarine blue, Payne's gray, cobalt, some burnt sienna, Mars red and yellow, and Quick Dry titanium white. He does not use white alone, only in a mixture.

To begin a painting, he mixes a batch of yellow ochre and white oil paint with medium and covers the entire canvas with it. This earthy pale yellow is about the color of sand. Moses likes the way it influences successive layers of paint. He builds paint in thin layers to allow this underpainting to show through. Color and texture are essentials in Moses's paintings.

Because Moses works large, he frequently mixes batches of paint in cans and paints broad areas smoothly. His aim, in addition to laying fields of color, is to enhance textures. For this he might crumple a rag and blot color on one layer and then glaze over it. He might take the blunt end of a pencil and drag it through fresh paint. He scrubs and scumbles and scrapes in an effort to make textures. He puts colors on and wipes them off, then glazes over that.

Moses is not a graphic artist but a painterly one. Line plays its part only as the delight we find in following the path of his brush. The painting grows in masses of color; the forms develop from adjacent masses. Much depends on the color contrasts.

Explaining his painting method, Moses says, "I tend to get more involved in a work that has a sense of movement in it." He leaves some areas unfinished, and you can see how his painting is built: "Sometimes I go back and define things with pencil, and I leave the pencil there. I let the process be clear. Things in process are more life-giving than work completely resolved."

Because immediacy and an unstudied effect are important to him, Moses does not finish things off smoothly. If a drip occurs, so be it, if it does not distract. He paints to the edge of the canvas. Strokes that may seem incidental are often deliberately placed on the outer edge. To allow for them he uses floater frames, which he constructs himself.

Paint for its own sake is respected by the painter, and he gives it its integrity. Though each form is built upon a number of layers, its surface appears to be composed of just a stroke or two. Brushwork indicating weeds or other detail of contours is very free and gives the viewer a kinesthetic connection with the hand of the artist in a most pleasant way. There is a panache to the whole affair that is sought by Moses as he paints.

"I like to think of my painting as recreational rather than intellectual. For me to consider them successful, my paintings must appeal intuitively. If I can't get it freshly and immediately, it loses something vital. I analyze my own work to see what it is about a particular painting that makes it special . . . that makes it communicate. The difference is a quality of spirit that makes one piece art and another not," he muses.

"The term art," he says, "might be redefined so we separate art and craft in a new way. What defines art from craft is that the piece of art has a life of its own, independent from its maker. A teapot can be so special that it is art. Objects known as art can be without this life spirit. A portrait can be just an image of a person—or it can be a timeless painting.

"Art has to do with what feeds and what depletes the spirit. Most of us live lives that are depleting. Man invented the arts to be spiritually fulfilling."

Moses deplores the intellectualizing of art history in this century, which has divorced art from emotions and turned it into a science. Each step away from the direct confrontation of the artist with his subject—away from his sensual reaction to it—has been heralded as a progressive one. A recent change, probably stemming from the public itself, reflects a broadening acceptance of a painterly approach, one which Moses shares. He attempts to deliver what he calls the essence of a virgin landscape, unpeopled, without manmade objects in it.

In his choice of ubiquitous forms, such as rocks, sand, weeds, and water, Moses ensures a kind of relationship to the viewer that is unaffected by the particulars of time and space. His shapes are recognizable universally. While he is conscious of the viewer, his initial effort is to paint images that please himself.

Light and reflections, the dynamics of contrasts—hard versus soft, moving versus static—have held Moses's interest throughout his career. "I can only intellectualize after the fact," he explains, "because art is intuitive with me while I am working. I am definitely conscious of a very structured work. I need to organize."

Much of his thinking about a painting is done by Moses beforehand, using his own photographs for a starter: "I don't have any feeling that a camera shouldn't be used. I've had to free myself from an attitude of what is proper and improper. Here in the Southwest the sun and wind make it difficult to stay out and paint. I used to do watercolors on location but have practically given it up. I rely on the camera now. When I paint I prefer more scale than I can achieve in a watercolor.

"The difficulty with the camera is that photographs are an abstraction just as the flat canvas is an abstraction; to guard against it I have to keep in touch physically with the land."

Moses found that when he worked only from memory or imagination he became repetitious. "Compositions found in nature itself are far more varied than the mind can conceive," he says. Having chosen a subject, Moses tries to respond to it as freely as possible. To capture a mountain stream he might work loosely, whereas he might paint rocks on the desert with a harder edge. In details he wants to suggest rather than describe.

The means Moses uses to compose a painting are his senses of space, scale, texture and color, and structure and discipline. These aspects of painting are basically unconscious, he believes. They are a part of the artist's vision. He does not think vision can be taught, but it can be nurtured in such a way that the artist becomes a channel of creativity.

It is the artist's task to find the means to develop his vision, and for this Moses needed a sanctuary. His view of it is separate from a condition of safety. He enlarged his conception of sanctuary by studying his own work—noticing its concern with opposites. Within his painting he creates filled and unfilled areas, intimate spaces surrounded by limitless spaces. Translating an acceptance of opposites from aesthetics to his philosophical concern with sanctuary, he believes one must accept one's own opposite qualities, the good and the bad. In this way one finds mental resting places akin to those areas of a painting that allow the eye to pause. Self-acceptance in itself is a kind of sanctuary.

Freeing himself from preconception has given Moses peace of mind and has become part of a synthesis he has created between his art and his life. Santa Fe has given him the energy and the ambience he needs to expand his vision. It is here that the environment, both the one he has built for himself and the natural one, provides the sanctuary he has sought. In his exuberant paintings he conveys the spirit of it to others.

CARL W. PETERS

BY CHARLES MOVALLI

YEARS AGO he used to summer at Rockport, Massachusetts. But now Carl Peters spends most of his time at his home and studio in Fairport, New York, and only visits New England for a few weeks in the late spring and early fall. He rents a cottage down one of the roads that ramble on and off the route between Gloucester and Rockport.

Dirt, ruts, and broken macadam make the going tough—a little like the Western Front, 1918. You climb a steep hill to find his cottage, and as you go up, you notice a white Cadillac, shining gaudily next to one of the rustic red cabins.

No—it isn't his. When you see him, you mention the Cadillac. He smiles and points out the screen door to his trusty Ford. "When I was in Woodstock with John Carlson, he always told us students: don't go into painting for the money!" He smiles at this memory. "It's a hard life, and I certainly wouldn't encourage anyone to enter it. Unless, that is, you have an ace in the hole.

"Most of the people I know came to art from something else: sign painting, scenery work, commercial jobs. I knew plenty of serious sculptors who supported themselves by working for decoration companies." He pauses. "Artists have to be great egotists, just to keep going. And if they're to get anywhere, they have to have support from the people around them—from a wife or a family. I'm lucky: I have an especially good wife, Blanche."

Carl Peters stands in the middle of the cottage as he talks. He isn't tall, and he isn't short. He isn't fat, and he isn't lean. Yet he's a substantial presence, and when you first see him, you notice his bushy eyebrows, his slight stoop, and a look that seems to come right from his farmboy background. He's sizing you up, putting you in the scales, and seeing if you come up light. It's a sober, even dour look—and one that completely belies the man's real character. When he raises those bushy brows, smiles, and starts to talk, you feel as if everything has suddenly been turned inside out.

"It was one of Carlson's pictures that turned me into a painter," he says, moving toward a sofa. It looks hard as he sits on it—while you practically disappear into a marshmallow-soft armchair. "It was a tree picture—the kind of subject I knew on the farm." He thinks for a second, the serious look returning to his face. "My life might have been different if I hadn't seen that picture."

Peters's voice is soft and halting, but there's a crispness here and there—and some of his phrases crackle like frozen snow underfoot. "My progress was slow. I grew up on a farm, and nobody had money for art school. I learned a little bit from everyone. The funniest things stick in your head," he says, stumbling over a memory. "I remember working with Charles Rosen when I was in Woodstock. I was only twenty or twenty-one at the time and barely knew how to put paint on the canvas. I was doing a view of a valley, a little house, and a tree. Rosen came by and said. 'You didn't get it.' 'I didn't?' " There's a slight tremor in Peters's voice as he imitates himself at twenty, naive and a little incredulous. "Then he turned my canvas over and did a rough version of the scene—a great little start. 'You didn't get a feeling of the building being under the tree,' Rosen said. And I could see that he was right. Then he looked back at the scene—a 'pretty' view—and asked me if I liked it. 'Sure!' I told him; and as I said that, he turned to the old tree behind me—gnarled, with broken limbs and lots of color in the bark. 'And do you like that?' he asked. Well, I told him I didn't. He was silent for a minute and said, 'Someday you will!' Then he turned and walked off."

Rosen's terseness obviously delighted Peters, who chuckles as he thinks about the incident. It's a terseness that matches his own conversational style. "Rosen knew that I'd understand the character of that tree someday. But you have to be familiar with a subject before you can paint it." He looks to see if you understand him. "When I was a kid, I visited Gloucester and tried to find a subject along the back shore. Boy, it all looked the same to my friends and me, just a jumble of rocks and water. We didn't see a painting anywhere. So we climbed over the rocks, looking for spots of paint. And wherever we found them, that's where we set up. We stayed there till we figured out where the painter before us had found his picture!"

Winter Shadows, oil, 30 x 32. The largest area of snow is in the foreground; this makes the area look near to the viewer and pushes the steep bank far into the background. Cover the lower quarter of the picture and see how it loses much of its depth.

He again smiles broadly.

"Later on, I paid another visit. A local painter told me to remember that I was dealing with salt water, now, not hard water." A questioning look crosses his face; he wants to share with you his original confusion. "Well," he continues, "he meant that I'd be dealing with ocean-going boats. They're built to take the wind and waves. They have weight. They're fat and settle deep in the water. Along the Atlantic Coast, even the dories bulge at the sides. Look down on them, and they're shaped just like eggs!" He smiles when he sees you smile at the comparison.

"So when I come to a new spot, I don't start painting. I look around and sketch in my notebook. When you work out a composition on paper, you remember it. And sometimes you discover that a thing may look good when you first see it, but that it really isn't paint-able." He pulls out a worn black notebook and begins to leaf through it. "As you sketch," he says, "you have to move around and see how the subject looks from different angles. I used to do careful, linear drawings. If I drew houses on a hill, I got all the architectural lines just right. But when I went back to the sketch later on, it was too set. It didn't interest me anymore. I couldn't dream as I looked at it." He pauses for a second. "You have to be able to dream as you work. You have to feel your way into a subject with the pencil." He turns the notebook in his hand. "So I don't try for finished pieces now; I just squiggle, looking for the main lines of the design, searching for the light and dark patterns. I shift the different 'weights' around till I get something that balances." And suddenly the apparently random lines come together.

He continues flipping through the notebook. On

one page there are seven or eight thumbnail sketches of the same subject. Then there are three consecutive half-page sketches, each exploring an aspect of a site. Some sketches are clear; some are almost indecipherable. "There's a good spot," he says, pointing to a bundle of lines that could describe anything from a bucket of worms to a day at the circus. As you squint quizzically, he adds, "That's quite a bridge; everyone has done it at one time or another."

As you look at the sketches, you're struck by Peters's free handling of the parts of the scene. A retaining wall towers in one picture and hugs the ground in another. Tree masses wax and wane. Roads slither to the right or the left. "Look for the way things come together," he says, firmly. "Search for the pattern and don't just draw individual subjects. If you look for the pattern, you'll find interest in ordinary subjects. I enjoy painting what everyone's done a hundred times—and finding my own mystery in it." He points to an especially loose drawing of Pigeon Cove, a very popular artists' subject. "I draw so that one area

works into another. I'm not interested in the individual buildings; everything has to work as a unit."

He closes the notebook and lays it on the small table in the corner of the room. "My wife and I have been in Rockport for four days now. I've spent the first three sketching—we call it 'fishing.' " He smiles and almost winks. "I couldn't get anything. The elms have been cut down; nothing looked right. Then yesterday something clicked. I drew and the pencil felt good in my hand. Once I've figured the idea out on paper," he continues, "I know it has a chance; I'll go back and paint it. But maybe not right away. If the sketch is good, I put an 'X' next to it—and I might go through the book next week or next year, reviewing all the marked sketches. They give me ideas. Then I may do a small oil outdoors and use the oil and the pencil sketch to develop a larger picture in the studio. I have to have the oil as a guide; I can't work from the pencil sketch alone. And I've never liked taking five or six sketches, pasting them together, and working from that."

Opposite page: *Low Tide,* oil, 25 x 30. By increasing the size of the distant headland (half as
big in reality), Peters uses the dark band to balance the strong darks in the foreground.

Above: *Pigeon Cove,* oil, 20 x 24. Peters had to
redesign the cove so the horizontal lines of the
stone pier didn't dominate the picture. The boats
are bulky, a characteristic of ocean vessels.

Left: *Study of Pigeon Cove,* pencil on paper, 6 x
7. In this preliminary sketch, Peters looks for the
way shape is connected to shape; he creates a
rhythmic movement by playing with the literal
"facts" of the scene.

Starting at the top right of the palette, Peters draws a series of circles, each representing a color. Cerulean blue is first, then ultramarine blue, then Prussian blue. At Prussian blue he lifts his pencil for a second and says, "This is Carlson's color. He told me: make a purple with Prussian blue, and it's always purple; make a green, and it's always green. It's also a very strong color. When I first used it, I got it on my clothes, hands, face, in my hair—everywhere!" He looks back at the diagram and lists alizarin crimson, cadmium red light, orange, cadmium yellow medium, cadmium yellow light, and, at the far end of the palette, permanent green deep. "Depending on the character of the day," he notes, "I may replace this green with viridian, a cooler, more transparent color. Both these greens are base colors: I add colors to them. And I mix a lot of my own greens by using the other yellows and blues." Down the left side of the palette, he lists ochre, raw sienna, and burnt sienna. To the far right he places zinc white. "I don't use titanium," he notes. "It's opaque. Zinc, on the other hand, is transparent, and when you add color to it, the resulting tone also has a transparent quality."

Peters lays the pencil on the table and takes a sip of his coffee. "When I start out," he continues, "I don't worry about matching the colors of nature. That's what you do when you copy an Old Master in the museum. Outdoors, you don't see individual colors; you look instead for the quality of light and the relationships of value and color that the light and atmosphere create. The real thrill in painting outdoors is the way the light constantly changes what's in front of you. I want to get the feeling of light on a particular day—to paint today, not yesterday! If you can feel that it's 2 p.m., I'm happy. If the drawing's good, but I missed the day—then the picture isn't a success."

Pigeon Cove, oil, 25 x 30. This is a particularly strong example of what Peters calls painting in terms of "patterns." The dark background buildings and wall form a weight that balances the large expanse of light foreground snow.

"The value of a color counts more than the color itself," he says, wiping away a few crumbs. "I may not get the exact color out of doors, but I try to get the right value." He punctuates his sentence with a raised finger and eyebrows. "The important thing to remember is that the air here"—he touches his chest lightly—"is one thing, and the air over there is something else. Try to show that air has volume; get the feeling of the color and value change from here to there. Get it?" he asks quietly. "From here to there."

He leans back, hooking his elbow around the top rung of the chair. "There was a time when I thought I could save myself some trouble by taking photos instead of using my notebook. But it didn't work. The color in the slides was terrible. The camera saw all the shadows as very cold and dark. The painter, on the other hand, tends to see the warmth in the shadows. He senses the atmosphere around everything—

and the light that bounces into the shadows, giving them color. Paint from a slide, and your pictures will look like slides."

He crouches forward, thinking of a few basic things to say about composition. "Don't paint twelve things in a picture; eliminate till you've got only one." He raises a finger and points it directly at you. "One thing! When a picture is full of objects, it shows the artist is confused. He doesn't know what he wants to paint. A painter always tries to make his work simpler. Get a few simple masses and learn to appreciate the beauty within that simplicity."

He smiles, and you feel you'd nod agreement even if you didn't understand English. "Oil painters should remember what the watercolorists already know: strength in a painting comes from the big black-and-white pattern. It's important to hold the pattern, to stick with the design once you've figured it

Winter Morning, oil, 20 x 24. By keeping the buildings large, Peters leaves no doubt as to the subject of his painting. The foreground snow simply serves to push the buildings back in space.

out. It's like painting flowers. You don't paint the individual petals. You go for the group: its shape and color. And then you play one group against another." He looks at you out of the corner of his eye. "Once you've figured out the pattern, put the darks down first—and then the lights. Go for the main color and value relationships right off the bat. During the afternoon, the water in a harbor might change color and value five times. You have to relate the water and its surroundings first, and then stick to that relation, no matter how much things change."

He pulls himself short, as if struck by another idea. "The hard part is getting everything to come together. Sometimes you work and work and no matter how hard you try, you still have 'holes' in the picture." He pauses. "A painter knows what I mean: parts that just don't fit. You've put too much paint on; your darks go opaque—and as you smear everything around, it's like working with soup. That's when you should stop. Back home, you might discover that just a few touches can pull things together. If you plan major changes, however, use the sketch as a study and do another picture *from* it. That way you don't lose the outdoor quality of the original."

He thinks about what he's just said and notes that "When I talk about pulling it together in the studio, I don't mean 'I can finish it at home.' Students say that all the time, and they usually mean they can take it home and 'make a picture of it.' There's a big difference between making pictures and looking for patterns. Commercial artists frequently have to think of the picture: they sharpen everything so it photographs well. But that isn't necessarily 'finished.' A picture's finished when you've caught the effect or feeling you want. I've seen plenty of pictures that were described as 'crude,' but that weren't crude at all. They were very sensitive! The painter simply got his effect and stopped. A friend had a favorite critical description for a picture: 'You had a nice thing there, but you went by it.' That's the trick: not 'going by it.' "

There's again an amused look on Peters's face, as if he were reviewing in his mind all the times he himself had "gone by" an effect. He probably has—but he's also known just when to stop. His long list of awards proves that, as do the almost unprecedented three Hallgarten prizes he's won at the National Academy. Yet he doesn't bother to talk about his honors. He's happier when discussing the joys of outdoor painting.

"After years of painting outdoors," he says, "you work more and more on impulse and emotion. I believe in emotional painting—in getting excited by what you see. Talent is really the ability to get excited. A lot depends on your mood. There are days when you're just not ready for a subject. But you also know when you've got something. It's hard to describe the feeling." He searches for a word. "You're tongue-tied. On the good days, everything comes easy. The picture falls into place. On the bad days, nothing's right. I feel clean when I take a bad picture and rub it off!" He chuckles to himself, hunching his shoulders a little.

Peters gets up and walks toward the door of the cottage. The outside door is open and you can feel the early fall coolness in the air. In the parking lot, new arrivals unload their cars and lug the bulging suitcases across the macadam.

"When you're painting, don't look back; look forward. Don't think about something you've done before. You can't repeat a success. That painting records the way you felt on that day—and only on that day. Maybe it was sunny. You were hot; you were sweating, and a little of that is in the picture. You can sometimes do your best work under the worst conditions—just because you're more involved in what's going on. I was doing a watercolor one day when it started to rain. I had to steady the paper with one hand and paint with the other. I finally stopped, soaking wet, and tossed the thing in the back of the car. I was sure I'd gotten a lemon. But when I looked at it back home, it was one of the best things I'd done!"

He stands near the door and puts his hands in his pockets. "You struggle with a subject—but that struggle's good. When you struggle, you become a student again. You're trying to learn—and that's when you really paint. Once you stop being a student, you might as well give up.

"We're all students," he says, looking out the front door at a clump of brilliant red flowers, beating silently against the screen. "And we should remain students all our lives."

DAVID LOEFFLER SMITH

BY PATRICIA EAKINS

DAVID LOEFFLER SMITH is a painter in search of heroic perspective on an unheroic age. When he was growing up in the '30s, many artists found a mythlike largeness in the living drama of the Depression, which for all its sordidness seemed epic in scope. This was the generation of artists that included David Smith's father, Jacob Getlar Smith, best known for his mastery of watercolor. As David Smith has pointed out, these artists hoped that the massive social and economic displacement of the era would yield images that could carry gestures as grand in their way as those portrayed by the Old Masters. Although the painters of the '30s did not achieve the moral dimensions of either tragedy or satire, they did succeed in distilling the essence of ordinary American life through the closeness of their scrutiny. It was the intimate observation they brought to their art that David Smith first made his own, and their interest in gesture was later to serve his own ambition for an art of high style.

"I'm not concerned with the social imagery of breadlines, but my concern with gesture was born in discussions of my father's work and the work of Reginald Marsh, among other artists. I'd go with my father to a gallery that was exhibiting Marsh's work, and my father would say, 'That's a crowded beach in that painting. Do you ever remember seeing Jones Beach that crowded?' I developed an ability to relate to the images I was seeing."

For all the strength of his early sense of connection to human subject matter, Smith rebelled against the figurative tradition while still in high school. Yet, curiously enough, the distinguished teacher and Abstract Expressionist Hans Hofmann, with whom he studied during both his high school and college years, was to give him the courage to go back to the figure at a time when abstraction was very much the dominant tendency.

"While we may have ended up with an abstract drawing or painting, Hofmann's criticisms were always concrete," Smith recalls now. "Other teachers I'd had had been more literary. They'd say, 'That's a sexy dame in that picture; give it more.' I wanted to know what 'more' was and how to achieve it. Hof-

mann, for all his abstraction, made me look at objects and figures respectfully."

Smith elaborated further on Hofmann's special force as a teacher during a series of formal discussions with a fellow painter, Benjamin Martinez: "Hofmann, while a thunderous painter, as an instructor demanded that every line or shape be explained in terms of the model. He made me work from the model longer than I ever had, and yet I'm hard put to say what more it was he taught. This was partly due to his language difficulties.

"Much of his best instruction was by erasing or drawing right over your study. Either that, or he would rip your drawing into four or more parts and rearrange them on the board. What you had in the end was a fairly simplified Cubist drawing. The unifying movements and balancing forms were obvious enough that further verbiage was not necessary. The ideal of a tautly constructed page was applicable to any direction the student went in."

Smith still delights in the analogous idea of the "well-made picture" but now feels a need to "loosen up" his figures, to let them "move naturally." He began attending Hofmann's night classes while still a high school student in New York City, but he only undertook intensive studies under Hofmann during his undergraduate years at Bard College in Annandale-on-Hudson, New York, using two work/study periods for the purpose.

Of his early attendance at Hofmann's night classes, Smith recalls, "The monthly 'crit' was a great bit of theater. The man would literally go through 200 or more pictures at a sitting. It was heady stuff. Not only was the majority of students there on the G.I. Bill and far older than I, but Hofmann had a manner of relating your painting problems to those of Matisse, Picasso (who didn't abandon the figure to the extent that later painters did), and other august spirits."

David Smith's youthful disillusionment with the figurative tradition also drew him away from color. While he was in high school he did a great deal of drawing, and most of his paintings were black and white. In those days, he remembers, he fought the idea of becoming a painter; he was fascinated by his-

View of the Backyard, 1971, oil, 16 x 20. Smith's shapes seem to be formed of light and shade rather than being modeled: the illusion of volume without weight.

tory and thought of becoming an architect, sculptor, or psychologist.

All these interests are evident in the work of the mature painter: architecture in the way the baroque restlessness of the composition moves within a structure of balances, thrusts, and subtle repetitions of form; sculpture in the way the contours of the figures speak volumes in both the geometric and the literary senses; history in the frequent choice of mythological subjects and the feeling for the traditions of Western painting; and psychology in the precise intuition of the meaning and impact of gesture and color.

Over the years, Smith's concern with the "drama of the psyche" has led him not only back to the figure but away from the objectivity of Hofmann's teaching and toward a more subjective approach. He was not alone in his drift back to the figurative tradition, but many of the painters who returned to it did so without seeming to question grounds on which much of 20th-century painting is based.

"Most of the painters who came from abstract painting back to figurative painting were dealing with landscape, still life, and figures as static objects.

They were working in the Cézannesque tradition, in which an apple is equal to a madonna as subject. This objectivity was useful, but I took another direction."

However much Smith's questioning of objectivity went against the grain of the times, it was very much in the tradition of skeptical inquiry that he had been taught by Stefan Hirsch, with whom he studied at Bard College.

"Hofmann taught me the relationship of the painting to the object or model in front of me," he says. "With Hirsch, I hardly worked from the model. Stefan's great contribution was a kind of constant questioning. He would point to a brush stroke—a little, mundane brush stroke—and he'd say, 'Why did you put that there? Why didn't you carry it an extra inch? Why that color? Why that shade?'

"As I began to work back into the figure from my earlier, more abstract style, there was constant questioning—poses, gestures, meaning of the picture. I've never bumped into another teacher who applied the Socratic method to the studio."

After graduate studies at Cranbrook (in Michigan), a hitch in the army that took him to Korea and Japan,

Above: *The Picnic,* 1970, oil on paper,
16 x 20. The artist uses the architecture of balances and thrusts and
subtle repetition of form to create a
tautly constructed painting.

Right: *Sleeping Figures,* 1973, oil
on paper, 13 x 20. Smith uses calligraphic line to build form and to
control composition.

Opposite page: *Jean Reading,*
1958, oil, 10 x 12. The artist's contours speak to the viewer in both
the sculptural and literary sense.

and a few months' study with Raphael Soyer (under-taken mostly for a chance to work from the model), Smith headed for Europe. He spent a good deal of his time in Italy, where he encountered the originals of works by the 16th-century Venetian school—especially by Tintoretto and Veronese—that were to influence many of his later thoughts about the direction of his painting.

The stylistic impact of the Venetians is patent in Smith's mature work. Tintoretto's use of calligraphic line to build form and to control complex composition is echoed in it. So are Veronese's bright forms and luminous color areas, although Smith's palette is far less sunnily factual than Veronese's. The figures of both Veronese and Smith have volume and density without weight and seem to be formed of light and shade rather than to have been modeled.

Even before Smith saw Tintoretto's large European works, the Old Master had become important to him for his example of grandeur, although Tintoretto was by no means the only painter whose works struck an answering chord to Smith's ambition for an art of high style: "While I was still in school, the Met-

ropolitan Museum bought the large Poussin painting of the Sabine women, which just thrilled me. The only modern painter who had an equivalent significance for me was Orozco, who tried for a heroic style and images of dramatic clarity. The social painters of the '30s dealt with sympathetic figures, but I wasn't concerned with painting tired people coming out of factories, people carousing in a bar; I wanted something grander than genre painting."

Smith's works might strike an uninitiated observer as small for an artist so interested in the possibilities of grandeur, and he is well aware of the seeming disparity between his stylistic ambition and the size of the completed works: "Sixteen by 20 is a big painting for me. My habit of working small is like that of a child playing with tin soldiers. There's a lot of identity associated with the game, but the scale of the toys assures everyone that the child is aware of the difference between imagination and 'reality. With our modern sophistication, we are distrustful of the heroic statement. Almost no modern painter has consistently worked on heroic terms in a large format."

Because he works small, Smith is able to paint on

Agamemnon, Series II: Agamemnon Returning with Cassandra, 1972-73, oil, 16 x 20. Here the artist uses subject matter from mythology to develop a modern image of epic scope.

Children's Party, 1972, oil on paper, 20 x 16. Smith's interwoven figures seem to be playing a game, yet at the same time suggest something ominous.

paper, which he feels can be as permanent as canvas and which takes up less storage space than stretched canvases. He uses pre-World War II 140-pound cold press watercolor paper he inherited from his father.

He not only works small, he works with a care that sometimes seems to him to be at odds with his sense of style: "I'd love to be able to dash off a painting with the bravura of a Fragonard. I like the sheer showmanship of that kind of painting. And it would save me a lot of time. I always start with full confidence that I'll get a painting done in three days. Then I begin to see problems. It takes time to feel I've finished the painting, gained the right measure of balance and control. I don't spend that many hours on each work. But I work in a series of revisits. I work on it, put it away, look at it again, work on it."

Although he grew up with the example of a father who drew extensively, using drawing as a kind of setting-up exercise before he began a painting session, David Smith does not do extensive drawing: "A painting may be constructed on the backs of envelopes. The drawing evolves on the surface of the painting. I may do some sketching with charcoal, but the painting develops through paint itself. I'm concerned that it read realistically, but I'm just as aware of the shapes my brushes make."

Smith's preliminary laying in of forms is done with a "heavy mass" of paint, or maybe a turpentine wash, but he works mostly with a drier brush, squeezing out the paint, sometimes pressing it onto the painting with his thumb, and spreading it in lieu of a glaze.

"I work with a big brush, massing in large areas when I'm beginning; then I use a smaller brush to straighten out an edge or a contour, to firm up small areas.

"I repaint a lot: little touches all over a painting; scumbling; laying down echoes; jumping back and forth, the brush loose and bouncing all over the place.

"During the last phase of painting, I like the idea of working toward a crust. Here I work with very broad brushes, almost dry, lightly touching over the painting with them. My paintings are built in many layers, but not in the sense of a minute rendering around a button hole.

"I make lots of nervous adjustments, some more calculated than others. I have a habit of walking around at the end of the day, trying to find a painting that could use some of the leftover colors. You can make some real blunders doing that, but it's a way to get a good crust on the painting."

Smith's description of revisiting pictures time and again, walking about and adding little touches to various paintings, suggests an artist who works at an easel or at several easels, eyeing near-vertical paintings from across a room with feline intensity, then moving in to pounce with his paintbrush. Yet Smith rarely works at an easel, although he keeps his father's in his studio:

"I tend to work at a table, which is ill-advised—lousy for the back—but working on a table with a small format, I find I can keep swinging the picture around. I'll work upside down; I'll work on it from the sides. Once I get it up to the easel, I just tend not to change it around."

For all the pains that have been taken with them—all the revisits and incursions from various angles—Smith's paintings breathe freely in the small spaces they occupy. There is more than enough room in them for grand gesture. The aura of grandness depends mostly, of course, on the aptness and resonance of the gestures themselves. Smith attributes much of his success at handling gesture to simple awareness: "I enjoy the theater and television. I respond to gestures that carry meaning with them."

But he is not content to let his awareness seep into his work as if feeling could be expressed without form.

"You begin on an emotional, expressionist level; then you start worrying about the formal aspects. I'm not an expressionist in the sense of letting free-wheeling brushwork do it. I'm very concerned with anatomy in space."

He does not do extensive sketching to fix in his mind a lexicon or repertory of gestures. "I don't use a sketchbook, because the translation is too immediate. If you carry your impressions in your mind, you edit, clarify, dramatize," he says.

One sees the direct result of this editorial process in, among other pictures, *Eros*, a painting inspired by a scene Smith observed in a student lounge at the Swain Art School in New Bedford, where he has been teaching for many years and which he once directed. The scene was a simple one, Smith recalls: one student was sleeping, another was tickling the sleeper, and a third was whispering in the tickler's ear.

In the finished painting, the facts of observation are subsumed in a dramatic statement. The student lounge has given way to a stage set, every element of which heightens the impact of the figures themselves. And it is the figures that seize the attention; their Veronesean luminosity—that curiously "built" lightness constructed in many revisits to the work—and the expressive outline of each contour transfigure the sheer bulbous nudity of the subjects and make of them a statement about a kind of love.

That David Loeffler Smith recreated the central figure as a nude was not meant as a challenging act. "The nude has survived into the 20th century. The nude has always and rightfully been a vehicle for expressing intimacy which is very different from much of the erotic art that is being done today." Smith feels that most of this is one-dimensional: "It is produced by young people who have not gone through the trials, the tribulations of courtship, of marriage, of raising children, of seeing one's own parents die—all of which are involved in male-female relationships."

Smith is as familiar with the work of young painters as with works that have become part of art history; before Swain, beginning right after he returned from Europe, he taught at Chatham, a women's col-

Beach Scene, 1969, oil, 20 x 16. The artist's bright forms, luminous color areas, and rolling surf create a scene that is magnified but familiar: grander than a day at the beach, but real.

lege in Pittsburgh, for seven years. He has now been teaching most of his adult life, and he is very aware of the difference in artistic perspective years can make.

"Of late, I find myself very interested in myself maturing, in what happens to other painters as they get older. It's not the biological aspect of aging that concerns me. There is a second sight, a ripeness that artists achieve only late in life. If Rembrandt had died before he was 50, I don't think he would have been considered a great master."

Ripeness may deepen the vision of individual artists as they work out the terms of their talents, but the age a painter lives in determines to some extent the terms in which it is possible to negotiate with absolute confidence in the outcome. Smith believes that some of the traditional and serious subjects that have occupied mature painters down through the ages are far more difficult to achieve nowadays than, say, erotic images of whatever complexity and depth.

"Some artists have attempted scenes based on war or the shooting at Kent State University, but with the exception of Picasso's *Guernica,* we have no great modern memorial or funeral pictures. And yet when you think of all the great crucifixion scenes, for instance, you realize that tragic subjects have produced much great art—but not in the 20th century.

"In the epilogue to *Death of a Salesman,* playwright Arthur Miller relates the whole problem that Aristotle raises of the tragic hero: the figure must be sufficient in importance, and for Aristotle this means a king or a queen. Miller discussed how you can interpret this in modern society: 'To find a valid modern image for the death scene—to make a memorial picture, if you will—is a constant problem for me. The hospital scene is an attempt to come to grips with what approaches a death scene.'"

Smith has dealt with the Aristotelian criterion of *sufficient importance* in both of his two kinds of pictures: those that use mythological subject matter and those that find their subject matter in contemporary culture.

He is modest about the works that have subjects drawn from myth: "While I'm very happy doing them, I think that's a little bit of an easy way out. I can't say I'm a great reader of James Joyce, but I would like to be able to do what Joyce does and find in modern society equivalents for the Odyssey, for Electra."

Easy way out or not, mythological subject matter is well suited to Smith's purposes. In pictures like those in his Agamemnon I series, there is a lucid congruity between subject and gesture; in fact, Smith's interest in classical figures like Agamemnon and Odysseus grew out of his instinct for this kind of congruity.

"I'd be thinking of a pose or gesture usually observed around me, but when I would draw it as a straightforward, realistic image, it all seemed overexaggerated and mannered. Without conscious thought, I began to relate certain of these ideas to mythological characters and painted them as such."

Even as the mythological paintings are partly drawn from gestures observed in contemporary life, so the paintings the subjects of which are contemporary are resonant in some of the ways mythology is. A work like *Children's Party* is straightforward enough in some ways. The canvas is exuberantly crowded yet tightly organized; a band of complexly interwoven figures playing a game moves back into the picture at a very theatrical diagonal.

Then the stillness of a woman in a chair rearranges the composition around her; this shift helps lend the picture an air of portent and mystery—qualities mostly generated by the subjectivity of the distortion.

It seems the very liveliness of the party has reminded the painter of death, just as the sight of an intense red often evokes the memory of green. The distortion, the portentousness, and the mystery of such a picture bring to mind the more flamboyant distortions of the modern English painter Francis Bacon, but Smith's work displays little of the psychological extremity found in Bacon's. The pudgy babies, the serene look on the face of the seated woman—these and other elements help to preserve a balance of emotion that verges on the classical. One feels a reticence in such paintings that brings to mind the presence of the artist himself.

David Loeffler Smith is a very educated painter, an "old soul" in something of the Hindu sense of having gone through several enlightening incarnations. This aspect of himself is one of which the painter is conscious and that he enjoys. He attributes it largely to having been the son of a painter, to having come full-cycle through a series of changes toward a realization that, as an artist, he is first and foremost the father of himself.

"The vision of a son continuing in his father's footsteps seems to please others, but my father did not want to encourage it, and I was a long time in accepting the role. I now enjoy the image, and I ofttimes take the stance of a man who has lived an exceedingly long life.

"Like so many adolescents before me, I tried to find my independence by embracing some pretty incongruous heroes, artistic rather than political, and it has only been in recent years that I've realized to what extent I came to painting on my own terms."

His own terms are realized in paintings that illustrate in many satisfying ways at least one of the dictionary definitions of heroic: "Larger than life but smaller than colossal." The close scrutiny the artist brings to bear redeems his work from an impetus towards sheer drama that might otherwise seem overwrought in an age of relative values. With its modestly subjective emphasis on magnified but real gesture, Smith's work fits very well indeed into the scale of appropriate concerns defined by the modern master Oskar Kokoschka, who has said (to Alan Levy, *Art News,* February 1974), "Man is the measure of all things. Whoever uses any other measure, measures falsely."

JOSEPH SOLMAN

BY EVE MEDOFF

AFTER MORE than 40 years of painting, Joseph Solman can look back on the past decades with gratification. There were hardships certainly, especially at the beginning, but there were also rewards: his work in distinguished collections, the subject of a definitive book and of numerous reviews and magazine articles, and winner of important awards.

More important to this artist than any recognition his work has earned, however, is the satisfaction in having held to a straight course in his development, neither straying into tempting bypaths nor seduced by fashionable trends. He has remained firm in the belief that, for him, figurative painting, as opposed to abstract or non-objective painting, continues to be the only viable means of expression. In his own words , quoted from *Arts* magazine, October 1955), "In my search for the deeper aspects of Nature, I found that the *subject* yields more pattern, more poetry, more drama, greater 'abstract' design and tension, than any shapes we may invent."

Solman cannot remember when his obsessive urge to draw began. His mother liked to say that he first put pencil to paper when he was still at the crawling age. Later he was to sketch fellow students and teachers in school and draw portraits of his family at home. By age twelve he was resolved to devote his life to the study of art.

It was not that easy. His parents had brought him to this country when he was three years old, leaving a small village in Russia to begin a new life in New York City. In their circumstances, an art career appeared as distant as the moon. Nevertheless, by working as a bookkeeper by day, Joseph, at age 17, was able to enroll in an evening class taught by portraitist Ivan Olinsky at the National Academy of Design.

It was a long subway ride to 109th Street, where the Academy was then located, but young Solman hardly noticed. He was busy filling his sketchbook with innumerable drawings of his fellow passengers, figures slumped in fatigue after the day's work. Their faces haunted him; he wanted to search out the real

Left: *Square,* 1936, oil, 25 x 34. Collection Mr. and Mrs. Max Margulis.

Opposite page: *Margie,* 1962, oil, 40 x 24. Collection Mr. and Mrs. Irwin Corey. The subject is just a starting point for the interplay of abstract elements.

Studio Interior, 1950, oil, 28 x 38. Collection Mrs. Ethel Elkind. Using the rhythmic squares of light to create a contrasting backdrop, the artist isolates each object and reveals its form. Compare the modeling of the coffeepot at the left with the flat teapot at the right.

life that went on behind the worn features and vacantly staring eyes.

On some Sundays, together with some of his fellow students at the Academy, he would go to the Museum of Modern Art. Afterwards they would talk about Cézanne, Van Gogh, Gauguin, Seurat. He began to feel that he was learning more from these discussions, from the sketching on the subway, from the hours spent before the Rembrandts at the Metropolitan, than from his classroom studies. He grew impatient with the conservatism of the Academy and longed for a studio of his own. At length he left school to take on a variety of odd jobs at night, rented a studio, and began painting in earnest.

His first efforts, a group of dark gouaches, were shown at a Washington Square open-air show and attracted the attention of Joseph Kling, a bookseller in Greenwich Village, who bought several of the paintings. Later on, Solman and his wife, Ruth, whom he married in 1933, were employed by this friend and benefactor in his bookstore.

Despite the Depression, the 1930s decade was a time of exciting challenges for Solman and his contemporaries. They were exhilarated by the heady new currents in art and voiced their theories with youthful ardor. In an effort to present a unified point of view, they formed a group, Expressionist in character, called The Ten, which included—besides Solman—Mark Rothko, Adolph Gottlieb, Ilya Bolotowsky, and Ben-Zion. Later the group expanded to include Earl Kerkham and John Graham. They staged a protest against the Whitney Museum's Annual in 1938, denouncing the "regionalist" painting it favored. The Ten gloried in challenging accepted criteria and in flouting the tradition of the academies.

All this fervor of rebellious activity is in odd contrast to Solman's personality today. He is now a more reflective man, though he still manages to write sharply critical letters to attack what he calls "the *new* Establishment in art."

Four years before the Whitney protest, Solman was given his first one-man show by Emily Frances, director of the Contemporary Arts Gallery. A review in *The New York Sun* ascribed to his work "... genuine feeling ... smouldering color, vague and haunting."

A year later, in 1935, Solman was taken on by the WPA Art Project at $21.50 a week. If poor paying the job at least offered the opportunity to work with the tools of his own trade, vastly preferable to the alternatives open to his generation.

A period of great productivity followed, and in 1937 he had his second one-man show. A.I. Chanin, in his book *The Art of Joseph Solman* (Crown, 1966), calls these works "the best of the street scenes." The small, dark gouaches of his first one-man show had given way to a series of brighter, tightly organized oils that exhibited a new, more assured approach.

Solman's street scenes offer a clear example of how an artist can separate the units of a subject and put them back together again in a new design of his own invention. Signposts and fences, fire escapes and railroad ties, traffic signs and lampposts—each is reduced to its essential form, becoming a calligraphic symbol in place of a literal image. Chanin calls them "a hypnotic medley of shapes and signs." Like other critics before him, Chanin observed the "sense of mystery" in these paintings. He says, "No people throng the streets. Nevertheless, these scenes are instinct with ... their presence. The effect ... is of a vivid stage set, a moment before it springs to life with actors."

In 1938 the late J. B. Neumann, the first American dealer to import the works of Picasso, Rouault, Beckmann, Klee, and other modern European artists, decided to present an exhibition called *Five New American Painters*. The five were Solman, Lee Gatch, Earl Kerkham, Karl Knaths, and Joseph di Martini. It was followed that same year by a three-man show of works by Solman, Mark Rothko, and Marcel Gromaire.

But while some of his contemporaries, notably Rothko and Gottlieb, were to move fast in the direction of complete abstraction, Solman continued to find in realism a rich source of pictorial ideas. In the mid 1940s he moved to a new studio, one admirably suited to his needs. It contained an entire wall of mullioned windows above a wide sill. These two features, plus the studio's spare furnishings, would fuel his creative engine over the next ten years.

Indeed, Solman considers this period of work to be a kind of homage to the artist's environment. Within the confines of a small universe, the studio, he found everything he needed, as he says, to "cultivate his garden": the ambient light with its changing colors, the studio objects, and planes and lines to "form, re-form, and transform," in his own words.

During this period he took time out to pay graphic homage to his favorite composer by doing a set of print variations on the theme of the Mozartian profile. He issued a folio edition of 200 sets, each consisting of twelve serigraphs, some of them in as many as 16 colors.

This period was also marked by large one-man shows in New York and in Washington, D.C. His work was purchased by notable collections, including the Phillips Memorial Gallery, Pepsi-Cola Company, Joseph Hirschhorn, and Brandeis University.

Solman's long association with the ACA Gallery began in 1950, and a year later Dorothy Seckler was to write of the Interior series ("Solman Paints A Picture," *Art News*, Summer 1951): "His characteristic bent-wire line—black mixed with green—was sensitive but never impulsive as he set down the contours of objects, feeling patiently for the most expressive relationship, the edge that would imply a plane, clarify space and provide a resonance to the big rhythms."

While the Interior series still held the attention of critics and public, the growing number of portraits issuing from his studio presaged an increasing preoccupation with this (by then) neglected form. His devotion to portraits at a time when commissions were hard to come by, struck his friends as a foolish pursuit. Portrait painting, they pointed out, was obsolete; the camera had seen to that.

Solman, however, appeared not to be listening. In his mind's eye he saw the construction of a painting that would use what he considered to be the greatest resource for any artist: the human figure. It was painting he was after, not a portrait as such. The sitter would be his model, not his patron; the model to be the raw stuff from which he would extract the elements—colors, pattern, texture, line, and space—all to be shaped into an expressive form.

Personality and individuality nevertheless did find their way into the portraits, because, whatever his announced intention, Solman cannot suppress his interest in people; a *connection* with the subject informs all his work. The heavy impasto of his earlier portraits has yielded to a greater delicacy in handling. He creates subtle harmonies over a thin, loose underpainting, building up color areas along the way, as it were. Solman never mixes a "flesh" tone as such. His way of working is, rather, to "push" or "float" pigment over the underpainting, moving units of color (which might be yellow and violet, orange and blue with perhaps a touch of turquoise) until he has positioned them where they satisfy. "If you hold a magnifying glass over any small area of the face," he told a visitor to his studio, "you could be looking at a miniature landscape or an abstract painting."

In *Portrait of Eddie* a network of lines, white against the dark field of the suit jacket, moves in zigzag cadences up the sloping shoulders and tight shirt collar toward the long column of the neck. The bright, tightly knotted tie is the central vertical support of this foundation, leading the eye directly up to the small, compact, red-orange head. The expression in the china-blue eyes is wary, the jaw thrust forward defensively, the mouth a thin, taut line. The racetrack man comes alive in this painting.

We begin to see how Solman, maintaining his regard for the great tradition of figure painting, brings to his work the insights gained from contemporary painting, using flat or patterned areas to hold the image to the picture plane, making color choices based on the demands of the total scheme, directing the viewer's eye by linear movement, and, finally, investing the whole with a forceful expression of his response to the subject.

John Sloan said something that can be applied to Solman's painting when he spoke of the problem of

Interior with Green Wall, 1949, oil, 16 x 24. Solman combines local color, atmospheric color, and synthetic color. Tension is developed by varying the effect of flat surfaces and modeled areas.

Eddie, 1950, oil, 20 x 16. Collection Dr. and Mrs. Fred Elias. Solman uses solid impasto and minute pigment variation to build his form.

East Villager, 1967, oil, 20 x 16. Collection ACA. Here the artist uses color thinned down with turpentine, creating a wash effect.

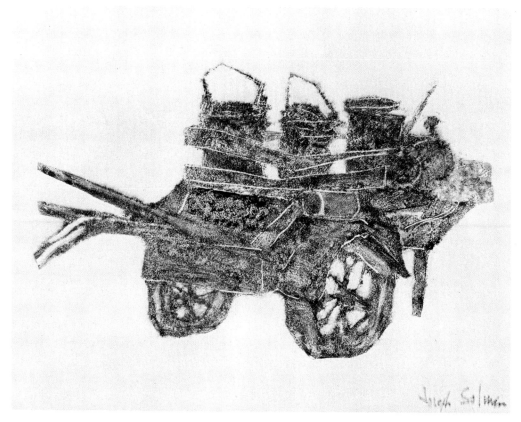

Tar-Cart, 1972, monotype, 9 x 12. Collection John Simon. Solman uses the traditional monotype technique of painting a complete picture on glass before transferring it to paper by overall pressure.

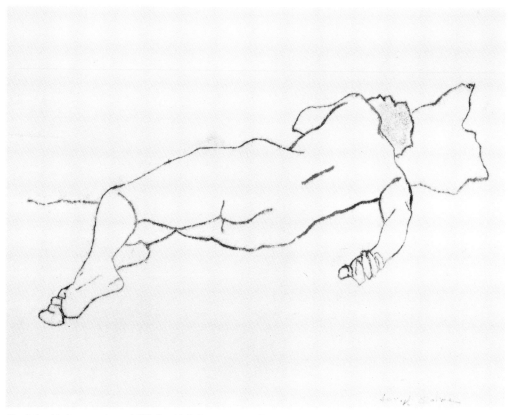

Reclining Nude, monotype, 1973, 9 x 12. In keeping with Solman's interest in the tension developed by contrasting modeled form with abstract patterns, the line in this drawing varies in color from contour to contour.

Dario, 1972, oil, 48 x 30. Collection Brandeis University. Solman's supple lines emphasize intricate planes of the coat
and shirt as opposed to the flat rendering of the socks and the flat planes of the background.

style that is "hidden under the cloak of representation."

Despite the gloomy predictions that an exhibition devoted solely to portraits could not hope for sales, the ACA Gallery's faith in Solman's work proved justified. The Hirschhorn Collection acquired four canvases from his 1954 show; six more went to other collectors. Solman felt then, and still does, that the public agrees with his view that his portraits are, first and foremost, *paintings*.

Ruth and Joseph Solman made their first pilgrimage to Europe's great museums with the money realized from those sales. At last the artist was face to face with the masterpieces he had waited so long to see. It was a deeply moving experience for him.

For a while, in the latter half of the 1950s, he limited his palette to tones of brown and sometimes blue-grays, creating somber images with strong, incisive delineations. He also produced at this time a series of "subway rider" pencil drawings, executed on newspaper pages while he was riding the trains, to which he later added gouache color—at first in monochrome, just to cover up the printed newspaper matter within the outlines of the drawings, and eventually adding color to these areas.

The '60s brought an influx of new young people to the neighborhood now called the East Village in New York City. Solman warmed to the colorful ensembles he passed on the street and would stop to ask an especially "paintable" subject to pose for him. The picturesque, nostalgic apparel that became so widespread had an exhilarating effect on Solman's work. The brown and blue-gray tonalities gave way to pure, high-keyed color; modeling all but disappeared, and his line, already identifiable as his signature, grew taut as a high-tension wire.

Several years ago, at his summer studio in Massachusetts, Solman tried making monotypes and found the form so congenial that he has been devoting at least three months of each year to working intensively in this medium. To the traditional method of transferring an image painted on glass to a sheet of rice paper, he has added some variations of his own.

As the name implies, monotype is limited to a single unique print. Although by definition any image transferred from a plate to paper is "printed," the monotype is more intimately related to the original sketch than are other forms of printmaking. In making his monotypes, Solman uses the following method.

First he places a drawing under a sheet of glass that is somewhat larger than the sketch, placing marks on the glass to indicate the top corners of the drawing. Then Solman tamps color with a bristle brush along and over the lines of the sketch as seen through the glass, varying the tones and colors as he sees fit. He allows the color to dry partially. The precise degree of dryness is a matter of judgment, gained only by experiment.

Next Solman places a sheet of rice paper over the glass and tapes it to the top edge. The sketch is removed from underneath and laid, with great care, face up on top of the rice paper, matching the original position by the registration marks.

Finally, Solman retraces the lines of the sketch with a stylus or other pointed tool sufficiently blunted to prevent tearing of the paper (his favorite instrument being the rounded point or back end of a clam fork), using enough pressure to assure that the paint on the glass will adhere to the rice paper in those areas where the tool has been applied. The resulting texture is not unlike that produced by soft ground in etching.

Joseph Solman's creative energy gives no sign of flagging after more than four decades of intensive, productive work. In the cool north light of his studio, he continues to paint like a man with a great deal left to do.

HAHN VIDAL

BY ELLYE BLOOM

HER MOTHER TENDED an informal garden of cultivated and wild flowers. Hahn Vidal remembers watching her cutting the fresh blossoms, wrapping them in wet newspapers, packing them gently in a carton, and finally covering the box with fancy paper. On special occasions . . . they would be sent to friends as gifts. The flowers could survive fairly long trips, and when they'd arrive at their destination they'd be revived in water and stay bright and crisp for days afterward.

It is understandable that Hahn Vidal loves flowers so completely. Her best childhood memories are associated with them. "I'm very deeply interested in flowers, and it is a subject that, for a painter, needs and deserves intense dedication." For 20 years Vidal has painted flowers, and she can't imagine being interested in any other subject.

Her understanding of flowers is not only deeply emotional, but deeply technical as well. To the serious flower painter she advises, "You have to know each flower, each of the varieties so well: how they grow, how they die, the leaves, the movement, and how they reflect the light. And the petals, the texture of the leaves . . . everything about them." Vidal endows each flower with humanlike quality. For instance, water lilies have "potent petals," while sunflowers are "virile." Her face glows as she visualizes them. "And they are even a good subject for the beginner. Their color and appeal can be easily translated."

Some of Vidal's favorite paintings hang on the walls of her New York apartment, their color harmony and mood echoed in the decor. A magenta gloxinia glows on a glass tabletop. Soft tones, curves, warm lights, and gleaming crystal glasses filled with wine set a mood of elegance. Beethoven's majestic Ninth Symphony sifts through speakers in the background. Margarita Hahn Vidal, the tiny, perfectly groomed woman who is a part of this rarified atmosphere of taste and refinement, does not at first reveal the core of strength that enabled her to reach a high degree of success and recognition. As a child in Germany, she had an overwhelming desire to draw. Her strongest memories of that time include a painfully strict education and, in contrast, the unre-

strained beauty of the free-growing flowers in her mother's garden. Just when Vidal was offered a hard-to-get art scholarship, her family moved to Argentina. This new home was strange to her, and in her early teens, a difficult time at best, she found that most of her energy was spent in adjusting to new surroundings. In her late teens she met and married an Argentinian artist, and they had two sons. When her husband became aware of her artistic ability, he decided to put her to work as his student. He taught her classical painting techniques and guided her to the subject of flowers with the advice, "You must always paint what you know and love best."

She made dozens of botanical drawings of every kind of flower and learned to know their stems, leaves, petals, and growing habits long before she ever thought of painting them. After the drawings she made watercolor sketches, which enhanced her understanding of the transparency of petals and also gave her the chance to use a brush to make quick impressions of each flower.

When Vidal was eventually ready to use oil paints, she used small brushes and painting knives to produce rather detailed, soft, romantic, low-key paintings. Her first exhibition opened in 1952 in Argentina. It was a complete sell-out on the first day, and each succeeding show was equally successful. "I was just lucky, I guess," she says. "But it was just too much. I found that I was painting to gratify others. Sometimes, even before a show would open, it would be sold out, and I started asking myself, what more can I do to satisfy the people but die for them?" Sensing that her further development as a painter was impossible under the circumstances, Vidal decided to leave Argentina. Her family stayed behind while she came to New York to test herself. (The children were grown by this time; her husband came to New York later.) Eventually she found a suitable studio at the Hotel des Artistes and began a fresh start.

In New York her work began to change. Colors became more vibrant, and their harmony became more daring. She was perfecting her knife-painting technique and applying less brush detail along with the broader knife strokes. Her work became more im-

Garden Glory, 1967, acrylic, 24 x 30. Private collection. When painting in acrylics, Vidal doesn't use an easel; instead, she paints on the floor. As to whether she prefers oils or acrylics, she only says, ''It's like playing two different instruments;'' her palette is exactly the same in both cases.

Blushing Roses, 1963, oil, 24 x 18. Private collection. Rather than a simple bouquet, Vidal uses a complex radiating composition of flower shapes, greenery shapes, and background to create the illusion of a garden environment.

pressionistic, and her goal in each work was generally the "simple synthesis of a complicated flower."

"Luck" was still with her, and one of the prestigious city galleries agreed to represent her. Again, success. She moved into a comfortable West Side apartment and converted one of its large rooms with a northwest exposure into a studio. For more than a decade she has painted there and has satisfied the need for change with trips to Europe and the Far East. With each trip came fresh inspiration to paint, yet the subject was always the same: the same flowers, painted over and over again with no trace of boredom.

While Andy Warhol, Jim Dine, and Claes Oldenburg, pioneers of the Pop Art movement, were breaking rules that would free the art world from tradition, Hahn Vidal was pulling away from the old tenets of flower painting. Her knife paintings were now bold, powerful flower expressions, and while many flower painters were still dabbing gingerly away at details, Hahn Vidal was slashing away with her big, springy painting knives loaded with big gobs of pure color.

Historically, flower paintings have been rated low on the popularity scale, and Vidal thinks the subject is still grossly neglected and underrated. "Flowers have never been given the position they deserve in art circles. I know this might sound a bit pretentious, but I hope to be one of the artists who will help to elevate them to their rightful place. You know, when you are a woman and you paint flowers—my back blushes, because I know exactly what people say: 'a little lady paints flowers'—it's absolutely a killer, because the flower is a very strong and difficult subject." Monet, Van Gogh, and Fantin-Latour are, in her opinion, the masters of flower painting who have brought vigor to a subject that many critics still consider strictly for women.

Vidal describes the level of consciousness that she must reach in order to work with her subjects: "While I'm painting, its almost like a transfiguration. It is such a spiritual thing. . . . I almost feel that I'm the flower." At its best this "transfiguration" is a highly productive one that excludes all sounds and all sights outside of the canvas. All her senses are concentrated on the painting, and the intensity with which she works leaves her totally exhausted after two or three hours.

Vidal is a hard-working, disciplined and organized artist who paints daily. Before starting a painting, she has a perfectly formed idea of what she is going to paint. Her favorite time to paint is either in the late afternoon or at night. The studio is as clean as an operating room. A large, sturdy wooden easel stands in front of a five-foot picture window, and three short, fat vases are stuffed with flat-tipped sable oil brushes in every available size. There are some flat bristles, too, "just in case," but they're rarely used, since approximately four-fifths of every canvas is worked with flexible painting knives. (These are not to be confused with the utilitarian palette knife that is used only to scrape paint off the palette.) The painting knives have pliable, triangular blades and stepped-up handles four to six inches long. Each knife has a particular function. Some are used for mixing paints, while others are shaped to facilitate painting petal shapes or stems or even highlights. Very large knives are used to paint in the backgrounds, and knives with tiny tips are used for sparing details. Vidal uses a variety of shapes and sizes, but prefers blade Nos. 3 to 5.

Hahn Vidal's oil palette is "classic" and includes lamp black, raw sienna, yellow ochre (or Indian yellow), burnt sienna, raw umber, burnt umber, magenta, and alizarin crimson (which she always combines with gel to reduce its transparency). The cadmium colors are red, yellow, and lightest yellow. The cools are thalo green, terre verte, French blue, cobalt blue, thalo blue, and violet. Titanium is the only white she will allow on her palette. Vidal uses mineral turpentine with a drop of damar varnish as her medium. Linseed oil is completely eliminated, because the artist finds that it yellows the whites, "which are, after all, the soul of the painting." She believes acrylics will be the most popular medium of the future because of their versatility and color intensity. Some of her paintings are executed in acrylics, but she invariably returns to oils, since she prefers their slower drying time.

The artist keeps a supply of unprimed linen canvases of varying grain stretched and ready in her studio: "The smaller the painting, the finer the grain. And I never stretch my own canvases, because I prefer all my energy to be directed to the painting itself rather than the back-breaking work involved in preparation." Occasionally she will use a Masonite panel, which she coats with two layers of acrylic paint, choosing from pale pink, Indian red, cool gray, light blue, or yellow ochre.

Getting down to work is just as tough for Hahn Vidal as it was for Winston Churchill, who would spend long periods with a loaded brush in his hand, paralyzed by the sight of the blank white canvas. Throughout the creation of the picture, Hahn Vidal does not use live flowers as models. Instead, she recreates the memory of them while working. But the memory, she claims, is very clear and precise as a result of so many years devoted to floral paintings. "Visions are stored away, but I don't want to paint them for fear that they will shatter like broken glass," says Vidal. The "visions" of flowers are structured and composed before the first knife stroke is made, but she knows that her best plans can go to pieces as the painting unfolds. Often, when the artist begins, she thinks, ". . . I know this will be great," but, halfway through the picture, the thought changes to ". . . This is not working out the way I had planned." And, when the painting is finished, the thought becomes ". . . This didn't work out the way I expected at all!"

Once Vidal gets through the initial period of "painter's block" she begins the first of three stages necessary to complete the painting. She roughly

Lotus Dream, 1973, oil, 20 x 30. Courtesy Hipola Gallery, Madrid. Vidal prefers a limited palette: "The less variety in colors, the greater the harmony."
Right: *Egyptian Lotus,* 1968, oil, 35 x 24. Private collection. The artist recreated her impressions of the elegance of the lotus she had seen in Taiwan.

blocks in a part of the background and the geometric forms that are the basis of the composition. In keeping with her love for informal gardens and flower arrangements, most of her compositions are of natural settings—usually three or four kinds of flowers in profuse groups. But, sometimes, as a dramatic change, she will paint just one flower against part of a landscape. In this step, pure colors are either brushed or knifed in, and some of the darks are established along with the understructure. After a three-day drying period, she begins the second stage, in which mixed pigments are knifed on over the first layer of paint, allowing areas of color to show through. "This gives the blossoms the effect of light and air." At this point the background will be completed. After a thorough drying period, Vidal begins the third step. Highlights and details are added to the painting with the painting knives.

"Knowing when the painting is finished is the most difficult thing, but I know," she says. And finally the finished canvas is propped against the studio wall where its quality can be judged on a daily basis by the artist while it dries. If the painting doesn't come up to her standards, she simply destroys it. "I find it abhorrent to rework a painting, and to paint over a used canvas would ruin the freshness. I've destroyed

many, many paintings because I don't want something I don't think is good coming back to haunt me. Once it is sold it's too late." After the finished painting passes the artist's critique, it receives a light coat of reduced damar varnish, "but not quite enough to make it glisten. The finished painting of the flower should never be something perfect. Rather, it should be a transfiguration of the artist that takes you away from reality—to another space, and to poetry and music. Always, everything is so interconnected," she says.

The major source of Hahn Vidal's inspiration comes not only from the memory and sight of live flowers, but from travel that provides the artist with a very necessary kind of stimulation. The newness of a foreign city, the excitement of the people, architecture, and galleries make it possible for her to produce enough work for three group exhibitions each year. "I am very affected and influenced by the city I'm in, and my paintings always reflect this," she says.

Is there symbolism in her flower paintings? "There is none, except in relation to poetry and beauty. The subject must almost flow through your hand; it has to be in your blood, and you have to be almost a reincarnation of a gardener."

Peonies, 1966, oil, 20 x 10. Private collection. Vidal's energetic impasto knifework creates a sensuous portrait.

Red Rose, oil on board, 11 x 8. The rose itself and the background merge as an application of oil, swiftly attacked with the palette knife.

Morning Sun, oil, 32 x 24. The sunlight heightens the form of the yellow chrysanthemums and the antique Spanish vase.

DUANE WAKEHAM

BY JEAN McCORD

HE IS A QUIET man. And peaceful. A sense of peacefulness wraps him like an aura. So it is the same with his paintings. And why not? Shouldn't a man's work reflect his personality like a mirror?

Stand before his paintings and lose yourself in quiet, gentle landscapes. There is no activity, no people, no machines, no buildings. The only movement is the wind blowing softly across the grasses of a meadow.

He shows us the quiet side of nature, the part of him that goes out, lost in contemplation, paying homage to mountains, ancient trees, perennial grasses, drifting clouds and fog.

"Look," he says through his paintings, hushed and rapt.

We look, and if we're quiet we can see clouds floating on the surface of infinitely still ponds, rivers winding off into the distance like ribbons of light laid down and lost. He offers us moments of tranquility, urging us not only to observe but to react to the moods of nature.

The painter of these poetic yet strong oil landscapes is Duane Wakeham. Born in Michigan, he now lives and paints in San Francisco. He also teaches art history at the College of San Mateo.

"Since junior high school, I had wanted to be a commercial artist and thought that getting started on a career meant that I couldn't spend four years going to college. Just as I started commercial art school in Detroit, the Korean war broke out, and six months later I found myself enlisting in the Navy for four years. I was not what you'd call a born sailor. In fact, the first time I boarded a ship, which was for transport to Japan, I became violently seasick almost before the ship had passed the Golden Gate Bridge."

Eighteen months in Japan and the remainder of his enlistment in Hawaii did not manage to transform him into a seasoned sailor. He still became ill every time he went to sea. But the four years were not wasted. That period in his life determined and shaped many of his later values.

He worked as a journalist and spent his liberty and leave time in Japan recording his impressions in sketches and a series of little watercolors, the size dictated by his small shipboard locker. In Hawaii he could expand the size of his paintings when he was offered studio space in the quonset hut home of a friend and his wife. "They received baby-sitting services in exchange," Wakeham explains. He also painted outdoors and used the colorful landscapes of the islands to stretch and grow into an accomplished watercolorist, exhibiting, receiving awards, and selling his paintings.

When his four years in the Navy were over, he requested discharge in Hawaii and gave himself a gift of several months on Maui, painting watercolors all day long while enjoying the luxury of tropical landscapes, ideal weather, and good friends. Finally the "Gauguin life" was over. It was time to go home.

As a veteran he was entitled to four years of educational benefits. In reappraising his goals, he realized he no longer wanted to be a commercial artist: "Somewhere along the line I realized that attending college was important to me, that I wanted a more complete education than an art school offered."

Back home he enrolled in Michigan State University. By applying for credit for his naval training and by taking extra courses by special examination, Wakeham earned his B.A. in three years, ensuring that he would have educational benefits left over for graduate school. While still an undergraduate he took a year off from school and worked as a technical illustrator at the University of Michigan Research Center. "It wasn't the kind of illustration work I had dreamed of doing years earlier, but I learned how to use a ruling pen, do paste-ups, and prepare artwork for reproduction, skills which have been very useful to me."

Wakeham moved to California for graduate work at Stanford University, where he had been awarded a teaching assistantship. After earning his M.A. in 1960, he was on his determined route in life as an artist and a teacher. Each occupation would support and buttress the other, since he had no urge to be a "starving artist," but neither would he allow himself to sacrifice his life and talent as a painter to be a teacher only. The two roles would have to co-exist. He has been able to make the arrangement work, with great

Marsh at Evening, 1976, oil, 34 x 54. Collection William Burke. Privately commissioned, the shape and colors of this painting were determined by the wall on which it was to be hung. Space within the painting was established by reducing the size of the water shapes instead of through value changes.

Spring Grass, Sonoma, 1976, oil, 30 x 50. Collection of William Burke. Wakeham departs from his customary square format to use a long, horizontal canvas for this scene of flat pasture land. To depict the full light of midday, he began his painting directly on the white canvas. The water areas in the foreground were added to pull some blue from the sky down into the lower half of the painting, to repeat the shape of the tree shadows, and to emphasize the long, horizontal shape of the canvas.

personal satisfaction derived from both activities.

Now a teacher of art history, Wakeham originally taught drawing and painting. His first assignment at Stanford was teaching a class in Expressive Drawing: "What I remember about that first class was my annoyance at students who attempted to justify bad drawing by calling it 'expressive.' And I've seen students devise some truly clever methods to avoid what seem to be difficult drawing problems. A student in a painting class once boasted to me that he had gotten through a life drawing class without ever having to draw heads, hands, or feet simply by making sure that those parts wouldn't fit on his paper."

In speaking of his belief in the need for a good foundation in drawing, Wakeham cites a statement by Henri Matisse in which that artist expressed his fear that "the young, seeing in my work only the apparent facility and negligence in the drawing, will use this as an excuse for dispensing with certain efforts I believe necessary."

Wakeham stresses drawing again: "Students seem so amazed to discover how beautifully, even academically, Picasso was able to draw. They aren't aware that Picasso, Matisse, Klee, Kandinsky, and Mondrian, some of the artists most directly responsible for the dramatic changes which occurred in 20th century painting, all had early conventional training." He states his firm conviction as a teacher: "I've always believed that knowing how to draw frees the artist to draw as he chooses."

In 1962 Wakeham left Stanford for what was to be a year-long "grand tour" of Europe and ended up staying another year to paint. To finance that second year he asked a number of friends and acquaintances to send him $100 each at some time during the year. "That amount was to be advance payment for a small painting which they would be able to select from the work I expected to do. Almost by return mail I was assured sufficient funds to live modestly for the year."

Originally he had planned to spend the year in Spain, but when he arrived in Florence, Italy, he knew instinctively that was where he should stay. He located a studio apartment in a reconstructed medieval tower house half a block from the Ponte Vecchio.

"It was on the seventh floor overlooking the Arno River," he recalls. "When I first saw the apartment and made arrangements to rent, there was an operating elevator. By the time I moved in, the elevator was not working and never was repaired during the year I lived there. But I soon got used to the 105 steps and thought nothing of running right back down to the street if I forgot something while shopping. And, of course, there were wonderful compensations. If I wanted to look at a particular painting at the Uffizi, the museum was only 105 steps and three blocks away. I did a lot of painting, studied Italian every day, and spent many hours in the incredible museums and churches of the city. In addition there were trips to Siena, Pisa, Assisi, Ravenna, Venice,

and Rome, both for study and pure enjoyment."

Wakeham's pleasure in his memories is obvious. He pauses for a laugh: "Two weeks before I left Florence I found out that the elevator was not really broken. It simply wasn't in use because of a disagreement between some tenants."

Back home the next year he was offered a job teaching art history at the College of San Mateo: "Perhaps one reason I was given the position, even though I had never taught art history, was because I had lived in Europe for those two years and had seen many of the works I'd be teaching about. Also, I had a pretty firm background from assisting with lecture classes in the history of painting and architecture at Stanford."

Wakeham says that he has learned something important about combining teaching and painting: "I get more painting done as a teacher of art history. When I was teaching the studio courses, my own studio was stacked with unfinished work. It was as though I was expending most of my creative energy on the student work. Now, teaching a historical survey of painting, sculpture, and architecture keeps me busy, happy, and seems to stimulate my painting activities."

The only difficulty he finds is adjusting his painting time to his teaching schedule. Except for sketches and some small outdoor studies, all of Wakeham's painting is done in his San Francisco studio. "It's too difficult to work on large canvases outside," he explains. "But even sketching can create problems. Every day, as I commute to school, I drive though beautiful country, constantly seeing scenes and effects that I want to paint. I try to hold on to those images until I can get them down on paper. Sometimes, however, I pull off the freeway to make a sketch, but it can never be more than a few scribbles, because it's awkward to have the highway patrol stopping to see what's wrong."

Wakeham's landscapes range in size from 8 x 10 inches to 4 x 5 feet. He paints on stretched single-primed canvas, which he tones with a middle-value turpentine wash. He explains that "just getting the canvas covered with a color makes me feel that something is happening. And it ensures that in the finished painting there will be color rather than raw white canvas in unpainted areas."

The actual painting starts with a broad, loose brush drawing in umber to establish major compositional lines and to begin to determine general size and shape relationships. He continues with a quick laying in of color, thinking in terms of light and dark. Everything is kept tentative. Subject, composition, forms, color, and value will all be refined as the painting progresses.

The reality of his landscapes comes from a combination of remembered impressions, sketches, small studies in watercolor, oil, or oil pastels, and from photographs. A countertop in his studio is covered with reference material: "Working in the studio, I

Morning Light, 1976, oil, 34 x 36. Collection of Mr. and Mrs. Jack Corey. Working on a canvas toned with a yellow ochre wash, Wakeham has used a limited palette and closely related values and intensity to depict the soft light of dawn.

November Morning, 1976, oil, 34 x 36. Collection of Daniel Butler. Utilizing alternating bands of light and dark receding into space, Wakeham introduces his brightest color on the far bank both to pull the viewer deep into the painting and to create a feeling of openness behind the tree mass at the upper right. This emphasis on distance is balanced by the more intense blue and the broken pattern of warm accents in the foreground.

January Morning, Big Sur, 1977, oil, 48 x 54. Courtesy Western Federal Savings and Loan. One of Wakeham's series of morning paintings. Of the paintings reproduced here, this one comes closest to being a portrait of a specific place. Working from sketches and slides, Wakeham has simplified the scene into broad patterns of light and dark, loosely suggesting foliage and grass patterns rather than attempting a meticulous rendering.

find photographs essential because the sketches and studies can't begin to provide all the information I might need."

Generally Wakeham begins a painting with something specific in mind, but he describes his approach to painting as one that allows change: "The stage I enjoy most is when the forms have been loosely indicated on the canvas. Then I sit back for a long time just looking to see if I can discover something more interesting than what I've begun. Nothing really is fixed at that point. It's easy to let shapes, color relationships, even the direction of brush strokes suggest other possibilities. If something else becomes apparent, I'm willing to try it. Painting in oils is perfect for me, for it allows me to change my mind."

As a watercolorist Wakeham learned to simplify and summarize forms, at the same time maintaining a sense of reality. He employs a similar technique in his oil landscapes. Shapes tend to be simplified and somewhat broadly painted. Details of textures and surfaces are lightly suggested.

His oil paintings are thinly painted and have almost no surface texture other than that of the canvas. He explains that he loses interest in a painting when he loses the texture of the canvas, which he uses to achieve a feeling of transparency. Rather than glazing, he creates transparency by scumbing or scrubbing with the side of his brush on the textured surface of the canvas.

Wakeham claims that recently he became conscious of a difference between his landscapes done before 1965 and his current work: "My earlier landscapes usually included houses, streets, fences, boats, and sometimes people. Now all evidence of man's occupation of the earth is missing. Only an occasional road or path suggest human presence."

Yet the landscapes are inviting. Empty foregrounds draw the viewer into the scene, and openings beyond allow movement into the distance. In even the smallest paintings, he is able to convey a sense of spaciousness.

He speaks slowly of his paintings. "The landscapes that I paint truly exist only on the canvas. Although they relate to places I have seen and know, rarely do I attempt to recreate a specific place accurately. Although people often think they can recognize the exact place, the paintings are based on remembered experiences. By being sensitive to qualities of light and atmosphere and the moods of Nature, I work to create an illusion of a real landscape, a tranquil place in which both I and the viewer can feel comfortable.

And when a painting becomes real for the viewer in terms of his own experience, I feel that I've succeeded."

When asked about influences in his work, Wakeham acknowledges his debt to 19th century landscape painters, pointing out that as a teacher of art history he has respect for past traditions. He notes that his most vivid memory of his first visit to the Detroit Institute of Arts was seeing Martin Johnson Heade's *Sunset*. He also speaks with admiration of the poetry and emotion that George Inness introduced into American landscape painting.

Concerning choice of subject matter and style of painting, Wakeham comments on the problem of acceptance. "When I was trying to become established as a painter in the early 1960s, traditional subject matter painted in a somewhat traditional manner was not very acceptable. So I kept trying to find an approach to painting that would be satisfying to me and also attract the attention of gallery directors, jurors, and critics. I didn't find it.

"It took a long time for me to decide that it was okay to be myself in my paintings, that I could paint just the way I wanted to without worrying about being fashionable. I was encouraged and supported in this decision by Professor Daniel Mendelowitz of Stanford, who stressed that it is essential for each artist to select the subject matter and form most meaningful to himself—that satisfaction comes from being honest with yourself.

"Dan was my graduate advisor at Stanford. I studied both art history and watercolor with him and assisted him with his History of Painting class. Though now retired, he was a fine lecturer and teacher. For nearly 20 years I've benefited from his guidance, criticism, and support and can honestly say that he has been one of the most important influences in my development both as a teacher and a painter."

Wakeham speaks of yet another teacher who made an impact on his painting. There was a time during his student days when he began to harbor doubts about becoming a painter, because he questioned whether he had anything to say, any message to communicate. "I finally confessed this fear to Abraham Rattner, with whom I was studying at the time. His answer was very short and direct. He said, 'Having something to say as an artist is simply sharing a way of seeing and feeling,' And that answer has followed me through my life. That's what I am doing today in my paintings."

Autumn Afternoon, 1977, oil, 35 x 35. Collection William Kelsey. The patterns of water and grass intermingle to form the basis for the composition in this painting.

PAUL WIESENFELD

BY DOREEN MANGAN

ANACHRONISM, NOSTALGIA, the musty flavor of decades long gone pervade Paul Wiesenfeld's paintings. Yet Paul Wiesenfeld has been around for not much more than three decades. What's more, he sports kinky hair in an Afro style, blue jeans, T-shirt, and grubby sneakers. His conversation is straight from the youth vernacular: "cool," "groovy," he says, and, "I'm really getting into plants."

It seems a paradox that this distinctly contemporary young man should depict in his interiors turn-of-the-century parlors replete with old-fashioned sofas and lamps, faded carpets, and assorted bric-a-brac. As he explains it, his choice of subject matter has to do with his personal vision. "We live in interiors. We can find in them a landscape, a world, a whole universe. The closer I look and the longer I look, the more I see—that universe just opens up."

The room—Wiesenfeld's universe—that appears in many of his paintings is the parlor of his rambling, 75-year-old barn of a house in Buffalo, New York where he lived prior to his move to Germany. The nude he sometimes includes is his wife; the pieces of furniture were acquired in Buffalo's thrift shops.

Wiesenfeld paints in his home "because painting is part of my life. I want to be together with my work and to be able to look at a painting in the middle of the night if necessary." He wryly points out one disadvantage to this arrangement: his two lively young children, who sometimes have to be admonished to be quiet because their daddy is painting. "How did Vermeer do it with eleven kids?" he asks with a grin. "His paintings are always so quiet, so serene."

This reference to Vermeer is only one of the many that pop up in a conversation with Wiesenfeld, whose style has been called academic. Indeed, he is a devout student of the Old Masters, evidenced by his use of light and abstraction, his tight, controlled brush strokes, the muted color of his earlier works, even in the highly glazed finish of his paintings. A well-marked book on Vermeer is always close by. "I can never stop learning from him," Wiesenfeld observes.

Like Vermeer, Wiesenfeld paints a whole world in one room. The low perspective he employs in several works is also reminiscent of the Dutch master. Wiesenfeld feels that this view lends dimension and unity. However, painting from a child's eye level can present the artist with a certain mechanical problem. "My handicap is that I'm too tall," explains Wiesenfeld, whose height approaches six feet. "On the other hand, I just can't work sitting on the floor." He solves the problem by sitting on a rattan armchair that's only about five or six inches off the floor and using a sliding easel that he can adjust to any level. He sits in the hallway of his house, "very inconsiderately blocking the front door," looking into the parlor—his interior.

Another touch of Vermeer is the inclusion of a figure in the still-life interior. The female nude, oddly enough, does not look out of place in its vaguely Victorian surroundings. Nor does it dominate the scene. There is complete harmony within the painting, each area retaining its own value and accent.

These similarities to Vermeer do not mean that Wiesenfeld slavishly imitates that artist. Rather he absorbs the traits he best admires and incorporates them into his own artistry. Wiesenfeld has his own goals. He is striking out in new directions; in his serene, intimate interiors he seeks a personal definition of the still life.

Wiesenfeld's interiors are indeed more than simple still lifes, more than mere studies. He takes the usual accoutrements of the still life—vases, fruit, knick-knacks—places them in the context of a room ("the floor is my still life table"), and creates a living, breathing space. Contemplation marks the execution of these paintings. They've been looked at, mulled over, and pondered over by the artist. Life has been breathed into them.

The atmosphere he captures is tranquil, often cozy and snug in the earlier ones, dignified in the later ones. The aura echoes the familiar, yet there is also the element of the unspoken. One perceives, as one critic stated, "a hint of humanity"; there is a sense of presence, as if someone had just left the room. The missing presence is suggested by a crushed sofa cushion, a lighted lamp, a half-open cigarette pack, or a mug on the floor within arm's reach of the sofa. The

Secrets #1, 1969, oil, 46 x 49. Courtesy Robert Schoelkopf Gallery. Wiesenfeld uses a thick, syrupy medium to obtain a smooth, glossy surface without visible brush strokes or canvas texture. Only his white highlights are ''loaded''—applied without medium.

Seated Nude, 1971, oil, 57 x 51. Courtesy Robert Schoelkopf Gallery. Here the artist contrasts his tightly painted controlled style and meticulous attention to details of patterns with a looser treatment of the figure.

Reclining Nude, 1971, oil, 46 x 61½. Collection Mr. and Mrs. Charles Balback. Wiesenfeld uses mirrors to convey depth and enhance the illusion.

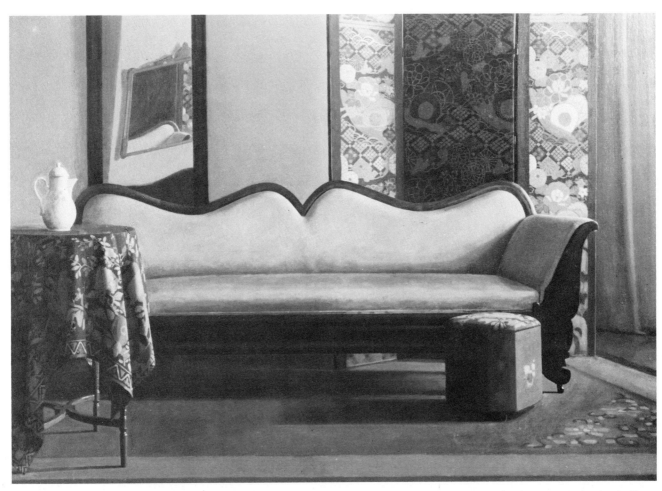

Untitled, 1972, oil, 48 x 60. Collection Robert Freudenheim. Regarding the furniture he uses, Wiesenfeld says, ''They're not antiques; they're like pieces of sculpture.''

Interior, 1972-73, oil, 40 x 60½. Collection Mr. Morton Z. Newman. The artist explores the play of flat, stylized flowers on the screen against the green forms of the real plants.

clues tantalize. Who has been here? The answer is simple: Wiesenfeld himself! "My paintings are lived in. I often step in and out of the scene I'm painting. I stretch out on the sofa, relax, maybe eat a piece of fruit." This practice affords him a more all-round view of his scene than if he were on the outside looking in.

Wiesenfeld compares his approach to composition to that of a chess player. The floor and walls of the room are the chessboard; the furniture, bric-a-brac, and nude are his pawns. His "game," however, is called abstraction—"to make all parts of the painting relate to each other until the painting 'sings'; to make a shimmering, vibrating painting that makes all others seem dull and dead." In the course of this endeavor, Wiesenfeld employs much variation on a theme. One painting literally grows out of another. For instance, in comparing two paintings shown here, *Untitled* and *Interior,* one can see that they are almost identical. However, the pitcher and hassock of *Untitled* have been omitted in the later painting. Instead, a plant on the table and a tall one beside the sofa have been added. The scene changes again, but again slightly, in *Interior with Rubber Plant,* also shown here. The sofa and rug are the same. The table is minus its covering and bears a rubber plant that is reflected in the mirror, this time placed above the center of the sofa.

Juggling of objects to show relationships, however, is not the sole *raison d'etre* behind Paul Wiesenfeld's work. He wants to study the effects of different lighting situations. Says Wiesenfeld, "I'm absolutely fascinated by light, the way it shines and shimmers." He is intrigued by the difficulties of achieving just the right light and has painted his drawing room as it looks by the soft, diffused glow of lamplight: golden, 19th century; in late afternoon: muted, nostalgic, almost indolent; at midday: brilliant, optimistic in the clear flood of daylight.

A Wiesenfeld painting is carefully nurtured from conception to execution. The artist begins with three or four scaled drawings that are also careful composition studies. ("I'm constantly refining," he says.) These drawings are done with lithographic pencil. "It's beautiful to shade with," Wiesenfeld explains. "Light and dark come out immediately, and the drawings are more three-dimensional than if done in lead pencil. I'm not a line man," he goes on; "more of a shader." Referring to another still-life painting nearby, Wiesenfeld comments, "I must have moved the compote with the pears 50 or 60 times before I found the right position." Then two careful studies were made with the plant in different positions.

Once he decides on the best drawing he transfers it very lightly in charcoal to the canvas. Transferring the drawing, however, does not mean the composition phase is over. Composing is something that goes on throughout the painting process. "When I put in a table," says Wiesenfeld, "I might think it's perfectly placed. Yet three weeks later I may move it. Five weeks later I might take out a whole wall."

It is only when the preliminary studies and the drawing are completed that Wiesenfeld turns his attention to color. On the whole, he has been reticent in his use of color. "My tendency has been to mute the colors; now I'm trying to be more brilliant." His palette has been and still is somewhat limited. It consists of "a combination of warm and cool"; burnt umber, raw umber, ultramarine blue, titanium white, ivory black, raw sienna, yellow ochre, alizarin crimson, old Holland yellow, and most lately, viridian green, inspired by the more common inclusion of plants in some of his paintings. Before his "plant period" Wiesenfeld hadn't used a green paint in five years, mixing instead any green he needed from blue and yellow. Another factor in his choice of colors is the use of daylight in his recent paintings. "Now I'm being forced to use colors I've never used before," he says.

Wiesenfeld paints in oil because of its vibrancy and glow. "It [the color] is closer than anything else to the predictable in terms of drying. Acrylics dry vastly different from what you expect." And for him they lack the sensitivity and glow of oils.

Using a variety of sable brushes, the artist applies his paint in hard-to-distinguish brush strokes on a very fine portrait linen canvas. "I don't want the texture of the linen to interfere with the surface of the painting. Likewise, if I showed the texture of the paint severely, if I slopped it on, I'd lose the illusionism, the smoothness." Wiesenfeld uses a medium composed of ½ turpentine, ¼ stand oil, and ¼ damar varnish. When mixed with the paint it makes "a honey-like, syrupy mixture." This contributes to the smooth, mirrorlike surface of a Wiesenfeld work. (Because of the amount of varnish in the medium, a final glaze is not needed.) His whites, however, are "loaded"—applied with very little medium—for highlights.

He begins a painting with earth colors—white, yellow ochre, black. "Then I start refining, heightening it; taking it from the fuzzy stage into focus by gradually pumping color into it." Wiesenfeld blends a lot: "A pear can be splotches of light yellow, green, darker green. Then I blend the splotches to resemble the real thing. Each time I go over an area I try to make it sensitive, brilliant, refined." He continues, "My paintings always look lousy at the beginning; they are a series of corrections. It takes a lot of looking and thinking."

"I'm a tight, controlled painter," he goes on; "that's my style." This is especially evident in his meticulous attention to details of patterns in sofas, rugs, wall hangings, and so on. His execution of the figure, however, reveals a departure from this. The flesh tones are handled in an abstract manner—more a collection of paints that suggests rather than precisely defines.

But because of the precision involved in his work as a whole, Wiesenfeld takes from two to four months to complete a painting. For a while Wiesenfeld divided his time between painting and teaching (as an assistant professor of fine arts at the State University College of New York at Buffalo). Wiesenfeld

enjoyed teaching but decided to devote more time to painting. So in 1974 he and his family moved to Germany, his wife's native country, for a stay of several years. What was he looking forward to doing there? Painting full time. Discovering the turquoise skies and mellow light of lower Bavaria. Enjoying the proximity of museums containing works of his much-revered Old Masters. Finding more furniture for his still lifes. It seemed likely that he would scour the thrift shops of Germany as he did in Buffalo, looking for "furniture that looks lived in; cast-offs from the attics of people who want modern furniture."

Wiesenfeld is no stranger to Germany. Part of his student days were spent in Munich, where he studied at the Kunstakademie. He began studying art in America, however, at the age of 11, attending the Chouinard Art Institute in Los Angeles in the evenings and on Saturdays. His college years were spent studying art at the University of California in Los Angeles and at Yale. Then he found himself in Munich on a Fulbright grant. "I loved being there," he says, "mainly because of Munich's art museum, the Alte Pinakothek, and its fine collection of Old Masters." The collection includes great Flemish paintings, such

as those by Rubens, that Wiesenfeld had never seen before. "In Munich I didn't study much," he admits, "just painted and painted."

Art has always meant realism to Wiesenfeld. But shortly after leaving Germany, he indulged briefly in a fling with surrealism. This was during his first year of graduate study at Indiana University. During his second year, he says, "I reordered my life" and came home to realism. Surrealism still interests him, however. "All strong realism becomes surrealism. It becomes so real that it's strange," he says, which is an apt comment on his own work.

Wiesenfeld's brand of realism exhibits none of the slickness, cynicism, disenchantment, or toughness of the New Realists. His paintings are beautiful, soft, poetic, mysterious. A 1969 German showing of his work was entitled "Poetic American Realism." "There is so much ugliness in the world." Wiesenfeld says; "I want to create a little more beauty."

Yet creation does not come easily. This artist admits to the difficulty of getting down to the task, a problem that plagues many an artist: "Sometimes I'd much rather do anything else than paint; I have to force myself to get to work." But once he does get going the experience is breathtaking: "I'm in a state where I exist no longer—my being responds to the incredible beauty I see. I'm just a vehicle. That's when I'm really hitting."

He must also come to terms with the self-doubts that torment any artist; he's never quite satisfied. "I always think the last painting is the best. Then two paintings later I think it's the worst. They're all disasters!" he exclaims, self-deprecatingly. Yet Wiesenfeld isn't really putting himself down, he's just facing what he feels are the facts: "An artist paints his best only a few times in his life," he feels, and he doesn't think he has reached that point yet.

Nonetheless, one of his "disasters" is now in the permanent collection of the Whitney Museum of American Art and another in the Virginia Museum of Fine Arts. He has had one-man exhibitions both in the United States and Germany, and the Robert Schoelkopf Gallery in New York City handles his work. Surely Paul Wiesenfeld is within close reach of that elusive masterpiece!

Opposite page: *Interior with Rubber Plant,* 1973, oil, 42 x 50. Collection Virginia Museum of Fine Arts. Wiesenfeld uses curves as a compositional device. Here the flowing curves of the sofa, table, and leaves of the plant echo one another. Sometimes—as in the case of the sofa—the artist feels the pieces of furniture become almost human.

Above: *Still Life,* 1970, oil, 60 x 60¼. Collection Mr. Edmund Pillsbury. The artist is fascinated by Oriental rugs. "They're like beautiful paintings in themselves," he says.

JANE WILSON

BY DIANE COCHRANE

THE EARLIEST AND MOST VIVID image Jane Wilson can remember is the afternoon sun pouring through a west window. Exactly when this scene first occurred in her childhood she doesn't know, but she has been reinventing this light in her paintings ever since. Her early landscapes were dominated by a western sun, and the same afternoon light diffuses her interiors now so that objects are seen in relative darkness rather than illuminated by the brash light of midday.

Another of Wilson's early memories is an overwhelming Midwestern landscape, empty and enormous. This visual recollection has also profoundly affected her work, although she has lived in New York for over 20 years. The influence of these early impressions seems to justify the rather fashionable theory that an artist spends his life reconstructing his first most intense images. But this theory is too limiting to describe Wilson. For, while it is true that remembrances of subdued golden light and a big sky have been profound and long lasting, it would be better to say that these early scenes led to an identification with environment itself. The result is that the size, the weight, and the light of any hospitable place or setting will trigger an emotional response that she can translate on canvas.

Sitting in her big East Side studio, a few stories above Manhattan's traffic-clogged Third Avenue, surrounded by a few of her favorite things—peonies from a nearby ship, croissants from a French bakery, posters of her friends' shows—Wilson, a casually elegant woman in her 40s, seems an unlikely farm girl. Yet she speaks of the Iowa of her youth with a surprising vividness: "The landscape was enormously meaningful to me. I used to roam around a lot by myself as a child, and when I think of a landscape, I think of the great weight of the sky and how it rests on the earth. And I remember the light. Light is specific to certain places, and what sort of light and landscape formation you grow up with is immensely influential to what you do later on."

This realization came gradually: "At first I thought I was influenced by French Impressionists or Dutch landscapists and was painting light and air I hadn't seen. But a conversation with a painter from Min-

nesota who had similar feelings to mine about a vast sky with a low band of clouds on the horizon changed my mind. He told me that at one point in his life he felt he had to find that particular landscape and live in it. So he spent a whole year searching for it in Scotland, where he was sure it was, only to find it back in Minnesota. The same thing happened to me. I went to the Midwest, and there was that particular sky I was looking for, trying to get into my paintings."

The place Wilson was born and raised was southern Iowa, where each family was a self-contained unit. "Everyone had their own stock and crops and made their own products. Today it seems as if these experiences were out of another century, but I suppose they made me want to make things myself."

Rural experiences continued to color her life until she entered the University of Iowa to study painting. There the traditional values she had known back on the farm and in the small towns where she lived were echoed to some extent. Representational still lifes and figures were the school's staples, but it was not provincial. Traveling shows from New York and other big cities were exhibited, and such avant-garde artists as Jackson Pollock and Willem DeKooning exploded on her horizons for the first time. ("To this day I can still remember exactly where a certain Pollock hung in an exhibit.") But as seductive as the message proclaimed by these leaders of the big-time art world was, she didn't immediately respond to its lure. She stayed on at the university, first earning her B.A. and M.A. and then teaching art history. Finally the time came when she had to make the break: "I wanted to see if I could be a painter, and I didn't think I could do it there, particularly while I was on the staff of the university."

After moving to New York she succumbed, as did so many other young painters of the 1940s and '50s, to Abstract Expressionism. The still lifes and figures that were the mainstays of her college days no longer worked for her. Abstraction seemed the only valid approach, and for several years she devoted all her energies to experimenting with it.

By the mid '50s, however, she had come to two realizations. One was that no matter what kind of ab-

India Silk, 1970, oil, 60 x 50. Collection Mrs. Alice Esty. Using a rich collection of colorful textured objects and fabrics, Wilson creates a still life environment that is full of objects and details yet maintains a light and airy feeling.

Above: *Gloxina, Begonia, Petunia,* 1970, oil, 50 x 70. Collection Kathrine Graham. Photo courtesy Graham Gallery. By selecting the most telling contour, Wilson portrays the specific energy and interval of each object.

Right: *Near Naples,* 1967, oil, 42 x 50. Courtesy Graham Gallery. Moving her approach to landscape away from the horizontal, Wilson fills her canvas with the patchwork effect of a Naples countryside.

straction she did, it seemed to have a horizontal construction that always referred back to the horizontal landscapes of her childhood: "It seemed to have planes, things were on it, above and below." Or, as she has written, "It was about gravity, let's say; the contact and the weight of air and color were going very definitely in the direction of landscape." The second realization was that subject matter was very important to her: "I am not gifted at pulling a composition whole cloth out of my head. For me, everything comes from the relationship between things, so I use nature or a setup as a point of departure."

Wilson considers these early years of experimenting most fruitful: "Looking back, I was trying to sort out what was useful from my past life so I could dump the extraneous things and establish a new direction." Her investigations resulted in a palette that, with modification, serves her today, and, more importantly, with a resolve to return to representational art. Not to still lifes or figures ("They were too claustrophobic, too close to what we had done at school," she says.), but to landscapes, which were not associated with training: "In Iowa no one ever went outside to paint that marvelous sky." Why? "Probably for the same reason I rejected still lifes and figures. My teachers were too close to the Regionalism of the '30s."

So in the middle of the abstract era, Wilson took up landscape painting. As she was always a fairly willful person, there may have been a certain amount of rebelliousness in her rejection of the then-accepted art form, but on a more fundamental level she believed that, "If I were going to do anything original at all, I knew I had to find the most meaningful thing for me and follow it."

Having decided to paint landscapes while in New York should have proved a disadvantage to a painter who finds it difficult to invent compositions. But in Wilson's case, it wasn't. She had her roots so firmly sunk into the land that she could invent imaginary landscapes. "My chain of memory is strongly related to the past." For example, she remembers a family trip taken out West by car when she was 13. On the way back, they crossed the Great Divide in the late afternoon. The eastern side of the mountains was already dark, but in front of them lay the Great Plains bathed in sun. Says Wilson, "I got a lot of paintings out of that golden landscape," which is probably another way of stating her preference for western light.

For ten years Wilson painted rural landscapes from memory. These paintings brought her her first recognition when she showed them at the Hansa Gallery, which led to purchases by such major museums as the Museum of Modern Art and the Whitney Museum of American Art. Today her works hang in the country's finest private and corporate collections, and she continues to receive invitations to show at the most prestigious national exhibitions.

Wilson follows each direction her art takes to its conclusion and no farther. Then, responding to a change of place or a symbiotic effect of a different lo-cation on a long-simmering idea, she takes up a new course. In 1965 this meant cityscapes replaced landscapes when she rented an apartment with large windows opening out onto Tompkins Square on Manhattan's Lower East Side. With the city brought into her living room, she turned to painting what she saw outside her windows, a scene of endless possibilities created by the changing seasons and light. She also added a Polaroid camera to her equipment for forays farther afield, because she doesn't paint on the street and, "I have no conscious memory of the city."

At first the construction of the cityscapes relied heavily on the horizontality of previous work, with the verticals of the city structures adding a geometric element: "I saw everything in terms of horizontals and verticals." But a trip to Europe destroyed this great geometry. The leaning buildings of Amsterdam and Venice accustomed her eye to asymmetry: "It gradually occurred to me that nothing is really vertical or horizontal, including things in New York: the streets arch, the buildings are set back." As she kept turning the idea over in her mind, she remembered a lecture given in art school about the difference between the heads of Greek and Roman sculpture: "The Greeks gave every feature a life of its own; no two were alike—eyebrows, ears, etc. But in an effort to copy the art of the Greeks perfectly, the Romans made their heads symmetrical and took the life out of them. I felt that all painting is an extension of this idea, and I developed a mania for asymmetry."

By 1969 Wilson, having satiated her appetite for painting places, entered "phase one" her still lifes. "Phase" is my word, because on the surface her work seems so neatly compartmentalized—rural landscapes, European scenes, cityscapes—but it really isn't an accurate description. She doesn't finish one body of work and say, "I must do something new." A change of direction is usually an interaction of ideas and events. The switch to still lifes, for example, resulted from three factors: a move from her airy Lower East Side apartment to a "very much indoors" flat where thoughts of the out-of-doors suffocated under dark woodwork and obsessive wallpaper; a decision to teach painting instead of art history; and the desire to solve a painting problem.

Art history had always been her forte: she taught it at the University of Iowa and in New York at Pratt Institute. But for some time friends had urged her to give private painting classes. Finally she agreed and set out to find a system to teach still life, which seemed the most convenient subject to paint in the city. "I began by putting big patterned cloths on the table to show how space moves between objects, and I asked them to supply their own objects with which they would be at ease." Expedience dictated that she, too, paint still lifes, since that was what was going on in the studio, and following her own advice she began to haunt the neighborhood vegetable and flower shops, looking for her own objects. Before long she was hooked: "I became absolutely mesmerized by the displays of fruits and vegetables."

Children's Playground, 1965, oil, 50 x 55. Collection Jacques Kaplan. Wilson's early cityscapes were essentially geometric.

Are They Smelts? 1973, oil, 13 x 15. Collection Mr. and Mrs. Leonard Bernstein. Without elaborate props, her still lifes have begun to reflect the natural silvery light and mood of her studio.

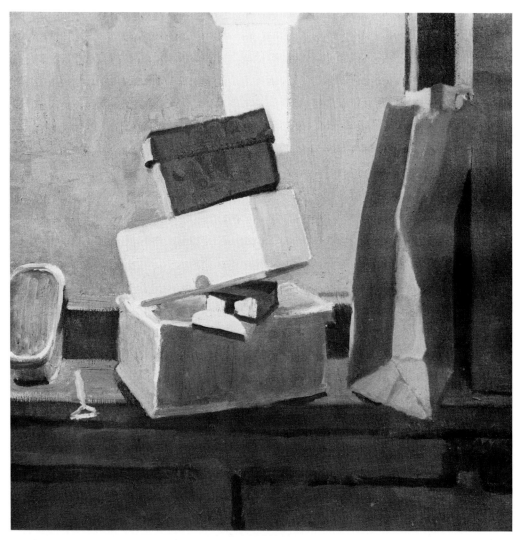

Tottering Boxes, 1972, oil, 21 x 21. Collection Mr. and Mrs. R. Meryman. Photo Courtesy Graham Gallery. Craving humbler subject matter for her still lifes, Wilson chose anxiety-producing objects arranged arbitrarily.

But she wasn't interested in painting simple still lifes. For some time Wilson had wondered why it was so hard for contemporary artists to include a lot of details in painting. It wasn't always so difficult. The Flemish painters and those of the Baroque and Renaissance managed quite handily to incorporate a wealth of tiny details. The more she thought about it, the more tempting the idea became of trying it herself. Furthermore, she was convinced that a painting should offer a number of visual experiences, depending on how close the viewer is to it: "The canvas is enormously seductive, and it can be read at different levels, not like many contemporary paintings that devastate you at 50 feet and then give you nothing as you walk toward them, wounded."

To accomplish her goal, Wilson created huge setups filled with more objects than could be contained on a canvas: "They forced me to find out what had to be simplified so I could incorporate as many of them as possible. Simplification develops by discovering the specific energy of each object and interval in a given situation and finding the simplest, strongest, most telling contour to carry them. This means forcing your experience into the contour and the objects. If they are carefully observed and intuitively felt, people will see not only the details of the objects that are depicted but others, too, because they bring their own specifics with them in their heads."

The obsession for imposing order based on masses of details began to pale in the early 1970s. "I began to crave plainer shapes and less of them. I also wanted to get away from the handsome objects I had been painting—the patterned cloths, the flowers, etc.—and describe objects that create anxiety in me. Fish heads do this; so do cleavers and empty boxes." She also wanted to wean her students away from their devotion to an arranged setup, and as usual she followed her own teaching. Still lifes were no longer deliberately set up. In *Are They Smelts?* for example, she picked up the fish by their tails and threw them on the table. The way they fell was the way she painted them.

The choice of subject matter and the lack of deliberate subject arrangements affected her palette. Objects seen without elaborate props began to reflect the true light and mood of her studio, a place she describes as "indoors, New York, wintery." So warm hues changed to silvery tones. The subdued palette was not new, however. "My choice of color swings like a pendulum. I change back and forth between a series of paintings in which value studies predominate, like the cityscapes, and a series in which color predominates, although I like mixing too much to work with pure color."

What sort of paintings will Wilson produce next? It's hard to say. And what about subject matter? Recently she has tended to paint less and to draw more, the result of a life course she has been teaching at Parsons School of Design: "I am trying to formulate ideas that will help students draw the figure." Does this indicate the figure might creep into her work? If so, she will have traveled full circle back to her student days. Or she might paint the Iowa landscape again. For Wilson went back to Iowa—this time as a visiting professor for a fall term at the University—back where it all started.

INDEX

Designed by Bob Fillie
Set in 10 point Medallion